Prison Pedagogies

PRISON PEDAGOGIES

Learning and Teaching with Imprisoned Writers

Edited by **Joe Lockard** and
Sherry Rankins-Robertson

SU
Syracuse University Press

Copyright © 2018 by Syracuse University Press
Syracuse, New York 13244-5290

All Rights Reserved

First Edition 2018

18 19 20 21 22 23   6 5 4 3 2 1

∞ The paper used in this publication meets the minimum requirements of the American National Standard for Information Sciences—Permanence of Paper for Printed Library Materials, ANSI Z39.48-1992.

For a listing of books published and distributed by Syracuse University Press,
visit www.SyracuseUniversityPress.syr.edu.

ISBN: 978-0-8156-3563-5 (hardcover)
       978-0-8156-3581-9 (paperback)
       978-0-8156-5428-5 (e-book)

Library of Congress Cataloging-in-Publication Data

Names: Lockard, Joe, 1953– editor. | Rankins-Robertson, Sherry, 1976– editor.
Title: Prison pedagogies : learning and teaching with imprisoned writers / edited by Joe Lockard and
    Sherry Rankins-Robertson.
Description: First Edition. | Syracuse, NY : Syracuse University Press, [2018] | Includes bibliographical
    references and index.
Identifiers: LCCN 2018017097 (print) | LCCN 2018017210 (ebook) | ISBN 9780815654285 (E-book) |
    ISBN 9780815635635 (hardback : alk. paper) | ISBN 9780815635819 (pbk. : alk. paper)
Subjects: LCSH: Prisoners—Education.
Classification: LCC HV8875 (ebook) | LCC HV8875 .P75 2018 (print) | DDC 808/.042071—dc23
LC record available at https://lccn.loc.gov/2018017097

Manufactured in the United States of America

supported by a word without wall
Figure Foundation

In the depths of a prison, dreams have no limits,
never held back by reality.

> —*Albert Camus,* The Rebel,
> *translated by Edward M. White*

Contents

Illustrations

Preface

CALEB SMITH

This volume appears in a time of economic and political disaster. Its contributors imagine various ways of bringing the intellectual resources of higher education, whose institutions are under assault, into a prison system that, already unprecedented in scale, seems destined to continue its nightmarish sprawl. There is no question anymore of a separation between theory and practice. The same monster that is building up the prisons with one hand is tearing down the schools with the other. One of the ironies of our predicament is that prisons are among the few places where education programs, public and private, are actually expanding. After the triumph of the carceral state, how will we teach? What is the use of what we have to give?

For a long time, Americans in captivity used to talk about education as something they had to steal. Take two examples, one from the plantation and one from the penitentiary. Here is Frederick Douglass on learning to read in slavery: "I was most narrowly watched. If I was in a separate room any considerable length of time, I was sure to be suspected of having a book, and was at once called to give an account of myself. All this, however, was too late. The first step had been taken. Mistress, in teaching me the alphabet, had given me the *inch*, and no precaution could prevent me from taking the *ell*" (1845, 38, emphasis in the original). And here is one of Douglass's contemporaries, the prison memoirist Austin Reed, telling a similar story about his time as a juvenile in the "colored" section of a New York reformatory: "I had such a greedy appetite for reading that I was called up before Mr. Williams the school teacher one day and laid across the stool, where I got fifteen cuts with the rattan for having more than one book in my desk" (2016, 26). Literacy in these narratives is a clandestine and contraband thing. Your hunger for it is a vice, and your satisfaction is a crime. To get it, you have to sneak around, risking exposure and punishment. Your overseers are not going to give it to you. You have to take it for yourself.

Thus, the scene of education can be imagined as a scene of self-liberation, even self-making, in opposition to regimes of legal violence. The prison, like the plantation whose place it takes, appears as a dehumanizing institution, a zone of exclusion and living death. Although its first task is to arrange and immobilize vast numbers of bodies, its harm goes deeper, into the minds it would numb or destroy. Inmates who educate themselves—think of Malcolm X making his way through the dictionary, starting with the weird beast *aardvark*—are working against the prison's annihilating designs. In solitude, they secret away resources of self-preservation, critical reflection, and expression. They steal a chance at a new identity, a new life.

So the story goes. But if you are reading this, if you have some interest in the dynamics of prison education, you may have noticed another figure in the scene—namely, the one who gets the lessons started. In Douglass, it is the paranoid mistress, so intoxicated by her power over the enslaved child that she becomes his relentless pursuer. In Reed, it is the schoolteacher who finds himself in the absurd position of punishing a student for reading too much. Both educators bring the rudiments of literacy to captives, and both see it turned to unexpected purposes, against their own authority. Such, in the tradition of literature from America's plantations and prisons, are our spiritual ancestors.

Douglass and Reed tell stories of their own self-education within institutions that would constrain their minds. To stage their dramas of stark antagonism, they align their teachers with the enforcement of ignorance and social death. Douglass's mistress becomes an agent of surveillance. Reed's schoolmaster doesn't teach at all; he puts down his pencil and picks up a rod, like an ordinary guard, to punish disobedience. Most of us who teach in prisons now, I imagine, would not like to think about our work this way. We would like to see ourselves as taking our students' side against the system that holds them. To the degree that prisons really do enforce a condition of social death and mental incapacitation, our teaching is an intervention against its designs. But the penal system is complex and heterogeneous. It has several, sometimes contradictory programs for the bodies and souls that it locks away. Our students are ensnared in its paradoxes, and so are we.

Defenses of prison education, crafted for administrators or funding agencies, tend not to pose fundamental questions about legitimacy. They accommodate the common sense of a system that many of us, in our hearts, would like to undermine. (In this way, they are a little like defenses of the humanities, whose pitch intensifies as the budgets dwindle.) It is said, for instance, that prison education brings about rehabilitation and cuts down on recidivism. As a matter of social scientific fact, the proposition does appear to have some validity. To think about our work this way, though, is to conceive of it as something other than resistance. Conscripted into the mission of reform, educators in prison become agents of social control, promising to make the institution more efficient in preventing future crimes.

The paradoxes of prison education are with us even before we make such public statements. They shape the very labors and the intimacies of the classroom. And they may become most vivid, most intense, when our topics are writing and the arts of expression. There is a strong temptation to describe this work in heroic terms—to paint a picture where the writing teacher enables incarcerated students to find their voices and speak out against the forces that would silence them. Pedagogy is the cultivation of humanity, even a kind of liberation.

But is it true that the penal system enforces a rule of silence? Does it not also demand, at every turn, that prisoners speak? Confessions, testimony, letters to judges and parole boards: these are some of its genres of first-person expression. They constitute in speech or writing the willful subject who can be held responsible and punished. "I was sure to be suspected . . . , and was at once called *to give an account of myself*" (Douglass 1845, 38, emphasis in the original). Douglass, nineteenth-century America's greatest autobiographer, had special insight into the dilemmas of first-person narrative; he remembered that some of his earliest first-person stories had been delivered out of compulsion, under the threat of punishment.

When we teach writing in prison, we are teaching other genres, other modes, and we may prefer not to see ourselves as figures of disciplinary authority. Part of the learning our students have to do is *unlearning*: setting aside habits—cultivated, sometimes, for very good reasons—of mistrust and self-restraint. We are not asking for confessions, but we can be heard to say that our task is to open up a space or provide a platform for our students to speak in their own voices. Such metaphors can make it sound as if we would prefer to disappear, to become little more than the free channels of their expression.

In the end, though, what the essays in this important volume show is how much thought and work it takes to teach writing in prison. They present a range of arguments and case studies, each animated by its own pedagogical philosophy. Along the way, the contributors take responsibility for their own authority, and they demonstrate that teaching incarcerated students (like teaching other students) means much more than simply allowing them to speak without restraint. It is not a matter of stepping outside discipline into free expression. The project instead is to grasp new rules and master new forms. Writing is its own discipline, and our classrooms in prisons are arenas of its instruction and practice.

References

Douglass, Frederick. 1845. *Narrative of the Life of Frederick Douglass.* Boston: Anti-Slavery Office.

Reed, Austin. [1858] 2016. *The Life and Adventures of a Haunted Convict.* Edited by Caleb Smith. New York: Random House.

Acknowledgments

Joe Lockard thanks Jianhua Zhang and Talia for their love, tenderness, and care; Jessica and David for sharing life's journey; his brother, David, and family—Adam, Noah, and Hannah—for their good cheer; and, as always, his mother, Ruth Klein, who began this story. He thanks the English Department at Arizona State University, his faculty colleagues across the university, and the deans and English Department chairs for their support of prison education programming.

Sherry Rankins-Robertson is grateful for the unwavering patience and presence of Neely and Madeline and their constant encouragement and support. She thanks her colleagues at the University of Arkansas at Little Rock and her former colleagues at Arizona State University, especially those in the Prison Education Program. Joe Lockard has been a trusted colleague and friend, and without his tireless dedication this book project and the Prison Education Program would not have been possible. Sherry would be remiss if she did not acknowledge the friendship and the life education of teaching in prisons shared with Michelle Riberio.

We thank Deborah Manion, the reviewers, and the editorial team at Syracuse University Press. We are grateful to the contributors not only for the considerable time and effort they invested on the words within the pages of this collection but also for their tireless dedication to prison education.

We also thank those readers who may be working in prisons or considering how to begin educational programs in prisons. We are grateful to the educational partners in the Arizona, New Mexico, and Arkansas prison systems who welcomed our presence and provided access to prison writers. Last, we thank the thousands of incarcerated writers who persist beyond the constraints of their environments to come to class and do the work.

Prison Pedagogies

Introduction

Prison Writing in a Dark Time

JOE LOCKARD AND
SHERRY RANKINS-ROBERTSON

When we began work on this book, the prospects for higher education in prison were improving. The Obama administration evidenced a policy concern for prison education, even if it was late developing, well into his second term. In 2015, President Barack Obama made a symbolism-charged visit to El Reno Federal Correctional Institution in Oklahoma, the first by a sitting US president to a prison, to press home this concern. At the state level, for different motivations there was strong cross-party political concern over recidivism and promoting education as an effective tool against it. The devastating effect of the ban on Pell grants for education in prison instituted in 1994 appeared to be eroding with a new experimental US Department of Education program.

The resurrected law-and-order policy environment under the Trump administration heralds retrogression. The movement toward renewed federal funding for higher education in prisons appears in serious jeopardy, as is funding for the Department of Education and the social budget. The Trump administration has renewed emphasis on prisons as instruments of state power. There has been a massive and growing roundup and deportation of undocumented immigrants: this requires prisons. Communities of color have endured rhetorical assaults that US Department of Justice policy in favor of renewed mandatory minimums and lengthier sentences are converting into practice: this will sustain prisons. President Donald Trump has stated that prisoners at Guantánamo Bay and other sites will face harsh torture: this involves fresh human rights violations. Private prisons, once in official disfavor and apparent decline, have seen a renewal of their fortunes: this will make prisons a source of increased corporate profit for private jailors such as GEO Group and Core Civic. The nature of US civil discourse itself changed during the presidential campaign of 2016, with thousands of Trump supporters chanting "Lock her up" and Trump promising to imprison his opponent.

The term *mass incarceration* is gaining new meanings. In consequence, the educational and research work that the contributors to this volume do within and around prisons will gain a new and especially vital importance. We represent diverse viewpoints but share a common belief that writing about prisons challenges their power over our lives and US society. Prison writing exposes stories of social injustice and helps us understand what must be accomplished to oppose poverty, racism, misogyny, mistreatment of mental illness, educational deprivation, and many associated causes of mass incarceration.

There is unquestionable public concern and interest in these issues. Michelle Alexander's book *The New Jim Crow: Mass Incarceration in the Age of Colorblindness* (2012) has remained on the *New York Times* bestseller list for nearly its entire shelf life. Our book highlights what Alexander calls the "redesigned" racial caste system in America through massive incarceration for poor minorities (2). The importance of prison writing and teaching writing in prisons cannot be underestimated as a contribution to social justice as the United States faces a dark period in its history.

The facts and figures of contemporary US incarceration, with proliferation of prisons, jails, and different holding facilities, are well known. The burgeoning growth of mass incarceration is equally well known, and though there is a vast amount more to be stated, that story needs no retelling here. Others have already told that history well. Our book sets out in a new direction, one that parallels our own involvement in prison teaching as we began the Prison English Program (now called Prison Education Program) at Arizona State University. As we began educational work in prisons, we discovered that prisons are not only material institutions but also equally a state of mind: prisons are immaterial sites as well as physical walls and razor wire. They contain emotions, memories, and lives spent. All of these immaterial attributes and qualities can be and are rendered into written words.

Mass incarceration has led to US prisons and jails becoming a major network of literary production. Unlike in Europe and elsewhere, in the United States prisons have not been given much regard as sites of intellectual work. In Europe, so the assertion goes, there were political prisoners who wrote; in America, there were only common criminals, and thus there was no American Aleksandr Solzhenitsyn. Such a claim ignores the fact that US prisons produced writers such as Malcolm X, George Jackson, and many more who confronted the racism that criminalized people of color. They read Solzhenitsyn, too, as Arthur Longworth's novel *Zek* (2016), written in a Washington State prison, witnesses. Mass incarceration pushes prisoners to engage with the terms of their diminished citizenship and social marginalization. That has turned US jails and prisons into centers of critical writing, and a need for attention on the teaching of writing has become more evident.

This wave of writing has remained largely invisible in a market economy that privileges the economic value of words. Contemporary prison writing remains almost entirely outside the commercial publishing market, with rare exceptions, such as Edward Bunker's novels. Only when prisons begin to intrude on the comforts of white middle-class life does much attention get paid to US prison writing, as in Smith College graduate Piper Kerman's overballyhooed story of her short-stay encounter with prison life in *Orange Is the New Black* (2010). The expressive aesthetics of writing from prisons places little value on market viability and more on writing as a means of existential statement from outcasts.

Inmates write for themselves, fellow inmates, family members, and teachers—like those in this collection. Too few write for college credit. In the dearth of well-organized higher education in US prisons, noncredit programs organized by colleges and universities have served as a leading means of informal higher education in prisons and jails. Thousands of teachers have entered prisons, many teaching writing or relying on writing practices when teaching other subjects. Yet these teachers have few pedagogical resources that address prisons, writing, and teaching. This collection of essays provides such a resource and begins to establish a conceptual matrix upon which to develop prison writing programs.

Although some might think of prison writing as a romantic pursuit of freedom from confinement, in truth many motivations drive prison writers, and writing pedagogies need to respond to these motivations. In shaping creative responses to students' needs or desires, teachers can find more freedom in prison than in the outside world, an ironic realization that draws more than a few volunteer teachers tired of neoliberal universities. There is further irony that, given the neglect of higher education in US prisons, informal, noncredit education has flourished through voluntary provision—meaning that the subordination of individuals into compliant national subjects, so visible in much public education, has little foothold in prisons. Prisoners are by definition noncompliant citizens. Some prison administrations treat postsecondary education programming as an unnecessary spare part in an educational salvage yard, one better dedicated to mandatory literacy and GED classes. Yet education, in prison or out, that does not provide a horizon has little if any meaning. Good prison pedagogies, like pedagogies anywhere else, offer a horizon of knowledge, the achievement of self-expression, the power and means for change, and hope.

Writing about the work of prison teaching requires experience, and a first-person voice can sometimes be the most appropriate one, but we have encouraged contributors to go beyond accounts of personal experience to incorporate pedagogical practices and theory that inform the teaching of writing in prisons. Narratives from well-meaning prison teachers too often amount to no more than a recitation of individual classroom experience. Such narratives focus on the "heroic" prison teacher rather than on the students and their writing. Self-centered teaching recitations contribute little to useable, transferrable pedagogies that function within prison environments. Finding a balance between individual teaching experience and collective educational direction can be difficult, but the essays here constitute an effort to achieve that balance.

This volume does not champion any one prescriptive approach to writing education. It recognizes a wide range of possibilities whose effectiveness relies on the immediate situation, institutionally determined limits, committed teaching, and available resources. The authors of the chapters in this volume share a belief that writing represents a form of intellectual and expressive self-development in prison, one whose pursuit has transformative potential. These pedagogies emerge from numerous praxis-based experiments attempted by teachers who have sought out the challenges of prison teaching. Writing education works well in prison environments because it translates memories or immediate surroundings into reactive language. The work is portable, although subject to search and seizure, which many of us have experienced firsthand. The work is satisfying for not only the teacher but also the writer as it turns time into meaningful language. Just as higher-education educators cannot make generalized assumptions about university writers, the authors of these pages do not make those projections about incarcerated writers; however, their collective voices offer an orchestra of commonalities in teaching within the confines of prison spaces.

This collection is a compilation of prison educators' pedagogical-situated teaching lore. The text is arranged in three parts. The first part, "Free Writing and Unfree Writers," situates readers in the broad social and cultural contexts of developing prison writing programs. The second part, "Jail and Juvenile Hall Writing," explores writing that occurs in temporary spaces, jail facilities, and juvenile halls. The third and final part, "Organized Prison Writing," offers essays on prison writing programs, past and present.

Part one considers prison writing education in terms of tensions between expressive freedom and absence of physical freedom. The initial essays address the politics that emerge from this conflict. In chapter 1, Joe Lockard treats prison writing as a claim by prisoners on full citizenship. US prisons have been overwhelmingly populated by the working class; mass incarceration has created a reserve labor pool; prison writing is heavily working-class literature. Integrating race, class, and gender consciousness into pedagogies, Lockard argues, responds to the social realities that create prisons. In chapter 2, Bidhan Chandra Roy writes about the WordsUncaged project located on a maximum-security yard of Lancaster State Prison in California. Roy uses reading from Michel Foucault, Paulo Freire, and Raymond Williams to help students imagine and develop practical possibilities to enlarge and empower their voices. In chapter 3, Juan Pablo Parchuc explores Argentinian prison writing and art as sites of confrontation with state and social violence. Using a series of texts and artworks, he illuminates how prisoners challenge dominant legal ideologies. Prison writing, Parchuc concludes, produces tactics and strategies that can counteract and resist penal institutions and their enabling political framework.

Continuing this joint consideration of prisons and social institutions, Ashwin J. Manthripragada argues in chapter 4 that prison and university classrooms differ across a range of institutional attributes but share a common ground in their efforts to produce intellectual freedom. Transparent and participatory methodologies, combined with classic questions of a liberal education, Manthripragada suggests, work well in prison settings. Facilitating a space and voice through which to speak back has also informed the teaching work of Anna Plemons in her writing classes. In chapter 5, Plemons writes against the economic logic that predominates as a programming rationale in mainstream prison education and calls for decolonized, antieconomistic approaches to education in prisons. She advocates for a relational ethics concerned with strengthening communities.

Part two delves into educational issues specific to teaching writing at shorter-stay jails and in youth facilities. Tobi Jacobi opens this part in chapter 6 with her SpeakOut! writing workshop model, part of a prison–university program that has been operating for more than a decade in northern Colorado youth and adult facilities. The SpeakOut! program works to create alternative counterpublics and counternarratives based on prison writing. In chapter 7, Tasha Golden discusses writing workshops conducted for incarcerated young women in Ohio, Indiana, and Kentucky; her text focuses on the pro-social benefits of personal narratives. She theorizes and exemplifies the praxis of group writing and sharing as a means of comprehending and overcoming psychological and social traumas. Authors Meghan G. McDowell and Alison Reed teach writing classes at Norfolk City Jail in Virginia. In chapter 8, they begin with a concept of "false teaching," described as "the deliberate, systemic omission of social identities and movement legacies that pose a challenge to the dominant social order of the US educational apparatus." They advocate for a "fugitive ethics" of prison teaching that seeks to subvert oppressive institutions as well as for a commitment to the abolition of prisons.

The chapters in part three detail the diverse practical experiences of writing teachers and the forms of social resistance they encounter in their classes within organized prison writing programs. These chapters' concerns include what ideologies and limitations inform the enterprise of teaching writing in prisons—in particular, how teaching behind the wire resembles or differs from teaching in college or university classrooms.

In chapter 9, Julie Rada and Rivka Rocchio introduce drama and performance as resistance to dehumanization in prison. As teachers, they have used poeticism and collaborative-writing work to create plays in their Arizona prison drama workshops. Their essay recounts these workshop performances and locates them as a means through which prisoners speak back to their prisons. In chapter 10, using oral history, Laura Rogers reconstructs the work of prison newspaper publishing at the Arthur Kill Correctional Facility in New York State in the 1980s. The prison newspaper, heavily subject to administrative censorship, nonetheless functioned as a useful outlet for writing workshops. In chapter 11, moving forward to the contemporary digital era, Sean Moxley-Kelly treats the American Prison Writing Archive at Hamilton College as a source of teaching texts for prison writing workshops and as a publication destination for the work of imprisoned writers. In the final chapter, Kimberley Benedict considers the usefulness of writing-about-writing pedagogies in prisons. This is a relatively new pedagogical concept in composition studies that seeks to expose students to the scholarly knowledge that informs the teaching of writing. Benedict reports on her use of a writing-about-writing approach in a prison class and its potential benefits.

This collection may serve educators in the facilitation of teacher preparation for teaching in prisons. It may be a useful resource for experienced prison educators. The volume offers a guide for starting new community writing endeavors. Our aim in assembling it was to offer scholarship that not only moves beyond firsthand accounts but also serves as a catalyst for additional prison–university partnerships to emerge.

Several years ago when we were giving a conference presentation, a young woman in the audience responded extemporaneously and passionately to a question from another audience member about how to establish a prison–university education program. "Just do it now!" she exclaimed. She was right. The essays in this book provide a range of perspectives and practical reports on prison education programs initiated by colleges, universities, and prison administrations. Nothing in the book can substitute, however, for the energy and commitment required to bring good education to US jails and prisons. Go do it now.

References

Alexander, Michelle. 2012. *The New Jim Crow: Mass Incarceration in the Age of Colorblindness*. New York: New Press.

Kerman, Piper. *Orange Is the New Black: My Year in a Women's Prison*. New York: Spiegel & Grau, 2010.

Longworth, Arthur. 2016. *Zek: An American Prison Story*. Seattle: Gabalfa Press.

Part One

Free Writing and Unfree Writers

1

Prison Writing Education and US Working-Class Consciousness

JOE LOCKARD

Writing programs in US prisons and jails function under an enabling assumption of political neutrality. The authorizing pedagogical goals of prison writing classes are commonly framed as promotion of individual self-expression, encouragement of literacy practices, or positive activity that will increase institutional security. In adopting putative neutral curricula aimed at achieving academic potential, prison education remains acceptable to state prison authorities. Education centers on rehabilitation and the easily quantifiable outcomes of adult basic education, the General Equivalency Diploma, or vocational training. Rarely do we stop to ask a crucial question: Education for what? We know the answer, repeated many times over: to prevent recidivism. Outside the walls or wire, education can speak to opening freedom; inside the walls, education satisfies demands made by a system that takes away freedom.

Education has been conscripted as a tool for perennially ineffective efforts to prevent the systemic problem of recidivism rather than as a means

I thank participants in the 2012–16 poetry workshop at the East Unit of Florence State Prison for their many contributions to better understanding. The unpublished poem "Ebola" by Jesús Lopez appears here with the author's permission and may not be reproduced. A shorter version of this paper was presented at an American Literature Association conference on May 27, 2016.

to engage with root social causes of incarceration that would challenge a circumscribed focus on personal responsibility. Larger questions of social responsibility do not disappear because of institutional, pedagogical, or personal avoidance. To be a prisoner is to be an element within an anathematized class. To be a prison writer is to be cognizant of this difficult-to-escape reality. As teachers, we address writing as the work of individual prisoners but need to take cognizance of prisoners as a class, of their class consciousness, and of our own class situation and privilege. In a carceral state characterized by general awareness that any unprivileged citizen is at risk of jail or prison, class status and the terms of citizenship are open to question. An enduring difference between incarcerated students and free teachers is an unwarranted assumption. So a prison writing pedagogy benefits from examining the citizenship that we share, including and refusing to distinguish the global citizenship we share with undocumented immigrants in prison.

Prison writing expresses a positive claim on citizenship, the fullness of which has been denied to incarcerated subcitizens. Whether the act of writing from the inside references prison directly, as in Chester Himes's stories of the 1930s, or avoids prison life entirely, as in Elizabeth Gurley Flynn's romantic poetry from the Alderson Federal Penitentiary in the 1950s, it involves an effort to bridge the wire and invoke a common citizenship. It is not the topical content that establishes this claim; it is the self-assertion of a literate civic presence that has not been invalidated or made to disappear. Prison writers may not consider themselves writers. They do consider themselves equal participants in humanity with a social voice not to be denied. Or as California prison writer Shawn Khalifa asks, "Can we write our way out of darkness?" (2015, 76)

In this work of enlightenment, prison writers constitute an ideological challenge to liberal or bourgeois universalist theories of citizenship. T. H. Marshall provided possibly the best-known postwar theoretical model of citizenship as composed of civil, political, and social domains that function together for mutual realization. The civil domain is composed of "liberty of the person[;] freedom of speech, thought and faith[;] the right to own property and conclude valid contracts[;] and the right to justice"

(1950, 10). The political domain refers to voting franchise and officehold-
ing, and the social domain comprehends a right to economic welfare,
education, and social services. Each of these domains is either absent or
severely curtailed in US prisons. Universalist models of citizenship, to the
extent they even address prison systems, usually treat prisons through exclusion from their theoretical paradigm on grounds of social protection
and inapplicability. Fran Buntman functions within this paradigm, where
she writes, "In denying liberty, prisons exist in antithesis to the freedom
that undergirds democracy and democratic citizenship. However, penal
sanctions also represent an important means to advance and maintain
democracy as majorities protect themselves from criminal threats which
undermine security and break the law" (2009, 402). Such positions pass
over issues of social causation and impute primary responsibility for crime
to individual actors, who lose liberties owing solely to their own choices.
Freedom becomes a reified and alienable property that an ill-educated
citizen can lose through bad behavior.

Individuation of imprisonment renders social causation a secondary
issue, not a promising starting point if pedagogy seeks to engage with incarceration as a collective experience. The realities of social causation—
the exact nature of which is beyond the present argument's ambit—cannot
be ignored in discussions of prisons, citizenship, and education to citizenship. Prisons in the United States function as systems that strip away
vestiges of citizenship, to the limited extent that these vestiges actually
existed for prisoners, whose preincarceration lives frequently were characterized by hollow social promises of equal citizenship. Education that
fails to acknowledge prior and probable future conditions of life risks irrel-
evance from the outset. Prison writers are intrinsically unintegrated subjects, those who have either violated the terms of a social contract or never
enjoyed its putative protections. A prison is the bare face of an illiberal
state, often the only version of the state that prisoners from racial, ethnic,
sexual, gendered, or disabled minorities have experienced. To write as a
disenfranchised subcitizen in such precarceral and then carceral environments is to write as an alienated voice seeking to establish self-validation
and to participate in open society despite exclusion and subordination.

Although many critiques have been advanced against Marshall's universalist model of citizenship—those by Iris Young, Martha Nussbaum, Will Kymlicka, Eamonn Callan, and Amy Gutmann are among the better-recognized arguments for disaggregated and pluralistic concepts of citizenship, multiculturalism, and educational justice—it is easily noticed that few of these critiques seriously address prisoners or the conditions of mass incarceration. Among writers on citizenship and democracy, prisons appear more often as a metaphor than as a lived daily reality. The scope of education for citizenship remains limited to schools. Prisons hide in the social background in these critiques, uncounted as educational institutions that work toward other, resistant, noncompliant versions of an alternative *civitas.*

Within this lacuna of citizenship ignored or denied, jail and prison writing and literature establish the assembled voice of a minority culture with its distinct claim on citizenship. It is a culture that controls little beyond its own thoughts and voice, and its voice and words function within the censorship established by prison authorities. Drawing on Julia Kristeva, Agnes Czajka argues that prison citizenship is "located at the nexus of superfluity, abjection, and dangerousness" (2005), 114). Incarceration is an exercise in social purification. Yet although prisoners have been excluded and expelled from society, as Czajka suggests, "they never become completely and absolutely undesirable, for they are never wholly politically and economically irrelevant" (114). This barely retained marginal relevance suggests several derived points for consideration.

First, the continuation of existential relevance is a given of prison writing; otherwise, there would be no impetus to write. Writing resists dismissal and social exile; it seeks to redefine an imposed sentence. One writer from the Penitentiary of New Mexico described this resistance in a succinct poem titled "Convicted":

> The hardest part
> was coming to the realization
> in the eyes of the Government
> I was no longer human.
> > (Aaron 1985, 18)

Second, prisoners implicitly affirming this relevance represent a foundation for the claims of citizenship advanced by prison writing. As a collective presence, prison writers voice positive claims toward citizenship. Third, the social reason for relevance, as I explore in the following section, lies in the role of US prisons and their mass incarceration in defining, shaping, and controlling the US working class. Where citizenship provides a legal paradigm, working-class status specifies the terms upon which citizenship is lived.

In a sociological definition of the term *working class*, we mean those adults and their families characterized by either manual labor or low-status clerical work; rental or low-value homes; low net worth or indebtedness; and little or no postsecondary education. These characteristics are attributes of class, but in the larger sense that we employ here the term *class* expresses an entire historical relationship that, following the arguments of E. P. Thompson, assembles and unifies social events into a discrete consciousness. The working class, the force of production, constitutes about 60 percent of workers in the United States today (Zweig 2012, 4) and provides the overwhelmingly larger share of prisoners. Under conditions of mass incarceration, a comprehensive understanding of the working class as a unified body of experience necessarily includes imprisonment. Prisoners are not a separable underclass but an inseparable element of the US working class. Just as important, prisons themselves are working-class institutions staffed primarily with low-paid prison officers. From a Marxist viewpoint, which defines the working class by the use of labor to produce value, the labor histories of prisoners and guards are inseparable (Thompson 2011). Prisons set the working class to guard the working class.

US Prisons, Working-Class Consciousness, and Writing

Why are prisons crucial to working-class writing? The most obvious answer is that US prisons not only are the second home of the working class but also contribute heavily to its formation. Those who were not working class or poverty class when they entered prison most likely will be when they get out. In 2014, 636,000 people were released from state and federal prisons, an annual number that remained relatively steady over the period

2004–14 (Carson 2015, 9). Approximately 20 million people in the United States have felony convictions, of which about two-thirds have served time in prison or jail. Race matters: black men are approximately 6.0 times as likely to be found in prison as white men, and Hispanics are 2.3 times as likely (Sentencing Project 2015, 5). Bruce Western observed more than two decades ago that on an average day in 1996 "more black male high school drop-outs aged 20 to 35 were in custody than in paid employment" (2002, 526), and that remains the case according to more recent data (Pew Charitable Trusts 2010, 8). Racially driven mass incarceration has only worsened in the past twenty years: it has become a major formative force of working-class life in the United States. If one escapes the cycle of recidivism, then prior incarceration for a felony cuts hourly wages for men by 11 percent, reduces annual employment by nine weeks, and slashes annual earnings by 40 percent (Pew Charitable Trusts 2010, 3). Economic mobility substantially disappears, with a heavy majority of released former prisoners remaining stuck at the bottom of the earnings ladder (Pew Charitable Trusts 2010, 16–17). Much of the take-off growth in mass incarceration came from the "criminalization of the working-class" (Kilgore 2013, 358–62) during the Reagan administration, especially through the war on drugs, police repression in poor urban communities of color, ideological and political attacks on welfare assistance to working-class people, the growth of the school-to-prison pipeline, and more.

Imprisonment is among the severest social disadvantages in US society, and those who have felony convictions or who were incarcerated pay for these convictions throughout their lives in terms of employment, occupational barriers, educational access, and political disenfranchisement. In an economy where nearly 15 percent of the US population—or more than 46 million people—remain below the poverty line (US Census Bureau 2015, 12–14) and the greatest job growth is in low-skill, poverty-level jobs (US Department of Labor 2016, table 1.4), the future for most released prisoners is clear. Their tenure in the free working class likely will be short, and they will recycle through a massive county and local jail population of some 650,000 held in pretrial detention, unable to meet bail owing to poverty (Rabuy and Kopf 2016). Jails and prisons are exchange sites where free-world labor becomes unfree labor, often at the service of prison industries. The US prison class and working class today are interchangeable and function in a circular labor economy. Prisoners do not need sociologists to tell them about class, race, and labor. Dortell Williams, writing from California State Prison–Lancaster, summarized the issue: "The truth is, you're in prison, not so much for what you did, but for the zip code you claimed; or the lack of digits on your paycheck, if you even earned one" (2009, 97). The congruence between the prison class and working class is not complete—there are the occasional Martha Stewarts, Bernard Madoffs, or well-off suburban white-collar or sex criminals—but it is overwhelming.

These objective conditions meld together the working class and the prison class. To avoid mechanistic readings of prison writing, we must go much further, toward the formation and expression of consciousness within prisons. Most prisoners understand their current and prospective class status very well, barring the significant population with severe mental illness who are imprisoned. Since their establishment in the United States, prisons have arguably become sites of poverty-class or working-class consciousness formation and consolidation, whether one posits such formation as fully self-aware, emergent, latent, or simply inchoate. Incarceration entails intense awareness of the processes of criminalization and a realization that one belongs to a state-enforced collective identity that cannot be discarded even upon release from prison. In his prison novel *Zek* (2016), Arthur Longworth describes this circle of release, alienation, and reincarceration, where prison is "the reproductive chamber of a malignant, stone-faced bitch who, despite how much her children avowed their hatred for her, was a mother who nurtured them in a manner that compelled them to return" (127). In short, prisons create a prison class. The locus of this class awareness frequently centers on multiple carceral institutions, a series that recidivating prisoners can recite as their social pedigree. A system rather than a single institution conditions this prison-class consciousness. The writing that emerges manifests a strong synecdocal quality, as in *Zek* and other prison novels that represent one institution as the concatenation of many social forces and institutions.

Two brief points from Georg Lukács serve in advancing this discussion of interlocking consciousness between the working class and the prisoner class. First, as Lukács reminds us, "class consciousness implies a class-conditioned *unconsciousness* of one's own socio-historical and economic condition" (1972, 52). For prisoners, that unconsciousness has been in forced and sustained transition since the beginning of their incarceration. In prison, unconsciousness cannot hold. A prison-class consciousness established upon shared status pervades an imprisoned existence, and it persists after release from prison even where parole rules forbid association with other former prisoners. Once released, prisoners are a class forbidden to be a class. Second and crucially with respect to comprehending prison writing, Lukács reminds us that "consciousness does not lie outside the real process of history. It does not have to be introduced into the world by philosophers" (1972, 77). As Ben Olguin discusses in reference to the imprisoned poet Raúl Salinas and others, prisons produce a consciousness that seeks to translate and explain the conditions of subaltern life (2010, 143–48). Olguin argues that "Pinto intellectuals deploy their prison-enhanced oppositional consciousness" (144) in signifying practices that link prisons and barrios. Opposition and its consciousness, however, have different meanings for those inside and those outside the wire. Prison writing reads differently inside and outside prisons. On the outside, we necessarily read through a dialectical awareness that citizenship can both produce and oppose mass incarceration. As free-world readers, discussants, and teachers of prison writing, we stand external to a consciousness of incarceration but function to produce that consciousness through our roles as taxpayers, voters, and citizens. We all are implicated. As teachers of prisoners, we are compradors despite any will otherwise.

There are different participatory modes of expressive production in US carceral systems. To read prison literature is to read about ourselves and potential selves; to write contemporary US prison literature is to write from within and about carceral systems focused on underclasses yet today encompassing ever-expanding social domains. What taking cognizance of Lukács reminds us of, then, is that working-class literature and prison literature share an impetus to transform class consciousness through expressive production. Literary imagination makes that opening and transformation of consciousness available to all, whether we are from the working class or the prison class.

Several relevant questions arise at the intersection of working-class literature and prison writing. How does this intersection manifest itself in the massive body of little-noticed new writing that constantly emerges from US prisons? How do the specific tropes and concerns of canonical working-class literature—such as labor; poverty; and class, gender, or race oppression—find expression in prison writings, especially by African Americans and Chicanas/os, who constitute the disproportionate majority of US prisoners? How do prisons and their social disciplinary threat mesh into working-class writing? What ideas and tools are available to create pedagogies that respond to the needs of prison teachers writing together with working-class students?

With the latter two questions as a starting point, it should be noticed that current working-class literature studies relatively seldom address prison writing. The still-tenuous canonization of US working-class literature, visible in a collection such as Nicholas Coles and Janet Zandy's *American Working-Class Literature: An Anthology* (2006), tends to center on public figures such as Eugene Debs, the near-mythological Joe Hill, and Bartolomeo Vanzetti as representative prison writers. Few if any imprisoned writers after the 1930s get mentioned as working-class writers. Other anthologies, such as Janet Zandy's *Calling Home: Working-Class Women's Writings* (1990) and Peter Oresick and Nicholas Coles's *Working Classics: Poems on Industrial Life* (1991), contain no prison literature. Prison literature anthologies such as Etheridge Knight's formative collection *Black Voices from Prison* (1970) for their part usually have taken working-class status for granted. As for critical literature that engages with both the working class and prisons, it remains quite limited despite great potential. In a recent brilliantly researched essay, Christina Heatherton (2014) calls attention to the radical writings, newspaper publishing, and self-education of antiwar dissenters, Wobblies, Reds, Mexican anarchosyndicalists—in particular Ricardo Flores Magón—African American socialists, and others in the federal penitentiary at Leavenworth from 1917 to 1922. But the norm in working-class studies remains an absent address to prison literature. If, as Magnus Nilsson and John Lennon observe, contemporary

US working-class studies have difficulty treating working-class writing as literary, there is even greater difficulty reading prison literature as integral to a working-class aesthetic (2016, 44).

Why does prison remain so often outside working-class narrative and editorial frames? At one time, this may have been owing to a desire to emphasize the heroic qualities of labor in early constructions of proletarian or working-class literature. But that separation between two literatures is not tenable under the social conditions of mass incarceration, if indeed it ever was in US society and culture. As one early film example of the parallel structures of industry and prison, *Modern Times* (Charlie Chaplin, 1936) illustrates in plot, scenes, and aesthetics how close factory floors and jails were to each other. Bosses and prison wardens were interchangeable cultural figurations.

In the literature of the civil rights movement of the 1950s and 1960s, jails and prisons were honored as sites of African American social protest. Margaret Walker's often anthologized poem "Girl Held without Bail" celebrates such imprisonment:

> I like it here just fine
> And I don't want no bail
> > (Walker 2014, 56)

Traumatic as such incarceration for civil rights protesting might have been, African American communities regarded the experience as honorable in the fight for social justice. Although prisons were central features of African American, Chicano, Puerto Rican, poor white, and Native American lives and disciplinary consciousness from the early nineteenth century until World War II, only with the massive growth of incarceration following the Attica uprising in 1971, the proliferation of law-and-order legislation, the war on drugs, the defunding of public mental-health services during the Reagan administration, the vastly disproportionate incarceration of people of color, and the rapid rise in the imprisonment of women have prisons become structurally inseparable from US working-class and poverty-class life.

This shift remains nearly invisible in working-class literature studies. When in 2005 John Russo and Sherry Lee Linkon announced a "new working-class studies" in their eponymous volume, the issues of prisons and prison writing did not figure into consideration. In the same volume, Paul Lauter suggested that definitional issues continue to "haunt" working-class literature studies and asked, "How do the distinctive *experiences* of working-class communities and their particular cultural traditions shape the forms and characteristics of literary expression?" (2005, 64, emphasis in original). A counterquestion might be posed: Given so many US working-class communities where prison is part of normal life experience and family histories, how did prison literature and arts disappear from view? These genre questions and definitional worries become obsolete under conditions of hyperincarceration. The roles of workers, prisoners, and writers become revolving and interchangeable. US working-class and prison writing now share an organic interpenetration that has gained continual strength from prolonged parallel social processes of class inequality, intensified impoverishment, racial inequality, and incarceration rates in the United States that rise far higher than in any other nation—processes likely to continue or expand during the presidency of Donald Trump. The marginalization of writing by prisoners is neither aesthetic nor political (Nilsson and Lennon 2016, 42); rather, it constitutes an integral part of the structural marginalization that characterizes both working-class and prison literatures.

Reading Class Consciousness in Prison Writing

So far I have discussed the economic integration of mass incarceration into working-class life, especially affecting communities of color; the production of consciousness through both poverty and incarceration; and the absent presence of prisons and prison writing in critical consideration of working-class writing. I want to ask now what it would look like to read prison writing as an expression of working-class experience. By focusing on manifest working-class identity in prison writing, we can employ both class and race consciousness as interpretive keys. To begin, consider these lines from "Poem for My Eighth Year in Prison" by Michael Hogan:

We name a thing and then we know it,
take possession and make it ours.
Poverty, I name you "freedom"
and I am free.
This cell in my eighth year I call "solitude"
and the darkness does not betray me.
The days I call "now"
and do not count them.
There is only one "now" not several.
My past binds the keepers more securely
than me.
It is, more than mine, *their* prison.
                    (Hogan 1976, 11–12)

If we understand working-class consciousness as recognition that a sub-
ordinated social class possesses no less right to claim historical agency
and that its labor makes human history happen, then awareness of individual agency is a necessary step in the establishment of that collective consciousness. Hogan's poem declares from the outset that it is the
prisoner who claims possession of experience and so achieves autonomous self-determination. Hogan states that although tightly confined—he
spent a substantial amount of time in solitary confinement—he remains
an autonomous subject within the prison. The fundamental quantifiable
product of a prison is time spent in confinement, and other production—
prison industries, for example—is derivative. This poem flies in the face
of confinement by declaring that it is the writer, the one who engages in
intellectual labor, who controls lived time and the prison administration
that remains bound by quotidian official time. In the act of naming, the
writer gains structure, freedom, and then power. The poem reverses the
terms of imprisonment.

Hogan's poem does more than provide a statement of individual consciousness. Expanded to a larger scale, it speaks to an adverse relationship
between working-class prisoners and the state. If Hogan transposes poverty
with freedom in order to assert self-determination, however, other prison
writers confront the absence of opportunity and impoverishment that has

defined their lives on the outside. Jesús Lopez, who served a seventeen-year sentence at Florence State Prison in Arizona, the same prison where Hogan served time in the 1960s and 1970s, wrote this poem:

Ebola

What do you take me for?
ebola?
media and politicians
point their dirty dickbeaters
with conviction
saying my name in full—
Pablo Escobar
like I own ships, semi-trucks
and planes
hell no, I walked here
I'm ebola
I'm taking all your shitty ass jobs
that you're too damn proud to do
I work twice as hard
for half the price
so try pointing your dirty dickbeater
at the asshole who hired me
he's a fucken traitor, a fucken sellout
ain't that what capitalism is all about?
I'm ebola
so pick your own fucken fruit
and clean your own damn yards
because I'm ebola

Lopez's poem boils with anger at the racism, labor exploitation, social exclusion, and impoverished futures that await Chicano prisoners as they emerge from prisons. His poem enunciates the terms of a racialized consciousness, possessed by a Chicano who revolts against subordination in a capitalist system that denominates labor according to skin color. The poem contends against stereotypes of criminality used to subordinate

Chicanos, such as pervasive accusations that they are drug dealers—"like I own ships, semi-trucks / and planes / hell no, I walked here"—and identifies with those who suffer labor exploitation in order to live at the meanest level. So although both Lopez and Hogan write from the marginalized status of prisoner, a racial and working-class self-awareness distinguishes Lopez from the more individualistic Hogan. What the comparison emphasizes is how individual and collective voices among prisoners can lead to very different senses of working-class identity. It is the act of specification, accomplished by Lopez in this poem, that opens the possibility of accomplishing more than setting rage to paper. Jimmy Santiago Baca stated about his own writing, filled with Chicano and working-class consciousness, "I used to hate blacks and whites. I used to hate my own kind. I've dealt with that" (in Stahura 2007, 28).

After tracing the poverty-destined lives of prisoners and released prisoners as well as their working-class consciousness and highlighting the inadequate reading reception of prison literature as somehow not coextensive with working-class literature, we are left with the powerful aesthetics of prison writing from its own yard. Those who teach writing to prisoners and are aware participants in the creation and fostering of prison literature ask the following question: How shall we carry forward this work?

Toward Pedagogies for Class-Conscious Prison Teachers

There are many pedagogies for students, but far fewer for teachers of prisoners. An initial pedagogical question for faculty or graduate students volunteering to teach writing in prisons does not concern prisoners but rather the teachers themselves. Why exactly are they there? Is teaching at a prison an exercise in counterhegemonic community education where they fulfill some higher political purpose than they find on a university or college campus teaching middle-class students? Is reform activism attempting to compensate for academic privilege? Or is there some element of desire to be known as a teacher who works at the heroic edge in a challenging environment? To walk in and out of a prison before and after classes manifests class privilege. How will teachers acknowledge and address this critical difference, a life built on class and racial inequalities in the free world that separates them from their students?

Teachers who fail to recognize how establishing questions of class and race function even before they enter a prison classroom are acting as educational missionaries, the charitable emissaries of pseudoenlightenment to the nominally unenlightened. Motives located in an announced passion for social transformation can be suspect. Sharon O'Dair argues that teachers who frame transformational anticlassist, antiracist purposes within their pedagogy for working-class students risk embarking on a project of attempted embourgeoisement (2003, 594–97). Such teachers fail to recognize or appreciate the presence of corrective powers within working-class culture. Some reasonable degree of self-comprehension, identification of teaching motives, and social self-location in terms of class, race, gender, and sexuality are necessary predicates to effective prison teaching. Certainty in motivation, however, is not a prerequisite. When the novelist Terry McMillan asked Richard Shelton, a distinguished writer who has run poetry workshops in Arizona prisons for decades, why he taught in prisons, he could answer only, "I do it because I do it. It's what I do" (Shelton 2007, viii). What Shelton finally identified within himself was a sense of loyalty to his students, one that might be read as human solidarity between students and their teacher. Our responses to this question will almost certainly change over time and with teaching experience, for there is no one definitive answer. What is important is that we continue to ask such questions of ourselves and find motivation in renewed responses.

From another vantage point toward a viable pedagogy for prison writing, we need to understand our teaching work as participation in an historic tradition of prisons as centers for writing or as "a school for writers" (Davies 1990, 3). This does not mean participating simply in romantic appreciation, as in Guillaume Apollinaire calling reason his cellmate ("Nous sommes seuls dans ma cellule / Belle clarté Chère raison" [in "À la santé"]) or according to the unrestrained hyperbole of H. Bruce Franklin's too often repeated claim that universities and prisons are the major competing centers of intellectual life in the United States. Rather, it means comprehending prisons as pushing many prisoners toward self-engagement and social reflection through writing practices, whether in letters, essays, poetry, drama, life writing, songs, or the work entailed in gaining adult literacy. Joy James reminds us that "the 'public intellectual' encompasses the oft-forgotten 'prison intellectual,'" and "the imprisoned intellectual reflects upon social meaning, ethics, and justice; only s/he does so in detention centres and prisons which function as intellectual and political sites unauthorised by the state" (2004, 37). Prison intellectual life can intensify confrontations between the state and its prisoners, just as it can shape a spiritual response to imprisonment. In terms of teachers, James argues that a contradicted relationship operates between "free" intellectuals and imprisoned intellectuals, "for it is the former who usually act as 'mules' or couriers, relaying the messages and texts of the latter. Yet the courier—as editor, translator, publisher, and critic—wields considerable power to influence or alter the text emanating from the incarcerated" (39). Prisoners remain the center of the prison writing tradition, and teachers who displace prisoners through control of writing engage in wrongful misappropriation.

Teachers benefit from being mindful that prisons, which are institutions planned, built, and operated through official writing, are also filled with subterranean levels of writings by prison intellectuals. What had been a relatively thin stream of literary production in US prisons throughout much of the twentieth century became a flood in the post-Attica era after 1971. Miguel Piñero, Edward Bunker, Etheridge Knight, Huey Newton, Piri Thomas, Angela Davis, Jack Henry Abbott, Jerome Washington, and Jimmy Santiago Baca gained large readerships in the United States and abroad in translation (Hogan 2005). Many lesser-known writers appeared in the boom genre of prison anthologies, journals, and hard-to-find, locally printed editions. Writing from and about prisons can and should inform prison pedagogies, and the United States provides a large selection of writers from which to choose.

Despite efforts by prison administrations and state legislatures to censor and limit speech and publication by prison writers (Novek 2005; Sweeney 2010, 35–36; Washington 1994, i–ii), writing from cells and barracks has continued to move out of prisons into the public sphere. An effective pedagogy for prison writing recognizes this history of prisons as sites of intellectual accomplishment, works to facilitate prisoner writings, and calls on teachers to participate in the publication and diffusion of these writings. Such a pedagogy comprehends that the complexities of prison writing have provided sites for self- and collective transformation from unconsciousness into consciousness and for an oppositional force that voices long-accumulated class, racial, and gender anger. Although some argue that US prison arts culture has witnessed an extended decline since Reagan-era budget cuts and the body blow from the cut-off of Pell grant funds for higher education in prisons in 1994 (Bernstein 2010, 173–84), it remains undeniable that today a massive but little-known body of contemporary prison writing exists: we can encounter such works as the *Dirty Tears* anthology from Folsom State Prison; the zine *Fanorama* in Rhode Island and the defunct Chairman of the Bored collective, also from Folsom Prison; and Levert Brookshire's handwritten journal *Celldweller*, written from a supermax unit of the Lewis Prison Complex in Arizona. A writing class in prison constitutes only a small element in the nationwide and global archipelago of human expression coming from confinement. It is writing teachers, those with privileged information access, who can research and draw together available connections within this archipelago and who can help classes locate their own work within the canon of historical and contemporary prison literature.

Given social loathing and fear of prisoners, there exists an undeniable fear of teaching prisoners. One prison teacher writes, "As a survivor of several encounters with criminal violence, including having my throat slashed during a robbery by a gang of teenagers wielding meat cleavers in a New York City subway, I had to set aside my prejudices—and my fears—to begin this task" (Evans 2001, 5). Family and friends often pressure prison teachers to quit, questioning their choice and expressing deep concern over their safety. Risk exists in prison classrooms, as it does throughout society: several years ago a prisoner raped and stabbed a teacher in one of the prisons where Arizona State University's prison programs operate. Security protocols need to be followed to mitigate risk to both teachers and their programs. Teachers represent neutral parties in the guard–prisoner conflict dynamic, and assaults on teachers are exceedingly rare in US prisons (so rare that no data exist). By comparison, thousands of student-on-teacher assaults occur annually in US high schools—with more than ten thousand reported incidents in 2013 (US Department of Education 2015). Fear of teaching in a prison represents a projection of social attitudes, not an evidence-based or realistic assessment of risk. A central objective in prison education lies in the humanization of systematically dehumanized prisoners. That cannot occur where a teacher manifests fear or reluctance to engage students or critique writing.

The absent parity between teachers and students creates a challenge to prison teaching. Student–teacher hierarchies that exist in free-world schools mutate into an insider–outsider relationship in prisons. In prison writing classes, this asymmetric insider–outsider relationship is not a power differential so much as a difference in experience. Because writing is located in lived experience, there exists an experiential chasm between prison students and visiting teachers who function in middle-class environments during the rest of their work lives. A weekly or fortnightly writing workshop that encourages life writing provides teachers with a window into prison life and working-class life before imprisonment, but the words prisoners write for class frame an inadequate simulacrum of lived experience. The pedagogical questions at stake concern not only the development of prisoners' writing but also the development of the politics, culture, and writing that emerge from the lives of prison teachers. Are writing teachers to be vultures feeding off the words of imprisoned students or simply occasional volunteers who take away reports to the free world? The work of prison teaching lies equally on the outside, in passionate commitment to change that opposes the educational deprivations, social environments, and political forces that have created the madness of mass incarceration and its ever-spreading prison system in the United States.

References

Aaron, Titus Edwin. 1985. "Convicted." In *Dog Blue Day: An Anthology of Writing from the Penitentiary of New Mexico*, edited by John Brandi, 18. Santa Fe, NM: Tooth of Time Press.

Bernstein, Lee. 2010. *America Is the Prison: Art and Politics in Prison in the 1970s.* Chapel Hill: Univ. of North Carolina Press.

Buntman, Fran. 2009. "Prison and Democracy: Lessons Learned and Not Learned, from 1989 to 2009." *International Journal of Politics, Culture, and Society* 22, no. 3: 401–18.

Carson, E. Ann. 2015. *Prisoners in 2014.* Washington, DC: Office of Justice Programs, Bureau of Justice Statistics, US Department of Justice.

Coles, Nicolas, and Janet Zandy, eds. 2006. *American Working-Class Literature: An Anthology.* Oxford: Oxford Univ. Press.

Czajka, Agnes. 2005. "Inclusive Exclusion: Citizenship and the American Prisoner and Prison." *Studies in Political Economy* 76, no. 1 (Autumn): 111–42.

Davies, Ioan. 1990. *Writers in Prison.* London: Blackwell.

Evans, Jeff. 2001. Introduction to *Undoing Time: American Prisoners in Their Own Words,* edited by Jeff Evans, 3–10. Boston: Northeastern Univ. Press.

Heatherton, Christina. 2014. "University of Radicalism: Ricardo Flores Magón and Leavenworth Penitentiary." *American Quarterly* 66, no. 3: 557–81.

Hogan, Michael. 1976. "Poem for My Eighth Year in Prison." *American Poetry Review* 5, no. 1 (Jan.–Feb.): 11–12.

———. 2005. "Blind Man with a Pistol: The Evolution of the Modern Police State as Seen by Prison Authors." *Monthly Review,* Dec. 16. At http://mrzine .monthlyreview.org/2005/hogan161205.html.

James, Joy. 2004. "American 'Prison Notebooks.'" *Race & Class* 45, no. 3: 35–47.

Khalifa, Shawn. 2015. *My Bleeding Pen: A Poem Book.* N.p.: self-published.

Kilgore, James. 2013. "Mass Incarceration and Working Class Interests: Which Side Are the Unions On?" *Labor Studies Journal* 37, no. 4: 356–72.

Knight, Etheridge. 1970. *Black Voices from Prison.* New York: Pathfinder Press.

Lauter, Paul. 2005. "Under Construction: Working-Class Writing." In *New Working-Class Studies,* edited by John Russo and Sherry Lee Linkon, 63–77. Ithaca, NY: Cornell Univ. Press.

Longworth, Arthur. 2016. *Zek: An American Prison Story.* Seattle: Gabalfa Press.

Lukács, Georg. 1972. *History and Class Consciousness.* London: Merlin Press.

Marshall, T. H. 1950. *Citizens and Social Class and Other Essays.* Cambridge: Cambridge Univ. Press.

Nilsson, Magnus, and John Lennon. 2016. "Defining Working-Class Literature(s): A Comparative Approach between U.S. Working-Class Studies and Swedish Literary History." *New Proposals* 8:39–46.

Novek, Eleanor. 2005. "'The Devil's Bargain': Censorship, Identity, and the Promise of Empowerment at a Prison Newspaper." *Journalism* 6, no. 1 (Feb.): 5–23.

O'Dair, Sharon. 2003. "Class Work: Site of Egalitarian Activism or Site of Embourgeoisement?" *College English* 65, no. 6 (July): 593–606.

Olguin, Ben V. 2010. *La Pinta: Chicana/o Prisoner Literature, Culture, and Politics*. Austin: Univ. of Texas Press.

Oresick, Peter, and Nicholas Coles, eds. 1991. *Working Classics: Poems on Industrial Life*. Urbana-Champaign, IL: Illini Books.

Pew Charitable Trusts. 2010. *Collateral Costs: Incarceration's Effect on Economic Mobility*. Washington, DC: Pew Charitable Trusts.

Rabuy, Bernadette, and Daniel Kopf. 2016. *Detaining the Poor: How Money Bail Perpetuates an Endless Cycle of Poverty and Jail Time*. Washington, DC: Prison Policy Initiative. At http://www.prisonpolicy.org/reports/incomejails.html.

Russo, John, and Sherry Lee Linkon, eds. 2005. *New Working-Class Studies*. Ithaca, NY: Cornell Univ. Press.

Sentencing Project. 2015. *Trends in U.S. Corrections*. Washington, DC: Sentencing Project.

Shelton, Richard. 2007. "Preface: Hard Ass and the Innocents." In *Freedom of Vision: Voices from behind Prison Walls*, edited by Stephen B. Gladish and Robert Yehling, vii–xi. Wesley Chapel, FL: Koboca.

Stahura, Barbara. 2007. "'I Can't Stand the Comfort Zone': Interview with Jimmy Santiago Baca." In *Freedom of Vision: Voices from behind Prison Walls*, edited by Stephen B. Gladish and Robert Yehling, 25–30. Wesley Chapel, FL: Koboca.

Sweeney, Martha. 2010. *Reading Is My Window: Books and the Art of Reading in Women's Prisons*. Chapel Hill: Univ. of North Carolina Press.

Thompson, Heather Ann. 2011. "Re-thinking Working-Class History through the Lens of the Carceral State: Toward a Labor History of Inmates and Guards." *Labor: Studies in Working Class Histories of the Americas* 8, no. 3 (Oct.): 15–45.

US Census Bureau. 2015. *Income and Poverty in the United States: 2014*. Washington, DC: US Department of Commerce. At https://www.census.gov/content/dam/Census/library/publications/2015/demo/p60-252.pdf.

US Department of Education. 2015. *US Department of Education, National Center for Education, Statistics, Schools, and Staffing Survey (SASS)*. Washington, DC: US Department of Education. At https://nces.ed.gov/programs/digest/d15/tables/dt15_228.70.asp.

US Department of Labor. 2016. "Employment Projections." At http://www.bls
.gov/emp/ep_table_104.htm.

Walker, Margaret. 2014. *This Is My Century: New and Collected Poems.* Athens:
Univ. of Georgia Press.

Washington, Jerome. 1994. *Iron House: Stories from the Yard.* New York: Vintage.

Western, Bruce. 2002. "The Impact of Incarceration on Wage Mobility and Inequality." *American Sociological Review* 67 (Aug.): 526–46.

Williams, Dortell. 2009. "You're Poor and in Prison." In *Honor Comes Hard:
Writings from the California Prison System's Honor Yard,* edited by Luis J.
Rodriguez and Lucinda Thomas, 93–97. Los Angeles: Tia Chucha Press.

Zandy, Janet, ed. 1990. *Calling Home: Working-Class Women's Writings.* New
Brunswick, NJ: Rutgers Univ. Press.

Zweig, Michael. 2012. *The Working Class Majority: America's Best-Kept Secret.*
2nd ed. Ithaca, NY: Cornell Univ. Press.

2

WordsUncaged

A Dialogical Approach to Empowering Voices

BIDHAN CHANDRA ROY

For the men of A-Yard,
California State Prison–Lancaster,
who continually inspire me.

In the winter quarter of 2016, I began teaching the first classroom-based BA degree class offered in a California prison since Pell grants were progressively denied to prisoners between 1988 and 1994. The students were all life and life-without-the-possibility-of-parole prisoners who had earned AA degrees through community-college correspondence courses (i.e., not face-to-face classroom courses). Although the students had previously received little or no formal writing instruction, they entered the class with a wealth of impressive, if unpolished, writing skills. Their hard-earned skills were the result of letters written to family and friends over the years and peer-organized self-help and study classes developed by the men at the maximum-security California State Prison–Lancaster.

We were on Yard A—known to the men, if not the institution, as the "honor yard." Many of the men at the prison were nervous entering the new BA degree program offered by California State University–Los Angeles (Calstate LA) because they had been in prison so long—anywhere from fifteen to thirty years—and questioned whether they would be able to meet the standards of a rigorous college class. They were nervous because the degree program they had thought a pipe dream for years had suddenly become a reality. They were proud of becoming college students; they had told their family and friends about the class and didn't want to let them—or themselves—down. In prison, where little changes across the years, this class was something new, something meaningful, and, as such, a cause of as much anxiety as excitement.

This official BA program at Lancaster grew out of my work with the men of Yard A developing the WordsUncaged project. WordsUncaged began as a writing component of the Paws for Life dog program. It later expanded into a larger project that collaborated with prisoners to develop new writing and literature classes, student writing exchange programs, as well as a biannual print publication and a website that would bring the voices of the men at Lancaster to a wider audience—all of which became collectively known as WordsUncaged. These dual tracks of formal education and platform for disseminating prisoner voices were initially largely parallel projects that complemented each other. From a pedagogical perspective, a significant part of my role was to bring the outside into the prison—both in the literal sense of bringing books into an environment that was largely cut off from the outside world and in the more subtle sense of exposing the men to new academic, literary, and social discourses to which they had previously not had access. On the dissemination side, I initially saw my role in helping to bring the men's voices to the outside world as centered upon procuring resources and facilitating production, while doing my best to be as transparent as possible in allowing the men to speak for themselves: it was similar to the approach Michel Foucault conceived in his work with French prisoners during the 1970s.

As the project began to take shape, however, I became increasingly aware of certain shortcomings in Foucault's approach and, at the same time, recognized how the praxis of prison education provided different possibilities for framing and thinking about prisoner voices. What had begun as disparate pedagogical and publication/dissemination aspects of the WordsUncaged project became increasingly enmeshed. The praxis of teaching formal issues of voice in prison literature classes offered different ways for the students to conceive of their voices and identities, to explore new possibilities of representing themselves, as well as to critically interrogate the constraints and limitations of bringing these self-representations into public discourse.

Foucault's Echo of Prison Voices

Foucault's work with the Groupe d'information sur les prisons (GIP) remains one of the best-known attempts to create a platform for prisoners to speak for themselves, bringing their voices into public discourse. Foucault articulated the group's objectives in an article published in 1971 in *J'accuse*:

> We want to break the double isolation in which prisoners are trapped: through our investigation, we want them to be able to talk to each other, to share what they know, and to communicate from prison to prison and from cell to cell. We want inmates to address the population, and for the population to speak to them. These individual experiences, these isolated rebellions must be transformed into a shared body of knowledge, and into coordinated action. (quoted in Brich 2008, 28)

In this way, the project sought to empower prisoners to speak for themselves rather than have public intellectuals, such as Foucault, speak on their behalf. Foucault envisioned a multidirectional dialogue between prisoners and other prisoners as well between prisoners and the public: a new prisoner discourse in which prisoners represented themselves and that formed the basis for a new form of social activism.

In recent years, the GIP's approach has largely been lauded by critics and understood as a project that achieved its objective. Leonard Lawlor and Jane Sholtz, for example, write that "the GIP re-sounded the inmates' voices, it produced a foundationless repetition, a recommencement of a commencement" (n.d., 20–21). From this perspective, the GIP is seen as successful in amplifying or echoing prisoner voices and in creating a space for prisoner's voices to be heard as *their* voices rather than as the GIP speaking for them. This assessment of the GIP as a transparent amplifier and echoer of prisoner voices is the prevailing view of most research on the GIP (Brich 2008, 27), whose work is generally seen as inaugurating a new form of activism. Cecile Brich sums up this prevailing view:

The announcement that the GIP wanted to give prisoners the opportunity to speak out without intermediary, for instance, has thus been
repeatedly commended as testimony to Foucault's ethics, endlessly
echoing Gilles Deleuze's claim that Foucault was "the first . . . to teach
us something absolutely fundamental: the indignity of speaking for others." Macey comments that: "The goal of Foucault's political activity
was the empowering of others by giving, for instance, prisoners the voice
they were denied." Halperin similarly argues that Foucault "consistently
refused to speak for others, working instead to create conditions in
which others could speak for themselves." The GIP's work is thus generally acknowledged as "the advent of a new form of activism, allowing
someone's speech to be heard directly, rather than speaking *on behalf
of.*" (2008, 27, emphasis in original)

Although this assessment of Foucault and the GIP's approach sounds relatively straightforward and laudable, Brich goes on to identify a number of
contradictions and complexities that call into question this evaluation of
the project. He notes, among them, the project's reliance on written narratives, which excluded a large contingent of prisoners who were illiterate
in French; the GIP questionnaire format's framing of prisoner responses
within the standardized knowledge of the social sciences (and the inherent power relations that come with this knowledge); and the GIP's shaping
of prisoner voices via the editorial decisions it made and the interpretative
framework in which it located them (2008, 30, 34–37). Adding to these
issues, Brich also recalls Gayatri Chakravorty Spivak's critique of Foucault
in her article "Can the Subaltern Speak?" (1988), which takes him to task
for reinforcing the constitutive subjectivity of prisoners as well as for con-
ceiving of the GIP as a transparent platform upon which prisoners can
speak for themselves (Brich 2008, 45).

Beyond these theoretical critiques of the project, what is rather curious about one of the best-known attempts to enable prisoners to speak
for themselves is how little contact the project had with *actual* prisoners. As Brich notes, the GIP was able to communicate with prisoners
only indirectly through questionnaires and documents smuggled into
prison by family members. Although the GIP claimed to have involved

the formerly incarcerated in the drafting process of the questions, the project engaged exclusively with prisoners via written discourse (2008, 30). Nevertheless, despite the textual nature of this engagement, the GIP approached voice solely in a representational sense. Prisoner voices were understood as the voices of subjects who had previously been excluded from direct representation within public and political discourse. What got lost in understanding prisoner voices narrowly within these terms were the formal ways that prisoner voices were constructed through writing in order to be able to participate in the project. Hence, voice within the GIP's project was a matter not only of content but also of form: what was said and *how* it was said.

Tellingly, one prisoner raised this question of *how* something is said—the formal aspects of written voice—in response to the question of whether he had been the victim of censorship in prison: "People don't write much in prison, because of spelling; they are ashamed of their spelling before the censors" (quoted in Brich 2008, 30). For this prisoner, the GIP's line of questioning missed the mark because it failed to recognize the more subtle constraints that prevent prisoner voices from reaching public discourse, bringing to light the GIP's lack of awareness of *actual* prison life. It was not the GIP's preconceived ideas of prison censorship that silenced prisoner voices in this case but rather their perceived lack of grammatical proficiency that prevented them from wanting to participate in written discourse. In other words, concerns and fears over *how* something is said play a significant role in determining who gets to speak. Hence, to empower prisoner voices is not simply a matter of creating a transparent platform from which they might speak (even if this were possible) but, perhaps more importantly, also a matter of understanding the extent to which many have been denied access to the formal tools of written expression that the GIP took for granted. The main shortcoming of the GIP's approach, then, was not its theoretical objectives but rather the methods with which it attempted to achieve these objectives. In theory, the GIP aimed to empower prisoners to *talk* and *speak*, but in practice, because of the restrictive environment of the prison, to talk and speak really meant to *write*.

Voice in a Los Angeles County Prison Classroom

Although the formal dimensions of voice did not factor significantly within the GIP's understanding of it, such formal analysis was something that we considered in the literature and writing classes at Lancaster. Students at Lancaster became extremely proficient in analyzing voice in a range of literary texts and were excited to use these tools in their reflective course writings to think about the development of their own academic and personal writing voices. Students very clearly understood voice within this prison classroom context to be connected with issues of power and the repressive state apparatuses that Foucault highlighted and that one student at Lancaster said denied him a "platform" from which to speak (Stein 2015). Yet as a second student put it, voice is also conceived of as a "writing muscle" developed through the process of thinking, drafting, and revising (Gilmore 2015). Whereas the former understanding is consistent with Foucault's political framing of voice, the latter highlights how voice gets constituted through the act of writing.

As students at Lancaster became proficient with the tools of literary and rhetorical analysis, they came to understand that *who speaks* in a text necessitates understanding how voice is shaped by context, discourse, genre, and a sense of audience. Importantly, students came to understand that the narrator of a text and the actual author are not one and the same. The very idea of the transparency of voice, from this formal perspective, was challenged because students saw written voice as constructed. Lancaster students forced a rethinking of the GIP's original goal of giving prisoners the means to express themselves by recognizing that their written voices are not fully formed products that simply need passage into public discourse, as the GIP's approach implied. Rather, voice speaks to a particular audience with all the entailed grammatical and stylistic choices as well as constraints and exclusions. If we take this fuller understanding of voice into account, an alternative to the GIP's transparency model necessitates creating the conditions in which prisoners might explore new possibilities of voice and expression as well as critically interrogate the power relations that shape self-representations. From the perspective of a prison classroom, one shortcoming of the GIP's approach is that it overlooked many of the complex constraints upon how written voices are produced within prisons. Although these constraints include issues such as censorship, it is often the more mundane issues of educational background, confidence in writing and self-expression, as well as prison culture that determine who gets to speak to a public audience and how they do so.

One problem with the GIP's approach is that although it theoretically attempted to challenge the hierarchy between academics and prisoners in producing knowledge, its method of transparency inadvertently reinforced a concept of the written voice as constitutive rather than constructed. One effect of this oversight was to unintentionally reinforce the power structures the project set out to challenge. For instance, the project's deafness to questionnaire respondents' comments about grammar overlooked how, as Mary Ehrenworth and Vicki Vinton argue, grammar is an aspect not only of language rules but also of cultural norms—in other words, "how knowledge of grammar grants access to power" (2005, 12). Hence, although censorship undoubtedly represents one way in which power is exercised over prisoner voices, as the French prisoner clearly articulated in his response to the GIP question about censorship, normative rules of grammar create a second form of control. The point is not whether the GIP held such views about normative grammar or whether it regarded grammar as an aspect of prisoners' voices that might add richness to the project. The point is that normative grammar conventions did matter *to the prisoners* within the project, exerting control over their written voices through a sense of shame and embarrassment.

Recognizing the constructed nature of the written voice in this way suggests that the GIP's theoretical platform of transparency unintentionally self-selected prisoners who were confident in their writing abilities and therefore willing to share their voices with an outside audience. To meaningfully empower a range of prisoner voices—to uncage their words—requires an approach that engages far more directly with prisoners: one that creates a critical pedagogical space that is dialogical rather than transparent. As Paolo Freire forcefully argues, foundational to the latter approach is the preposition *with*: how to empower prisoner voices becomes a problem to be worked out *with* prisoners (1993, 36). For example, to approach the issue of grammar in prison from a Freirian perspective would necessitate listening to the prisoner's comment seriously and then allowing it to shape the direction of the project: How might *we, together*, address the grammatical issues that silence many prisoners' written voices? This is not to suggest that teachers should then bestow their grammatical expertise upon prisoners by teaching normative grammar in order to empower prisoners' voices—an approach that would follow what Freire famously called the "banking" model of education that dehumanizes students by treating them as objects, vessels to be filled with information (1993, 60). Rather, as Freire elucidates, democratic education means that both students and teachers are open to transformation by each other through the exploration of a common problem. The content of this dialogue is neither "imposition" nor "gift" but an "organized" and "systemized approach to individuals of the things about which they want to know more" (1993, 74).

A Freirean approach toward empowering prisoner voices necessitates dialogue and understands voice as neither static nor constitutive but rather as a state of constant becoming. This understanding of voice is particularly important within the context of contemporary maximum-security prisons such as Lancaster because such prisons are extremely isolated from the outside world and, as such, are exposed to a limited range of narratives and voices: as many prisoners at Lancaster repeatedly tell me, "Prison is a universe unto itself." Within such an environment, not surprisingly, there are hegemonic narratives—on the one hand, those enforced by the institution, such as confession narratives and narratives of individual character reform; on the other hand, those enforced by prison culture, such as hardened expressions of masculine toughness—that are powerfully limiting forces upon prisoner voices and what they might become. The idea of echoing these voices serves to reinforce such narratives and does not speak to the desire for transformation that so many at Lancaster express. But as Freire (1993) points out, "authentic dialogue" means that this process of transformation must act both ways, that the voices from the prison must be able to transform those people working with them on the outside if the project is to avoid the paternalistic savior or charitable form of engagement, of which both Foucault and Freire were rightly critical.

This dialogic process results in an increasing blurring of boundaries between theory and praxis, between pedagogy and knowledge, between reason and affect, between prison students and university students, and between the boundaries of voices. It produced new understandings of voice at Lancaster that in turn produced new readings of texts at Calstate LA. A striking example of this process was when Lancaster students were asked to examine voice in two well-known texts written while their authors were incarcerated—the poem "A WASP Woman Visits a Black Junkie in Jail" by Etheridge Knight (1986) and "Letter from Birmingham City Jail" by Martin Luther King Jr. ([1963] 1991). In analyzing King's text, prisoner-students came to understand how the voice of the narrator and the tone of letter were shaped, to a large extent, by King's sophisticated use of punctuation. They noted in one remarkable passage how King's repeated use of the semicolon produced a particular rhythm and sense of frustration that intensified the content of the passage. They then experimented with using these syntactical models in their own writing, exploring how the humble semicolon could dramatically change a passage of writing and become a powerful tool in the expression of their own voices.

Students went on to explore voice in these texts by reading them from their own subject positions as prisoners. For instance, in analyzing how voice is constructed in both texts, one student at Lancaster, Duncan Martinez, provided the following, particularly rich reading:

> For starters, the Junkie is either a long-term prisoner or someone serving on what many of us call the installment plan. Dr. King, on the other hand, is clearly just passing through. There is a huge difference between the two from our perspective. Years in prison mean a different type of person, whereas the passerby really knows nothing of what incarceration is. There are thousands of things to navigate and languages (or version thereof) to learn in prison. This distinction between prison and jail is huge when we think of voice: most people cannot understand the voice of the long-term prisoner. We are, in simple fact, alien creatures. (Martinez 2015)

When we discussed Martinez's comments in my class at Calstate LA, none of us had considered the significance of this distinction between jail and prison. Martinez's reading provided us all with not only a much richer understanding of the texts (the initial sense of alienation between the Black Junkie and the Wasp Woman in Knight's poem, for example) but also a deeper understanding of how the use of words such as *prison* and *jail* matter. In ways such as this, Lancaster students shaped and enriched our learning at the university.

If attention to voice asks us to examine who speaks in a text, then Duncan Martinez shows that voice, far from being constitutive and individual, is in part socially produced. At the same time, he also indicates the importance of audience and the extent to which prison voices are not heard both because they lack a platform and because they emerge from a context and culture that most people outside of prison have little understanding of. This perspective provides a nuanced way of understanding Foucault's approach with the GIP because it suggests that simply echoing or amplifying prison voices is not enough: voices must also be *heard* meaningfully. For this hearing to take place, prisoners and teachers must be aware of the language and cultural differences between prison and the outside world. This understanding of voice that Duncan Martinez elaborated may be understood through Raymond Williams's concept of critical literacy.

Developing Critical Literacy

Raymond Williams developed an approach to reading and writing about texts that emerged from his experience teaching working-class adults in evening classes in Britain as part of the Workers Education Association (1989, 161–64). What emerged from this experience was a rejection of the F. R. Leavis tradition in which Williams was trained and of which he noted in an interview with the *New Left Review*, "What you were told to do is forget yourself, to forget your situation, to be in a naked relation—but with your training of course—to the text" (Williams 1989, 315). As a corrective to this method, Williams developed an approach to reading literature that aimed to make learning part of social transformation through the development of what he called "social consciousness" grounded in a "real understanding of the world" (1989, 166). Critical literacy is a much more active and dynamic process than the passivity of evaluation, revealing how Williams regarded critical literacy as a method for reading the world as a text. The reader does not escape from the messiness of the social and political world into an aesthetic realm but rather seeks to examine the complex interplay between the two. To be critically literate is to understand how historical constraints and conventions shape both literature and the material world. Moreover, one can understand how literature attempts to articulate desires and social possibilities that have yet to be realized.

Developing critical literacy among Lancaster students played an important role in expanding concepts of voice by offering students new ways of reading literary texts, the world, and their own lives. The importance of this approach becomes evident if we recall that Williams developed it as a rejection of the subservience to the Leavis tradition, in which readers must submit themselves to the rules of the literary establishment upon which aesthetic judgments are made and must remove their background and subjectivity from the process. Prison, of course, is a system built upon subservience, and prisoners are required to follow a litany of rules and orders from the minute they awake to the minute they go to sleep. One of the greatest challenges to Freirian dialogue in prison lies in exploring problems, such as voice, without a predefined answer that reinforces normative understandings. Williams's concept of critical literacy provides a method of reading that encourages students to enter into texts and to challenge the authoritarian structures that they encounter in all other parts of their lives. Critical literacy contributed a tangible way through which Lancaster students were able to use their personal experience to read texts and explore voice from their own subject positions.

Perhaps more importantly, critical literacy is an approach to reading and thinking that encourages incarcerated students not only to use their experiences to offer innovative readings of literary texts but also to use literary texts to produce new descriptions. Much of the force of developing critical literacy at Lancaster came from students using the tools of literary analysis to read their own lives and contexts. As one Lancaster student put it,

It's like we're being encouraged to think about where we would like to go—we are working through the assignments but also being challenged not only to do the assignment but also figure out how it relates to us as prisoners. . . . I really like this focus a lot. A lot of the assignments thus far are calling for us to critically think about who we are as prisoners. It's like us trying to figure out who we are as prisoners and then figure out where we would like to go. (Anonymous 2015)

In this understanding of academic writing, critical literacy and voice are conceptualized as a possibility of both critical self-reflection ("who we are as prisoners") and becoming ("where we would like to go"). This conceptualization provides a stark contrast not only to the banking model of education that is common in much prison education but also to many of the hegemonic narratives through which prisoners are encouraged to frame their sense of self and understanding of the world. These hegemonic narratives frequently include ideas such as conversion (Rolston 2011) and redemptive suffering (Graber 2012) that shoehorn a heterogeneity of contexts and experiences into predetermined forms while privileging individual character over social context.

Yet as powerful a tool as critical literacy is in a prison classroom, it does not address the impetus behind Foucault's GIP project that was repeated by the Lancaster students—a desire to have their voices heard. What emerged from the WordsUncaged project was that the most effective way to achieve this goal was collaboratively as Freirian dialogue, in which we worked *with* prisoners to develop new ways of bringing their voices to the public. The GIP's approach toward creating a platform for prisoners' speech was very much a top-down model insofar as it relied on the public status of intellectuals such as Foucault and Gilles Deleuze and had little direct input from prisoners within this process. By contrast, students at Calstate LA were partnered with Lancaster students for an entire quarter, during which time they corresponded about the same literary texts, read each other's papers, and reflected on commonalities and differences. By collaborating with each other, both populations were able to reflect on the different resources available to students at the university and to students at the prison and to think through how these resources could be mobilized in the service of a common project. For example, one way this collaboration took place was when students at Calstate LA enabled students at Lancaster, who did not have access to research materials, to gain access to the university library and databases via their correspondence. Sometimes this process involved a student suggesting an article that he or she thought might be useful to his or her partner and printing it for me to take to class at Lancaster; other times, Lancaster students would make requests to their partners at Calstate LA for research about specific areas or issues.

For their final projects, students at Calstate LA were required, after reading Foucault, Freire, Williams, and others, to work through the problem of how to empower prisoner voices by collaborating with their partners at Lancaster. These projects ranged from producing double-voiced collaborative poems, which were read at various poetry events throughout Los Angeles, to recording a music album using lyrics from the writing of the men at Lancaster, creating blogs and social media projects, coauthoring op-ed pieces for local newspapers, and producing a cover story for the university newspaper. Many of these collaborations continued after the class was over, creating lasting dialogues between Lancaster and Calstate LA students and producing ways of empowering prisoner voices that I could not have imagined.

There are a number of important differences between this dialogic Freirean approach to empowering prisoner voices and the GIP's attempt to transparently echo prisoner voices. First, technology has changed significantly since the GIP project in the 1970s, resulting in decreased dependence on public intellectuals to amplify marginalized voices. Calstate LA students were able to use a variety of new media platforms, such as Facebook, SoundCloud, and Twitter, as well as various blogs to reach new audiences in ways that were not possible forty years ago. And although the students were, perhaps, not able to reach as large an audience as the GIP, they were able to engage in a more direct, interactive relationship. The advantage of this type of direct engagement is that it does not rely on a central figurehead such as Foucault and is therefore more decentered and egalitarian. Prisoners participate much more directly in the process of disseminating their voices. The concept of transparently echoing a voice produces a rather disconnected experience for a prisoner because it offers no feedback loop and, as such, gives him or her no chance to respond, engage, or understand how his or her voice is being received. Working with university student partners, however, allows prisoners to experience the ways in which these new audiences receive their voices and to clarify, shape, or reframe what they want to say in response. The process of dialogue offers opportunities for Lancaster students to develop their voices in contexts outside prison and, in this respect, provides a method for addressing the alienation that Duncan identifies between the discourse community of prisoners and the general public.

Second, the process used for the WordsUncaged project allows for a qualitatively different experience in how prisoner voices are produced. Students at Lancaster and Calstate LA approached the problem of how to bring voices from prison to the public together through shared reading, research, dialogue, and reflection, which produced considerable transformation on both sides. For prisoners, in particular those who did not have families or friends on the outside who wrote or visited them, the directness of this experience and the significance of having an actual student with whom to collaborate were powerfully humanizing. As one Lancaster student put it, "All of this has led to the re-awakening of my own humanity" (Stein 2015). For students, the process is also transformative because it enriches their own sense of critical literacy with an affective dimension that far exceeds the current administrative frameworks and metrics that measure "high impact." Rather, it is better understood as an "embodied experience of learning that is not predetermined but that rather offers a new 'feeling' of learning" that challenges students to think and read texts as well as their own social context in new ways (Hickey-Moody and Page 2016, 9).

Third, by connecting the pedagogical exploration of voice in prison to the concrete praxis of bringing these voices to new audiences, the dialogic approach achieves not only a deeper learning experience at both prison and university but also new, lasting platforms from which prisoner voices might speak. These platforms importantly offered tangible ways through which the men in the BA program could share their learning with others in the yard via preexisting peer groups and workshops, ensuring that the BA program became neither exclusionary nor elitist but rather an inclusive catalyst for transformation for the entire yard. This inclusivity created opportunities for all men on the yard to explore new educational possibilities as well as continued collaborations with Calstate LA students via work on the WordsUncaged biannual journal, exhibitions, website, and other social media projects. In this respect, the publication dimension of the project proved to be important to the formal BA education program at Lancaster by creating an inclusive environment. The hope is that these platforms and networks will help create pathways into formal education for those at Lancaster who had previously not thought this possible.

The sum of these outcomes suggests that the concept of transparently echoing prisoner voices misses opportunities for deeper, more meaningful interactions between prisoners and the outside world. A Freirean dialogical approach to empowering voices not only enables prisoners to conceive of their written voices as constructed rather than constitutive but also offers a context in which they can explore what their voices might become. At the heart of this process is the collaboration between students at Lancaster and Calstate LA in which shared reading, critical thinking, and correspondence produces collective explorations of how to bring voices from the prison to new public audiences. Such a process is not a traditional mentoring model or a traditional pedagogical or research model. It is not a process *for* or *about* prisoners but a process *with* prisoners. The pedagogical component of the project is important because it enables writing within a maximum-security environment while at the same time addressing some of the formal constraints that prevent many prisoners from sharing with the public. The publication or dissemination dimension of the project is equally important because it offers a context in which peer groups can explore, beyond the formal educational programs at Lancaster, new possibilities of voice together and in collaboration with Calstate LA students and provides innovative ways to bring these voices to public audiences. Both aspects of the program inform and enrich each other.

As the humanities find themselves needing to demonstrate their value in an increasingly neoliberal educational context, the Lancaster students reaffirm the desires and energies that brought many of us to teaching in the first place. They remind us that how we imagine ourselves and others in the world as well as how we express ourselves play important roles in shaping our worlds. As one Lancaster student wrote, "This process of growth as a writer and a human being has enabled me to put language forms that I have learned, as well as the literature that I have read, into an evolving outlook of the world. I feel this intellectual growth has not only changed me as a person, but . . . has also changed what I once considered possible" (Cain 2015).

Voices from prison have much to teach us.

References

Brich, Cecile. 2008. "The Groupe d'information sur les prisons: The Voice of Prisoners? Or Foucault's?" *Foucault Studies*, no. 5: 26–47.

Cain, James. 2015. Unpublished narrative. California State Prison–Lancaster.

Ehrenworth, Mary, and Vicki Vinton. 2005. *The Power of Grammar.* Portsmouth, NH: Heinemann.

Freire, Paolo. 1993. *The Pedagogy of the Oppressed.* London: Penguin.

Gilmore, Jimmy. 2015. Unpublished journal. California State Prison–Lancaster.

Graber, Jennifer. 2012. "Engaging the Trope of Redemptive Suffering: Inmate Voices in the Antebellum Prison Debates." *Pennsylvania History* 79:209–33.

Hickey-Moody, Anna, and Tara Page. 2016. *Arts, Pedagogy, and Cultural Resistance: New Materialism.* London: Rowman and Littlefield.

Anonymous. 2015. Unpublished journal. California State Prison–Lancaster.

King, Martin Luther, Jr. [1963] 1991. "Letter from Birmingham City Jail (1963)." In *A Testament of Hope: The Essential Writings and Speeches of Martin Luther King, Jr.,* 298–302. New York: HarperCollins.

Knight, Etheridge. 1986. "A WASP Woman Visits a Black Junkie in Jail." In *The Essential Etheridge Knight,* 15–16. Pittsburgh: Univ. of Pittsburgh Press.

Lawlor, Leonard, and Jane Sholtz. n.d. "Speaking Out for Others: Philosophy's Activity in Deleuze and Foucault (and Heidegger)." At https://www.academia.edu/2362582/_Speaking_Out_For_Others_Philosophy_s_Activity_in_Deleuze_and_Foucault_and_Heidegger_co-author_Leonard_Lawlor_. Accessed Mar. 5, 2018.

Martinez, Duncan 2015. Unpublished essay. California State Prison–Lancaster.

Rolston, Simon. 2011. "Conversion and the Story of the American Prison." *Critical Survey* 23:103–18.

Spivak, Gayatri Chakravorty. 1988. "Can the Subaltern Speak?" In *Marxism and the Interpretation of Culture*, edited by Cary Nelson and Lawrence Grossberg, 271–314. London: Macmillan.

Stein, Jeff. 2015. Unpublished journal. California State Prison–Lancaster.

Williams, Raymond. 1989. *What I Came to Say*. London: Hutchinson, Radius.

———. 2015. *Politics and Letters: Interviews with the* New Left Review. London: Verso.

3

Prison Writing

Creating Literature and Community Organization

JUAN PABLO PARCHUC

Over the past decade, there has been a manifold increase in writing workshops and projects in prisons in Argentina. These activities are carried out by universities and educational programs as well as civil associations and social organizations. They are part of public policies to promote reading and education behind bars or independent cultural, craft projects. The resulting writing has been published in books, magazines, brochures, and blogs. These publications and activities share a common interest in writing and art as a path for social and political involvement as well as in the promotion of human rights and social inclusion.

This chapter highlights the main characteristics and issues of this writing movement in Argentinian prisons, based especially on the projects in which I participate or am connected to as a teacher and an activist (Parchuc 2014). I examine how state and social violence are articulated through disciplinary frames but are also contested by collective scenes of interaction. Then I propose questions about how these artistic materials formulate the experience of criminal law, punishment, and imprisonment. These questions allow us to think about the importance of teaching literature and writing in prison as well as about the possibilities opened by it. I focus

Thanks to Ximena Federman for the translation of this chapter (including quotations from non-English text) as well as to Silvia Delfino, Fabricio Forastelli, and Diana Tussie for suggestions and editing.

especially on the way these materials, including fictional ones, help record prison experiences and report in their own way questions of legality and violence. A poem, a story, a photo, or a drawing[1] can be turned into records or memories as well as powerful catalyzers of strategies and actions against stigmatization, discrimination, torture, and mistreatment. Art, literature, and education behind bars then become a gateway to coming up with new forms of confronting those problems and creating new horizons.

There are around 70,000 people in prison in Argentina, or 162 prisoners per 100,000 residents (Sistema Nacional de Estadísticas 2014). This rate is lower than in the United States and many Latin American countries. Argentina's incarcerated population has grown steadily for the past two decades. About 94 percent of inmates are Argentine; the rest are mostly from neighboring countries. More than half have been accused or convicted of robbery, theft, or other crimes against property.[2] Around 51 percent are in custody awaiting trial and have not yet been sentenced. Almost one-fourth of the prison population is between eighteen and twenty-four years of age. For those ages twenty-five to thirty-four, the share jumps to 63 percent. At time of arrest, many were or had a history of living in poverty and came from socially marginalized groups.[3] In other words, most prisoners are young and poor.

Most published research remains limited to statistical data on living conditions and characteristics of correctional populations. Reports from

1. For purposes of this chapter, "writing" is understood as not only the written word but also any action that leaves inscriptions or marks in any kind of format or media (paper, film, tape, canvas, walls).

2. Six out of ten women are incarcerated for crimes related to minor trafficking or retailing of illegal drugs (Procuración Penitenciaria de la Nación 2013, 319–29).

3. All statistics are from Sistema Nacional de Estadísticas 2014. Only 7 percent completed high school; more than one-third have not finished primary school. Forty-four percent were unemployed when arrested. Combined with part-time workers, the unemployed account for 87 percent of all prisoners. Almost half have no trade or profession. Fifty-nine percent do not have paid work in prison. Of the rest, only one-third are allowed to work forty hours a week, and very few are paid fairly. In some institutions, they receive no compensation. Eighty percent of prisoners do not participate in job-training programs, and more than half do not take part in educational programs.

the government and mainstream media adopt their own point of view as a valid source of information on prison conditions. Thus, programs that aim at intensifying practices of collective organization to resist these prison conditions face silencing and censorship. As the Comisión Provincial por la Memoria (Provincial Commission of Memory) states,

> Giving credibility to inmates' reports on institutional violence must be an inescapable starting point. This possibility allows a clear positioning in favor of human rights together with the perspective of the persons living in prison. In this sense, we believe that no other actor is more qualified to describe the violence and deterioration of conditions. Although this statement might seem obvious, it must be made explicit since the penal system, and especially the judicial system, downplays and/or undervalues the spoken word of prisoners and their families, in accordance to its own sense of social belonging and the penal accusation that singles them out as "criminals" or "families of" criminals. (2013, 71)[4]

Studies have documented overcrowded and degrading living conditions in Argentine prisons. Worse, there has been generalized and systematic torture, violence, and mistreatment.[5] Torture and mistreatment

4. "Dar valor a la palabra de las personas detenidas como relato sobre las violencias institucionales que las atraviesan es un primer e ineludible punto de partida, que supone un posicionamiento claro en la defensa de los derechos humanos y la perspectiva de las víctimas. En este sentido, creemos que no hay otro actor más calificado que ellas para describir los hechos de violencia y los agravamientos que padecen. Esta aclaración, aunque resulte obvia, se torna necesaria considerando que el sistema penal, y especialmente el sistema judicial, relativiza y/o desvaloriza el discurso de las personas privadas de libertad y de sus familiares, con arreglo a las marcas propias de su pertenencia social y la imputación penal que los sindica como 'delincuentes' o 'familiares de' delincuentes."

5. Complaints and reports are published by the Prosecutor General's Office of Institutional Violence, the National Penitentiary Office, and the Buenos Aires Provincial Memory Commission's Committee against Torture. Some of these agencies, along with the Penal System and Human Rights Study Group at the Gino Germani Institute, Social Sciences Faculty, University of Buenos Aires, have developed a national register of cases of torture and mistreatment since 2010. For further information, see the Inter-American

are not limited to physical aggression but also involve abusive practices such as isolation, inhumane living conditions, lack of food and means to maintain personal hygiene, deficient health care, restricted access to education or work, threats, humiliating searches, theft or damage to personal effects, and constant transfers inside the same facility or from one prison to another.

A look inside this "black hole into which the detritus of contemporary capitalism is deposited" (Davis 2003, 15–16) not only exposes the failures, flaws, and dark side of the rule of law but also questions the morality of laws that by default or omission enable and even legitimize such violence. Allowing people who endure imprisonment to speak out contributes not only to learning about prisons as part of social order but also to resisting naturalized senses of law, crime, and punishment.

From this point of view, those of us who have entered prisons as teachers or social activists cannot turn a blind eye to restrictions or violations of rights we witness or come to know about. We have a duty to report them. But we also have a fundamental task in the cultural battle for the recognition of the voices of those who bear the stigma of incarceration and are discriminated against as "criminals."

Teaching literature and creative writing behind bars is one way of listening and recognizing inmates' voices. Creating opportunities for collective interaction (workshops and outlets) where inmates can talk and where their words get heard and taken into account is part of this task. In these spaces, words circulate, make sense, and have a special value. They are not a mechanism for discipline and control. Traumatic events, stories about institutionalized violence, and personal and group situations get processed and put into words, which works against the isolation and depersonalization produced by the rules and prohibitions of prison life.

Commission on Human Rights reports about prison in Argentina at http://www.mpf .gob.ar/procuvin/; http://www.ppn.gov.ar/?q=documentos, http://www.comisionporlamem oria.org/project/informes-anuales/, and http://gespydhiigg.sociales.uba.ar/rnct/informes -anuales/.

At the Second National Conference on Writing in Prison in 2015,[6] a former convict told how he managed to finally get a judge's attention by writing a letter in verse, requesting him to order the replacement of another prisoner's dentures, which had been destroyed in a search. All previous requests, written in correct judicial language, had not gotten attention or response. After receiving this request in octosyllabic verses, the judge finally responded. This example, of course, is atypical, but it shows just how far learning literature and writing in prison can go, especially in defending rights.

Writing in prison not only contributes to making claims or providing testimony but also helps to imagine other worlds and realities and is a powerful weapon to counteract the "ideological work that the prison performs" (Davis 2003, 16). Considered from that liminal position at the margins of a legal system, voices turned into written works in prison provide clues to thinking critically, aid in communicating and acting on the prison experience, and add sarcasm, humor, and irony to this reality. They can even transform violence into something new, as discussed in the next section.

Uses of Literature

"Your sticks: have become ink for my pen,"[7] writes Gastón Brossio behind his alter ego "Waiki" or "Wk" in one of the poems in his first book, 79 (Wk 2015, 115). Brossio is an advanced literature student at the Devoto University Center, where I teach literary theory and have been coordinating creative writing and human rights workshops for the past ten years. He studies in the UBAXXII Program of Higher Education in Prisons of the University of Buenos Aires. He has already published one book and has five more ready for print: an anthology of short stories, a book of letters, one of aphorisms, another of essays, and his autobiography. He is also a painter, a muralist, a songwriter, and a mentor of an artistic, philosophical,

---

6. Organized by the Prison Extension Program at the University of Buenos Aires.

7. "Tus palos: / Pasaron a ser el alimento de mi pluma."

and literary group that came together in the space known as Pensadores Villeros Contemporáneos (Contemporary Slum Thinkers).

The walls of the university center bear Brossio's lyrics and artistic interventions. The following words from him have been inscribed in red and black ink in the auditorium:

> Breaking metaphor and lyric
> I nurture myself like a lycanthrope
> Tearing apart morphemes and phonemes
> To finalize in empiricism . . .
> Just writing torn apart
> What tears me apart and kills me . . .
> Meddlesome culture in my gut.[8]

Brossio establishes an intense relation between writing and subjectivity that repeats, displaced, the cultural action that hurts him but also feeds his literature. In a recent interview, he explained how literature has helped him to cope with his fourteen years in prison and to rethink his life project (Fava and Parchuc 2016, 38–46). He said that books and painting are not just a hobby but "tools" and that thanks to them he will no longer resort to that "other tool" (45) he knows, weapons, when he regains his freedom.

In a similar sense, Liliana Cabrera—another author who began writing behind bars—says in public readings that she found in poetry the safety that weapons used to give her. She used to stutter except during robberies because under those circumstances a wrong word or an unnecessary delay could cost her life. When I met her in Unit 31 of the Federal

---

8. Rompiendo la metáfora y la lírica
   Me voy nutriendo como licántropo
   Despedazando morfemas y fonemas
   Para terminar en el empirismo . . .
   Solo escribiendo despedazado
   Lo que me despedaza y me mata . . .
   Cultura entrometida en mis entrañas.

Detention Center for Women in Ezeiza, Buenos Aires, she stuttered. Although she could make herself understood, her impediment was obviously debilitating. After she began writing and working with literature, Cabrera stopped stuttering. Today her voice, soft yet determined, is confident. She is now free yet keeps visiting the same prison where she was an inmate in order to teach poetry workshops with the civic association Yo No Fui (I Didn't Do It).

Cabrera's poems have a defiant tone. They are harsh, raw, at times full of irony—a show of her intelligence, courage, and sensibility. They depict situations and life stories mostly in the first person. One of my favorite poems, which I often use in classes and conferences, is from Cabrera's collection *Bancame y punto* (Support Me, Period):

> I was
> all that I was accused of
> and also the reasons
> that you do not know.
> I was the thistle
> the stone in your shoe
> the crown of thorns
> the sword in your side
> the ghost that haunted
> the city
> leaving no tracks behind
> but also something else besides
> the bold letters
> of a file.
> Even though you do not know
> or you don't even imagine.
> I was
> I have been
> I will not be anymore.
>   (Cabrera 2013, 5)[9]

9. Yo fui
   todo lo que se me imputa

The documentary film *Lunas cautivas* (Captive Moons [Paradiso 2012])
shows that a first version of this text was the result of a reading exercise
with a poem by Luis Cernuda from 1933. However, Cabrera's poem has
a completely different tone and temporality. There is no nostalgic remi-
niscence, as in Cernuda's poem, of a past bright adolescence that "undoes
the shadow" and falls "into blackness" (Cernuda 1993, 200). Rather, it reconstructs the past from the remains not captured by moral condemnation
and the law. To demonstrate this reconstruction, Cabrera lets religious and
literary images speak for themselves and defiantly challenges the word of
the other, both the bearer and the person who condemns her, as well as of
legal institutions. She does not deny the accusations but rewrites the words
of those who judge her without knowing the causes or conditions of her actions. She puts that other in a place of absent knowledge, with the arms of a
justice that is neither human nor divine. Her poem constructs a justice we
might call poetic. In the end, she introduces denial as a projection into the
future ("I will not be anymore"), reinventing herself in a script that reviews
and remarks, in a different way, the bold letters of her case file.

---

y también las razones
que no conocés.
Fui cardo
piedra en tu zapato
corona de espinas
lanza en tu costado
fantasma que rondaba
la ciudad
sin huellas que lo identifiquen
pero también algo más
que las letras en negrita
de un expediente.
Aunque no lo sepas
o ni siquiera lo imagines.
Yo fui
he sido
ya no seré.

Josefina Ludmer coined the phrase "tricks of the weak" to describe the tactics of subaltern subjects that change "not only the meaning of [an assigned and accepted] place but the meaning of what . . . is established in that place" (1984, 53). When Cabrera writes, she separates the oral word, based on the law and the word of the other, from the field of knowledge that supports it and then builds on the writing itself. She combines, as do other tactics of resistance, "submission and acceptance assigned by the other with antagonism and confrontation and denial of cooperation" (Ludmer 1984, 51–52). Halfway through that path of enunciation, the subjective position changes. Cabrera's poem shows in a very concrete manner that acceptance of an assigned place does not entail submission to authority but instead becomes an answer, while words are unmoored from their prior context and used for a labor of self-definition (Butler 2009, 261).

Many texts written by prisoners question the failures and flaws of the penal system when the law confronts the individual and his or her history with the mystical pillars of authority (Derrida 2002). The "encounter with literature" (Panesi 2009) opens the door to narrating prison from the inside, widening horizons of self. At the same time, it gives us the opportunity to show the uses of literature in extreme situations.

An Oblique Document

In a poem entitled "Prison," Waldemar Cubillas—currently a tutor of literature and former student of the San Martín University Center in Unit 48 of the Buenos Aires Province Prison Service as well as founder of the Library La Carcova in the slum where he grew up—writes,

> Living anomalies
> reinforce the rite
> impact
> perplex
> the brightness wields
> the taut thread

that comes up
bringing flesh.
                    (Cubillas 2010, 29)[10]

The violence contained in these few lines is disturbing. The poem is evidently an indirect testimony of the violence of prison and its guards. However, it is also an effective vehicle to translate that violence, materialize it in words, and denounce it. We might even ask: *What kind of record or testimony does this type of writing produce? What does it tell us? What does it silence? And what can we read between the lines about the conditions in which that text was written and circulated?* In the cases of Brossio and Cabrera, writing is a tool and at the same time an opportunity for change or subjective transformation acting on the conditioning dominant ideology. Cubillas's poem allows us to think of writing as a record or testimony to the conditions of prison life.

The volume in which this poem appears, *Ondas de Hiroshima* (Hiroshima Waves [Albornoz et al. 2010]), is an anthology of the works of different authors and was produced in prison. It is a handcrafted product: its printed pages were sewn in a bookbindery workshop in the facilities of San Martín University. The cover, corrugated cardboard, painted by hand, without inscriptions, drips with red, yellow, and green paint, and stitches frame the missing title.

In reference to the photos and poetry produced by prisoners held by the US government at Guantánamo Bay, Judith Butler writes that these images and texts "are incendiary as much for what they depict as for the limitations imposed on their circulation (and very often for the way those

---

10. Anomalías vivientes
    refuerzan el rito
    impactan
    perplejan
    el brillo esgrime
    el hilo tenso
    que se arranca y
    lleva consigo la carne.

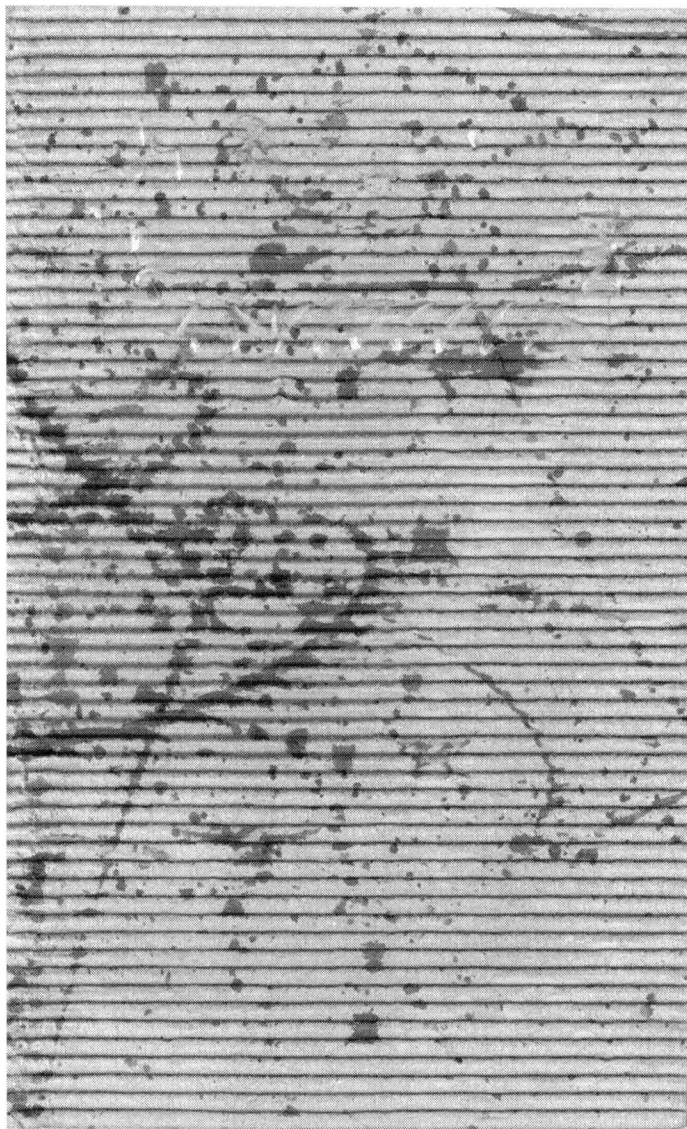

1. Book cover, Ignacio Abornoz, Marcelo Ameijeiras, Fernando Matias Basualdo, Emanuel Benítez Peralta, Ariel Bianco, Mauro Contreras, Mario Cruz, et al., *Ondas de Hiroshima* (Hiroshima Waves) (San Martín, Argentina: Azucena Villaflor Univ. Center, Va de Vuelta Civil Association, San Martín National Univ., 2010). Made in Unit 48, San Martin Prison, Buenos Aires Province, Argentina. Used with permission.

limitations register in the images and writing themselves)" (2009, 10). *Hiroshima Waves* speaks forcefully about the conditions in which it was produced: seemingly harmless to the eyes of the prison guards who see it leave in the hands or bag of a teacher or occasional visitor. The splashes, like bloodstains, tell of its content, just as the stiches—as in Cubillas's poem—refer to wounds or scars. As a rite that is named but not shown, these stitches on the cover frame the absence of words to name the violence that screams from inside.

The stitches try to suture and do in fact keep the book together. They try to heal, to end by picking at the skin, repeating, denouncing, and transforming words into action. The cut or stab marks the wound. In this sense, we might also ask, What do those threads sew and unsew? What plot or scene do they point at, aim at, or make possible once they are written?

When writing manages to escape confinement, when it has not been seized or torn apart by requisitions, it also filters, avoids, and goes beyond frames that usually define and contain the way prison is regarded. The frame that seeks to contain, convey, and determine what is seen depends on the conditions of reproducibility in order to succeed. However, as Butler argues, this process involves a constant rupture with the context (2009, 10). This self-rupture shows the effectiveness of as well as the vulnerability to reversal, subversion, and critical instrumentalization.

> The movement of the image or the text outside of confinement is a kind of "breaking out," so that even though neither the image nor the poetry can free anyone from prison, or stop a bomb or, indeed, reverse the course of the war, they nevertheless do provide the conditions for breaking out of the quotidian acceptance of war and for a more generalized horror and outrage that will support and impel calls for justice and an end to violence. (Butler 2009, 11)

The issue is, Butler adds, not only finding new content but also working with received renditions of reality to show how they can and do break with themselves. That is to say, a taken-for-granted reality can be "called into question, exposing the orchestrating designs of the authority who sought to control the frame" (2009, 12).

In this sense, it is interesting to study texts written behind bars, especially when they move the usual frames, breaking with expectations and confronting readers with images and representations that do not concur with what they would expect from someone who denounces torture and abuses of power in prison. Unexpected multiple windows open.

In December 2015, at one of the trials being carried out for the crimes against humanity committed at the Escuela de Mecánica de la Armada (Navy Mechanical School)—known as "Megacause ESMA"—between 1976 and 1983 during the military dictatorship in Argentina,[11] the prosecution introduced into evidence drawings made by a disappeared prisoner, Lelia Margarita Bicocca, during her captivity. One is a cartoon entitled *Il capuchino*.[12] The cartoon had been kept for almost thirty years in the archives of the National Commission on the Disappearance of Persons. Drawings of silhouettes, bones, and skeletons with shackles and handcuffs came to light with the testimony of survivors. They were rescued and then exhibited during the trial not only to help visualize what occurred at ESMA but also to provide proof of the presence of prisoners at the detention center. For the prosecutor, those drawings were "powerful speakers": they spoke of the experiences of resistance in the prison and were also an unprecedented window into the clandestine detention center (Dandan 2015, 10).

The act of creative writing implies a register not only of the harsh conditions of life but also of alternative experiences that can be imagined and lived collectively. To account for these experiences, Mikhail Bakhtin's concept of an "oblique document" helps explain the interrelationship between the ideological horizon reflected and the artistic structure within the unity of a literary work (Bakhtin and Medvedev 1991, 21–23). This theory considers point of view and the ideological context in which a work of art is produced or read. It also provides a framework to understand the

11. During the dictatorship, ESMA was the largest clandestine detention and extermination center in the country, under the command of the Argentine navy.

12. As in the term *cappuccino* but also referring to a hood (*capucha* in Spanish), a term describing the use of hoods during torture.

conditions and effects of a work as an utterance or speech-act produced in a given social and historical context. The apparently homogeneous sequence of history or society can then be altered according to the staging of the conflict of values and disputes of the language that the work of art absorbed.

If, as Jacques Derrida contends, the guarantee of legality is a force based on a belief and establishes a convention based on repetition (2002, 241, 249), it is therefore not exempt from the critical moment that opens the interval or spacing in which transformations take place, including juridical and political revolutions. Prison writing provides oblique proof of the failure of prison as a place of resocialization. Moreover, prison writing makes us aware that correctional institutions are a "criminal factory" and show the flawed arguments for a firm hand on crime coming from a state that tortures and kills.

When produced in extreme circumstances or by voices on the margins of the law, writing opens a space for experimentation that performatively challenges representations as well as frames,[13] norms, and regulations in which violence develops. Such linguistic actions have the potential to mark the language, affect and produce new possibilities, and contribute to the transformation of subjects and institutions. From a marginal place of resistance, they help to highlight contradictions and questions or at least to disrupt the ideological foundations of hegemonic interpretations of law, crime, and punishment.

Horizons

Prison writing and the circulation of "such mute" voices (Galeano 2012, 16) build a new point of view from which to look at prisons and their contradictions. They provide forms to give meaning to the practices exercised

---

13. Derrida uses the figure of the *parergon* to read Immanuel Kant's *Critique of Judgment*, (un)marking the limits not only of the object and aesthetic judgment but also of the "theoretical fiction" that involves reading and writing as such (1987, 82).

by correctional agents and highlight the excesses and flaws of penal institutions. At the same time, they generate tactics and strategies to combat, counteract, and at the very least resist such violence or reduce its damage. They produce alliances, gain ground, weave and unweave the hidden plots on which the law and its devices of power and domination are based.

To explain this idea, let us refer to a photograph. The image was taken as part of the Light on the Skin stenopeic photography workshop organized by Yo No Fui in Unit 31 of the Federal Detention Center for Women.[14] Stenopeic photography is a technique of capturing images with a homemade device: a pinhole camera—in this case made of cardboard—using 35-mm film. It produces blurry images—a ghostly aura—because of the absence of a lens and the long periods of exposure.

The photograph in question (Cabrera et al. 2015, 11) was taken with a camera made from a Frigate-brand matchbox in the courtyard of Unit 31's education sector. The photo was published in the collection *Iluminaciones* (Cabrera et al. 2015) and was part of an exhibition in July–August 2015 in the Haroldo Conti Cultural Center on the premises of what was once ESMA. The image is a shot of a large section of a bright yet cloudy sky over a patch of grass and prison buildings as well as a booth, a watchtower, and a water tank. The "landscape" is interrupted by an enlarged and twisted grid of wires that frame the buildings. Circles of razor wire seem to cut the sky. The effect of the shot and its subsequent development is that the clouds appear to be striped, and part of the image is "burned," which darkens the sky in the larger section of the image. Below the sky, red spots splash over the lawn and buildings.

Just as in Cubillas's poem quoted earlier, the photo produces an oblique register of prison. The image creates a kind of counterpanoptic that returns the attentive gaze of the tower belittled by the luminous sky, which in turn is cut by bars that frame and restrict horizons as well as

14. For security reasons, cameras are not allowed onto the premises, so only such prison-built devices can be used in these art workshops.

bodies. It silently shows the violence contained in the space of the shot. From there, it talks to us in a way that seems to be denied outside. If the effects of prison imply a loss of perspective, of time and depth, Cabrera's photo gives that loss back to us, transformed into an image. As Theodor Adorno writes, technique allows a work of art to negate the world as a given fact and, in consequence, to negate conciliation as a value (2002, 4–5).

A brief text by Jorge Actis Caporale in the journal *La Resistencia*[15] tells of an everyday situation such as going to bed:

> I dropped my humanity on the bunk where I sleep, my heaven consists of infinite perfectly aligned diamonds from left to right and top to bottom. I can mold infinite ways but none is familiar. The sky is the underside of my cellmate's bed, who surely sees a different sky. Can he form other images?, I wonder. . . . This muddled thinking showed me reality. That was not my sky, it had no stars, moon, breeze, nor the sounds of the river. That is what I miss. (2013, 10)[16]

The story, titled "Estrangement,"[17] makes associations and plays with words and puns. It breaks the Spanish word *extrañamiento* in two: *extraño* (strange) and *miento* (I lie). Again, the pattern of the wires appears to cut out a horizon that is not familiar: the story is full not only of memories and absences but also of the possibilities that Jorge imagines lying in his bed.

15. *La Resistencia* is one of the journals produced in our workshops and published by the University of Buenos Aires Publishing House. For more information, see *La Resistencia* and its sister journal *Los Monstruos Tienen Miedo* at https://tallercolectivoedicion.wordpress.com/.

16. "Dejé caer mi humanidad en la litera donde duermo, mi cielo está formado por infinitos rombos perfectamente alineados de izquierda a derecha y de arriba a abajo. En él puedo moldear infinitas formas pero ninguna me es familiar. Este cielo es el elástico de la cama de mi compañero, que seguramente ve otro cielo distinto al mío; ¿podrá formar otras imágenes?, me pregunto. . . . Este pensamiento confuso me mostró la realidad: ese no era mi cielo, no tenía estrellas, luna, brisas, ni el ruido de las olas del río; eso es lo que más extraño."

17. Like the famous concept developed by Russian formalism (Shklovsky 1965).

2. Education unit courtyard, Unit 31, Federal Detention Center for Women, Ezeiza, Buenos Aires, 2013. Photograph created with 35-mm film and a matchbox pinhole camera. Photograph by Liliana Cabrera. Used with permission.

From the bleak perspective of prison, writing becomes a place of estrangement that does not exceed simple wordplay, a place from which to imagine the future outside and not become consumed by the confinement.

Like all the texts published in *La Resistencia*, Jorge's story was discussed in an open workshop on reading and writing in Devoto Prison. These kinds of workshops are an exercise in and of themselves but also provide training with words. As suggested earlier, the objects constructed in the workshops produce a register or memory of the prison that differs from the institutional one and contradicts the voices of repression. This memory, as Rita Segato writes, provides an archive of specific knowledge that could contribute to understanding and disabling state and social violence that defines and permeates prison (2003, 29).

Writing can be an opportunity to expose a violent culture that silences and imposes hierarchies in the use of the word. It can change an enunciative position as a necessary starting point to recompose subjectivity—not denying the past but reading situations and life stories, recontextualizing and displacing plots and conditions. As we have seen, art and literature can offer an oblique document of the reality of prison and the criminal justice system and propose a new advantage for transformation. This sort of *copy* of reality mediated by the artistic technique taught, explored, and exercised in class is the other side of the naturalized representations of subjects and institutions that make up the grim experience of prison. Participation in the writing exercise opens a new world of possibilities, reprocessing past experiences with the same words and images that shaped it.

Despite such transformational potential, one of the main problems facing written production in prison is the difficulty of preserving, circulating, and giving value and visibility to it. This chapter recovers some of the materials and projects that constitute those archives of knowledge, experiences, and practices behind bars in an attempt to prevent them from being lost or forgotten. For this reason, over and above teaching, we also edit books, magazines, and blogs; compile information from different projects; and promote work agreements to develop mechanisms for cooperation and cultural exchanges with other institutions and social organizations.

In this way, we enable forms of collective production and circulation of knowledge, materials, and educational resources.[18]

Prison writing teaches that the margin is never a limit but a border and very often a platform from which new frames give shape to other worlds and horizons. Teaching literature and writing behind bars provides visibility to events and situations experienced by prisoners. It can strengthen processes of organization aimed at defending rights and expanding social inclusion for prisoners and former prisoners. Prison writing triggers new thought processes, widening the horizons of self. Other worlds and realities come into being. Writing becomes an opportunity not only for establishing claims but also for shaping new allegiances and thereby constructing community.

References

Actis Caporale, Jorge. 2013. "Extrañamiento" (Estrangement). *La Resistencia* (The Resistance) 9:10.

Adorno, Theodor W. 2002. *Aesthetic Theory.* London: Continuum.

Albornoz, Ignacio, Marcelo Ameijeiras, Fernando Matias Basualdo, Emanuel Benítez Peralta, Ariel Bianco, Mauro Contreras, Mario Cruz, et al. 2010. *Ondas de Hiroshima* (Hiroshima Waves). San Martín, Argentina: Azucena Villaflor Univ. Center, Va de Vuelta Civil Association, San Martín National Univ.

Bakhtin Mikhail M., and Pavel N. Medvedev. 1991. *The Formal Method in Literary Scholarship: A Critical Introduction to Sociological Poetics.* Baltimore: Johns Hopkins Univ. Press.

Butler, Judith. 2009. *Frames of War.* New York: Verso.

Cabrera, Liliana. 2013. *Bancame y punto* (Support Me, Period). Buenos Aires: Bancame y Punto.

Cabrera, Liliana, Celeste Moyano, Ana Fernández, Alejandra Marín, Constanza Cantero, María Medrano, et al. 2015. *Iluminaciones* (Illuminations). Buenos Aires: Yo No Fui.

18. One of our most ambitious projects was the creation of the nationwide Writing in Prison Network, with the potential of expanding to the region and beyond.

Cernuda, Luis. 1993. "Donde habite el olvido" (Where Oblivion Dwells). In *Poesía completa* (Complete Poetry), vol. 1, 200. Madrid: Siruela.

Comisión Provincial por la Memoria (Provincial Commission for Memory). 2013. *Informe anual* (Annual Report). La Plata, Argentina: Comisión Provincial por la Memoria.

Cubillas, Waldemar. 2010. "Cárcel" (Prison). In Ignacio Albornoz, Marcelo Ameijeiras, Fernando Matías Basualdo, Emanuel Benítez Peralta, Ariel Bianco, Mauro Contreras, Mario Cruz, et al., *Ondas de Hiroshima* (Hiroshima Waves), 29. San Martín, Argentina: Azucena Villaflor Univ. Center, Va de Vuelta Civil Association, San Martín National Univ.

Dandan, Alejandra. 2015. "El humor negro como testimonio del horror" (Black Humor as a Testimony of Horror). *Pagina*, Dec. 28, 10–11.

Davis, Angela. 2003. *Are Prisons Obsolete?* Toronto: Seven Stories Press.

Derrida, Jacques. 1987. *The Truth in Painting.* Chicago: Univ. of Chicago Press.

———. 2002. "Force of Law." In *Acts of Religion*, edited by Gil Anidjar, 230–98. New York: Routledge.

Fava, Julián, and Juan Pablo Parchuc. 2016. "De este lado y otro lado . . ." (On This Side and the Other Side . . .). *Espacios de Crítica y Producción* (Critical and Production Spaces) 42:15–78. At http://revistascientificas.filo.uba.ar/index.php/espacios/article/view/2287.

Galeano, Julián. 2012. "Continúa la batalla" (The Battle Continues). In Rodrigo Alfonso, Mario Cruz, Walter Díaz, Nicolás Dorado, Julián Galeano, Miguel Gamarra Acuña, José Antonio Gómez Giménez, et al., *Puertas salvajes* (Wild Doors), edited by Pablo Tolosa, et al., 12. La Plata, Argentina: La Fraternidad.

Ludmer, Josefina. 1984. "Las tretas del débil" (The Tricks of the Weak). In *La sartén por el mango* (The Upper Hand), edited by Eliana Ortega and Patricia González, 47–54. Puerto Rico: Ediciones Huracán.

Panesi, Jorge. 2009. "Los chicos imposibles" (Impossible Boys). At http://portal.educ.ar/debates/contratapa/recomendados-educar/donde-esta-el-nino-que-yo-fui.php.

Paradiso, Marcia, dir. 2012. *Lunas cautivas* (Captive Moons). DVD. Buenos Aires: Yo No Fui.

Parchuc, Juan Pablo. 2014. "Escribir en la cárcel: Acciones, marcos, políticas" (Writing in Prison: Actions, Frames, Policies). *Boletín de la Biblioteca del Congreso de la Nación* (National Congress Library Bulletin) 128:67–81.

Procuración Penitenciaria de la Nación (National Penitentiary Office). 2013. *Informe anual: La situación de los derechos humanos en las cárceles federales de la Argentina* (Annual Report: Situation of Human Rights in Federal Prisons in Argentina). Buenos Aires: Procuración Penitenciaria de la Nación.

Segato, Rita. 2003. *El sistema penal como pedagogía de la irresponsabilidad y el proyecto "Habla preso: El derecho humano a la palabra en la cárcel"* (The Penal System as Pedagogy of Irresponsibility and the Project "Interns Speaks Out: The Human Right to Word in Prison"). Brasilia, Brazil: Anthropology Department, Brasilia Univ. At http://lanic.utexas.edu/project/etext/llilas/cpa/spring03/culturaypaz/segato.pdf.

Shklovsky, Viktor. 1965. "Art as Technique." In *Russian Formalist Criticism: Four Essays*, edited by Lee T. Lemon and Marion J. Reis, 3–24. Lincoln: Univ. of Nebraska Press.

Sistema Nacional de Estadísticas sobre el Sistema Ejecución de la Pena (National Statistics System on Execution of Sentences). 2014. *Informe anual* (Annual Report). At http://www.jus.gob.ar/media/3074134/informe_sneep_argentina_2014.pdf.

Wk. 2015. 79. *El ladrón que escribe poesías* (The Thief Who Writes Poetry). Temperley, Argentina: Tren en Movimiento.

4

Freedom within Limits

The Pen(cil) Is Mightier

ASHWIN J. MANTHRIPRAGADA

There are few places outside the prison classroom where teaching critical thinking and writing, especially at the college level, is more exigent. Why work with a prisoner through a poem or through a philosophical treatise? Why teach a prisoner how to write an academic essay? Critical inquiry can serve not just as an instrument for intellectual growth but as a vehicle for improved social interaction. Indeed, any course engaging with critical inquiry in any setting contains the potential to empower students to be autonomous thinkers in compassionate interaction with their peers and society at large. But the prison setting sets up the conditions of unique exigency, where improved social interaction on the heels of critical thinking practically serves to shorten sentences and decrease recidivism.[1]

Further, critical inquiry in the prison classroom serves not just future freedoms but also freedoms in the present. The prison classroom becomes a safe space and training ground for peaceful interaction behind bars. As one student remarked to me, "I learned how to take criticism and not want to punch the guy in the face." I open this essay with

1. Numerous studies explain the relationship between prison education programs and reduced recidivism. A RAND Institute study (Davis et al. 2013) and a Pew Charitable Trusts study (Public Safety Performance Project 2011) are comprehensive. A recent NPR interview distills the information well ("Measuring the Power of a Prison Education" 2016).

a study of the limits and conditions of the prison classroom because this particular epistemological frame determines the kind of education that can and does occur in prison. Although our goal is to re-create the college classroom within the compound and offer students the opportunity to set mind, if not foot, into college, the parameters of prison nevertheless delineate a distinct environment from the college campus. The unique parameters of the prison classroom thus determine education. Naturally, prison classrooms will differ depending on specific institutional differences—state or private, security level, gender, region, funding—and even similar institutions may vary drastically in what they prohibit or allow, but the underlying enforcement of limits connects all prison classroom settings. In this chapter, based on my experience teaching in a maximum-security men's correctional facility in New York State, I explore the technological and curricular limits of teaching in prison and, using social justice pedagogy, present ways to convert these limits into opportunities for intellectual growth. Such limits are impediments to teaching how we usually teach in the twenty-first-century classroom, but the anachronism of the prison classroom—infantilizing and oppressive as it may be—facilitates a site-specific approach to pedagogy, where slow processes of information making and knowledge transfer offer freedoms vital for a population otherwise bereft of them.

Technological Limits

Allow me to redefine the "smart classroom." In this classroom, there are no phones to silence, no Internet to access, no computers to key. As far as writing utensils go, there are only pencils and paper, chalk and a blackboard; the occasional rebellious pen is usually confiscated by a guard. The "smartness" of the classroom is honed through feverish devotion to readings, active listening to lecture, and discerning engagement in debate and discussion. In a setting with such limited access to the diversity of information that a Google-reliant world, let alone a world outside, offers and with students hungry to learn, it becomes ever more imperative that teachers pay close attention to how the limits of the prison classroom shape education.

In *Discourse Networks* (1990), Friedrich A. Kittler correlates the development of systems of writing to the development of possibilities of thought. According to David Wellbery in his foreword to Kittler's work, notational "technologies are not mere instruments with which 'man' produces his meanings. . . . Rather, they set the framework within which something like 'meaning,' indeed, something like 'man,' become[s] possible at all" (1990). In other words, modes of inscription (longhand versus typing) and cultures of reading (reading a handwritten letter from a distant family member once a month versus skimming Facebook posts multiple times a day) determine not only meaning but also who we are. Accordingly, how a student organizes his[2] thought in the computerless setting; how he takes notes and plans out his essay in longhand; how he revises draft after draft without the delete key or the save and copy/paste functions; how he relies on an eraser to remove graphite mistakes; how he relies on ink to pen the final draft; how he reads all texts off-screen, devoid of prospects to hyperlink; how these simple writing instruments are cost prohibitive in the prison setting—all determine the realm of possibility for his ideas and the methodologies of their emergence.

Although one might be tempted to romanticize the technological restrictions of a webless yesteryear, one must remember that the choice to unplug is not the prisoner-students' and may have never been. The forced disavowal of computer technology is in most cases a protraction of scholastic poverty these students experienced prior to lockup. It is a widening of the already gaping digital divide. By barring prisoners from access to technological advancements, correctional facilities are failing to provide them with skills that could keep them from criminal activity once they are released.[3] Thus, with great hesitance I draw out a causal link between

2. Even when my statements may apply to incarcerated students in general, I use masculine pronouns because I have worked only with incarcerated students identified as male, and my observations, reflections, and critique stem from having worked with them.

3. There are no conclusive data to suggest that digital literacy alone reduces criminality. Given the data, the combination of college education with technology education (a combination yet to be examined) would, I hypothesize, lead to favorable results. See Moule, Pyrooz, and Decker 2013 as well as Public Safety Performance Project 2011.

technological paucity and intellectual progress among prison students. Nevertheless, I argue for redemption by means of the processes of slow reading and writing that technological limits require and foster: in spite of such restrictions on notational technologies, prison students produce some of the best student work I have ever encountered.

Some students have special privileges to use a typewriter, a word processor, or a closed-circuit computer, but the hurdles to access are so great that they spend more time and effort procuring the use of this equipment than in using the equipment itself. Once I learned this, I adjusted my own requirements for essay submission. Instead of spending precious class time discussing access to the computer room, I now begin every course with a discussion about notational technologies and how they influence how we think and who we are. This discussion allows students first to vent their frustrations about longhand, the tedium of writing drafts without a computer, and the incapacity to cross-reference (their library is scant save for religious texts, popular paperbacks, and the occasional manual on law). But the very same discussion allows students to embrace the limit of their education, if determinant, and use it for meaning making. Every word a student composes in an essay takes more time to place, and thus he imbues it with decisive significance. Every draft a student writes without the copy/paste function gives him the opportunity to revise from the very first sentence to the very last. The dearth of cross-references affords students closer and closer readings of the material at hand, such that they emerge experts, able to cite page and line number or to recite a quote without second thought when providing evidence to their claims. Handwritten work encourages physical and emotional closeness with classmates because they work together through at times indecipherable scrawls during peer-review activities. They must also withstand vulnerability when they relinquish a complete draft to a classmate, only to receive numerous marginal comments signaling yet another rewrite.

According to my students, sometimes with teary reflection, the sense of family that arises when they lower their guard in the classroom is one they find rarely, if ever, behind bars. In time, penmanship and spelling improve, contributing to overall improvement in confidence. The poetics of limited technology is also not lost on them, especially because many of them are poets and writers of creative fiction. We speak of the sound of pencil on paper and the tactile immediacy of writing what is on one's mind; we joke about the grind of the pencil sharpener: although a useful break in thought for the person sharpening, this activity is often a disruption to the rest of the class. And we agree on appreciating the historical record of collaborative writing as essays are marked with classmates' thoughts.

The dawn of hidden writing[4] is yet to break within these walls (unless of course through illicit posts on contraband cellphones). Given the bradytelic evolutionary pace of technology in prisons,[5] the necessary classroom discussion of the pitfalls of imposed computer illiteracy for a population removed from technological advancement must be followed by a hopeful—and deliberately ironic—embrace of the Luddite sensibility. In other words, in every prison classroom one must acknowledge the technological limit and then reclaim it. Yearned-for technological advancements developing at a maddening pace in the world outside prison will always remain out of reach (barring an unprecedented revolution in practices of incarceration), but the basic tools of language and writing and thinking are in front of us, so we consciously turn our attention instead to the beauty of these simple instruments and the creative potential they afford. To be clear, such an embrace does not mean throwing in the towel in the fight for computer literacy in a digital age. It does not mean complacency in the face of prison reform. It means remaining competitive thinkers even

4. *Hidden writing* is a term derived from Kittler's analysis of computerized writing: "The bulk of written texts—including the paper I am actually reading to you—no longer exist in perceivable time and space, but in a computer memory's transistor cells. The state of affairs does not only make a difference to history. . . . It also seems to hide the very act of writing" (Kittler and Johnston 1997, 147).

5. On exceptional basis, some progressive programs allow access to computers for courses in documentary filmmaking or computer code (Roose and Harshaw 2015a). According to Michael Santos, a former prisoner and prison-reform advocate, "[Prisons] try and keep people in the Stone Age, and they emerge from prison with no real possibility of functioning on the outside" (quoted in Roose and Harshaw 2015b).

in the most challenging of environments. Thus, challenges encountered upon release, such as reintegration into a hyperconnected world, can be faced with emotional confidence rooted in practiced methodologies of patient reasoning. In a report on prisoners' digital illiteracy, a student on the outside stated regarding his education behind bars, "I didn't have any tech skills, but I had bust-my-ass skills" (quoted in Roose and Harshaw 2015a). An embrace of the basic tools of language and writing and thinking means finding freedoms of thought and expression behind bars despite the consistent policing of physical bodies and prohibition on virtual bodies.

The body that remains can think thoughts and complete assignments that are protected from scrutiny by security guards. Even material that may be confiscated is shielded by esotericism: the most radical papers—if in relation to, say, a Nietzschean aphorism or a postmodern feminist sonnet—will likely be returned without comprehension of its inestimable value. In this way, we create within the prison's hermetic seal a seal of our own. And in this space roaring with heated debates, lively discussion, compelling arguments, constructive criticisms during peer review, poetry recitation, project presentation, burning questions, and insightful answers, the restriction to pencil and paper, chalk and blackboard slips into the background like the announcement for four o'clock meds blaring over the squeaky loudspeaker.

Curricular Limits

In order for this space to remain hermetic, instructors must abide by certain curricular limits. We must gain the trust of the prison educational board as well as of prisoners. Limits on course offerings and course content are stringent. Every text that we provide students must be screened, and many texts are censored by the board or are censored by instructors with full knowledge of board demands. The texts that we provide do not compete with the latest Netflix series or smart-phone app, but they become key players in the prison students' day-to-day life, especially because students rely on these courses as gateways to knowledge. On multiple occasions, students have told me that they take the discussion of course texts to the yard or mess hall. They even share texts with other prisoners in the style of an underground book club and in some cases share lessons learned from texts with at-risk children who are learning about the indigence of prison life. The students in my course on philosophical literature were known to other prisoners as "the philosophers" because they would not let go of topics discussed in class. These quixotic reports prove how significant these texts can be to prisoners in transforming the hostility of interactions in the yard and the unappetizing haste of meals in the mess hall into memorable encounters with knowledge. If the texts that we provide are such gateways to knowledge, then it becomes ever more imperative that we, as teachers, pay close attention to our course curriculum. What content will inspire and guide students to become empowered thinkers and writers? What role can textual selection play in fostering compassion, love, and forgiveness? How can the texts we select change toxic behavior? How can the assignments we give embolden contemplative practices of nonviolence? How can our classroom management build confidence in the clichéd belief that the pen(cil) is mightier than the sword?

A successful method of getting prison students to trust in education is to hand them the reins to steer it themselves. As with respect to technological limits, students respond affirmatively to the transparency of curricular limits. I inform students that the course material has been vetted and that certain texts have not passed through censorship. Texts filled with violence, sexuality, and contemporary politics are the first flagged. The educational board explains such censorship as an attempt at reducing volatile responses to known triggers. At the same time, I tell students of the great care taken in text selection. Although censorship does enforce limits, it also places pronounced emphasis on text selection and thereby pronounced emphasis on the purpose of education. John McPeck (1990) explains how curriculum selection is at the core of critical-thinking practice. We are not merely offering skills but adding value to chosen ideas by virtue of the time and thought spent on them. McPeck describes how putting into practice the Jeffersonian ideal of an informed citizenry "capable of making intelligent decisions about the problems which may face it" will inevitably face fundamental curriculum questions (1990, 29). Is it enough to teach critical-thinking skills under the assumption that they are transferable to any problem? McPeck writes:

> Since we could not possibly provide the requisite knowledge for every kind of problem, we are forced to ask the most fundamental of all curriculum questions: what kind of knowledge is most worthwhile for our students? . . . [This is] a question about what kinds of knowledge we consider to possess the most value. Will it be, for example, how to repair one's automobile, or the study of history? Will it be public speaking or literature? These are the sorts of questions that must be faced for education in general and *a fortiori* for critical thinking in particular. (1990, 30)

The freedoms afforded the liberal arts professor regarding course content are limited by disciplinary considerations, departmental requirements, campus-wide requirements and approvals, appropriate class level, and even personal penchant. Such limits notwithstanding, creativity in course content remains explosive. In my prison courses, I begin with a discussion on censorship to reveal that censorship occurs at all levels and locales of education, externally and internally. I share with students the questions that I ask when putting together course content, thus revealing my agenda. Students initially resistant to this agenda learn eventually that the texts I choose and the discussions I facilitate do not spoon-feed answers with moralistic directives. On the contrary, they push students to think critically about concepts ranging from censorship itself to knowledge, compassion, toxic masculinity, and nonviolence. Curricular limits do not prevent limitless discourse. It guides the discourse toward issues vital for their growth.

Curriculum in prison classes is limited unfortunately by much more than course content. Student–teacher interaction and even student–student interaction are restricted. Students finding each other to discuss course content or to work together on assignments outside of class proves difficult owing to cell block location, other jobs and duties, and restrictions placed on prisoners by the occasional guard who holds a grudge against prison education. There are sometimes opportunities to attend study hall, when provided, but the paperwork required to gain this privilege, though simple, is often disordered; students may walk to study hall, only to be removed after a few minutes because the paperwork is not complete, through no fault of the student. Student–teacher interaction is essentially limited to the one 3-hour class meeting per week. Even this class period is often truncated because we must wait for all students to file in. At times, students are "forgotten" in their cells, not released punctually for class. At other times, guards will end class early, with no explanation. Time is precious not only in the face of such uncertainty but also given the lack of curricular scaffolding. There are no office hours. There is no email contact, no way of asking for clarification about "cellwork" assignments (upon student request, we decided to strike the term *homework* from our course vocabulary). There is no remedial help. There is no library staff to help with research questions; no writing colleague to assist with thesis development; no dean or counselor to inquire about balancing personal issues with scholarly pursuits. In spite of these restrictions to the contemporary American college experience, the students in prison embrace our courses as true extensions of the college campus. For those (approximately) three hours, they feel transported out of their confinement, a transportation that has less to do with setting than with atmosphere. Setting is nonetheless important for an uplifting sense of accomplishment: students proudly carry their folders with embossed college insignia on their walk to and from class, commanding respect and curiosity from peers not in the college program.

Strategies for Empowerment

Incarceration in the United States is tied to institutionalized racism, poverty, and classism. Education programs within prisons, many of which are now receiving national attention and support, are helping to break down prejudice at two major junctures: first, within each student and, second, between students and their world. Learning how to read and write at the college level, prison students unmoor themselves from the heavy anchors of internalized prejudice, thereby changing the relationship each student has with himself. Even the unassuming title of "student" is highly prized, awarded only after years of good behavior and a willingness to learn. Students find in the practice of critical thinking and analytical writing a powerful, intellectual form of compassion. They thereby learn to break down institutional prejudice at the second juncture, between student and his world. In learning to listen before speaking and to deliberate before reacting, students develop the critical skills that will earn them respect behind and beyond prison walls.

An instructor's awareness of theories and practices of social justice education can help shape the transformation of prison students into both self-determining beings with a sense of their own agency and interdependent beings with a sense of social responsibility (Bell 2016, 3). Although arrival at the prison classroom is in itself a step toward social justice education, a theoretical grounding in understanding oppression and the conscious effort to create an equitable classroom are necessary factors in realizing greater change, wherein "individuals [are enabled] to develop the critical analytical tools necessary to understand the structural features of oppression and their own socialization within oppressive systems" (Bell 2016, 4). bell hooks alludes to the imperative that instructors in the prison setting abide by when she writes, "Within complex and ever shifting realms of power relations, do we position ourselves on the side of colonizing mentality? Or de we continue to stand in political resistance with the oppressed, ready to offer our ways of seeing and theorizing, of making culture, towards that revolutionary effort which seeks to create space where there is unlimited access to the pleasure and power of knowing, where transformation is possible? The choice is crucial" (1990, 145). If I have made this crucial choice to work in prison education, how can I now rethink my own pedagogy with an eye toward "political resistance with the oppressed"?

As with textual selection, transparency of theoretical grounding is key in teaching practice. For students to feel like and be full participants in their education, they need to know the goals of all assignments and how the instructor's modes of assessment attain those goals. An example here illustrates what I mean specifically by transparency in social justice education. Most courses in the humanities rely on written essays to assess students' ability to process and analyze information. Students need to understand why the essay—with its linear format and academic language and tone and thus coded with power prison students often do not possess—is the mode of writing we demand.

At the critical juncture before a first official writing assignment, I hold a discussion on *linguicism*, "prejudice and discrimination based on language." As Lee Anne Bell and her colleagues explain, "Linguicism, like racism, can be overt or covert, conscious or unconscious, and reflects dominant attitudes and beliefs about the value of and relative ranking of languages, accents, and ways of speaking" (2016, 147). Together, my students and I discuss the role of language in establishing power and recognize how it is used systematically as a gatekeeper. We think through the benefits and drawbacks of standardized language as well as through the problematic processes of standardization. We encounter in this discussion the various genres of writing and agree upon the existence of rules of convention in a world where power is real. One wouldn't open a letter to the president with the greeting "Wassup, G?" or write a children's storybook about the atomic bomb, unless in very unique contexts or with the clear intent of uprooting systems of convention. The effective upheaval of convention and problematic standardization, however, necessitates learning languages of power that are in place. Students have already been made aware of this necessity as they have learned legalese to counteract their disenfranchisement in court. They thus begin to understand the role that rules of composition play, and they learn that after mastering these rules, they can then skillfully break them. In so doing, we are stating that we are aware of the hegemonies of writing practice, are able to enter into conversation with those who hold power, and can create reform through language.[6] Practices of transparency become shorter and are less frequent as the semester progresses because

6. Namulundah Florence states that "Ira Shor and [Paolo] Freire (1987) strongly urge marginalized students to acquire the skill of Standard English, in view of the fact that one's ability to function effectively and/or critique social practices hinges on the command of the English language" (1998, 104). This reading of Shor and Freire, although appropriate especially in the context of a prison classroom, does not account for Shor and Freire's insistence that writers also learn to resist simple assimilation into dominant language forms.

students, who have come to understand instruction as democratic, begin to feel the participatory nature of the class.

If transparency is the first step in creating an equitable learning environment, the next step is classroom management. How can one make the atmosphere of the classroom conducive to open discussion, even heated disagreement? Gradually expanding in-class group work, a methodology I learned from teaching introductory German-language courses, lowers the affective filter, or the set of affective variables—for instance, motivation, self-confidence, anxiety, boredom, alienation, trust—that contribute to student acquisition, processing, and analysis of as well as verbal response to information. To build the trust in the classroom and lower the affective filter, I first have students discuss in pairs any question that I pose, then have them gather in groups of four to repeat and expand upon their conversation. Each group of four assigns a spokesperson to then share the group's findings with the entire class, and then we enter larger class discussion. In cases where the assignment is written work—for example, writing a thesis statement—the members of the group learn to compromise to create one piece that includes input from each person.

This gradually expanding group-work method builds confidence in student participation, provides every student with a sense of inclusion, and gains trust in the classroom as a democratic space. Given such practice, students are well prepared to share their ideas with the whole class, even when called to the front to give a presentation. When students give presentations, or when their ideas could benefit from a visual aid during discussions, I invite them to use the chalkboard. This practice breaks the hierarchical divisions of space within the classroom. During the copious group activities, students rearrange their seats to be able to huddle together over a problem. Such alterations of classroom architecture, perhaps commonplace in a normal college setting, provide the comfort to think without fear of repression. On occasion, guards file past the classroom looking inquisitively at our mode of interaction for clues of disobedience or the suggestion of an impending altercation, only to find peaceful, albeit boisterous, cooperation and collaboration.

Because the structure of the prison impedes assistance from peers or tutors outside of class, in-class collaboration is necessary to raise the quality of the students' work and to afford them the environment to receive feedback. Their intellectual discovery thus grows in response to criticism, invaluable for interaction in any social setting. There are countless methods of fostering collaboration, with peer review among the most useful. Peer review requires students to relinquish control of their work to the scrutiny of a peer. Before our first peer review, we hold a long discussion about constructive criticism: "Don't stop at finding fault; suggest ways to improvement." Students map out each other's ideas on paper, experiment with completing an essay using another student's thesis statement, and challenge each other to make their arguments more compelling. In addition to collaborative work, the occasional shift—at least once in the middle of the semester and once at the end—from content-based work to reflection on general progress helps students gauge their accomplishments, which feeds their motivation for further study.

Reflection also serves as an opportunity to observe the role of critical thinking and analytical writing in behavioral change. Students have voiced on multiple occasions that the skills they learn in these college courses transfer directly to their interactions outside of the classroom. The college course is not merely a means for better chances at survival upon release but also a means to develop skills to survive prison. Some students mention that they have averted fights not just because they want to avoid being kicked out of the prison college program, which maintains strict behavioral criteria, but also because they have learned to deliberate before reacting on impulse. Other students boast about their ability to express themselves diplomatically to prison authority, even when in grave disagreement with them. And all students articulate their joy of reading, writing, learning, discussing, and thinking together on topics otherwise never within their reach. For a few precious hours per week, they are in college, a place our society otherwise forecloses to them both before and after prison.

Exploring the Cave of Western Thought

The final two sections in this chapter share some anecdotes from courses taught in a prison setting. In "Exploring the Cave of Western Thought," a sophomore-level course in philosophical literature, we followed the idea of the "cave" from Plato's allegory to romantic-era poetry, the modern no-vella, and contemporary film. I had originally designed this course for nonincarcerated students, but it won approval for the prison college pro-gram. In the second course, "Writing from the Inside," a first-year writing course, we encountered the writings of Mahatma Gandhi, Martin Luther King Jr., and Anne Frank as fodder for theses on topics ranging from non-violence to social responsibility to agency. After the success of the first course in philosophical literature, in large part owing to the subject mat-ter's resonance to the concept of confinement, I built the second course intentionally around writers who honed their voice in confinement.

I learned from these two courses that a tailored education—a curricu-lum crafted to meet the needs and interests of the student body—brings students closer to the material. They invest more of themselves in their work, thereby revealing inherent self-reflexivity in their reading. Upon observing this self-reflexivity, we work through the distinctions between, on the one hand, personal experience and opinions born from that ex-perience and, on the other hand, critical analysis and conclusions drawn from that analysis. During analytical work, students learn quickly to wear different critical, theoretical lenses to correct the myopia of singular ex-perience. To tailor an education does not mean to pander to students or to undercut a discipline. On the contrary, a well-tailored curriculum can open critical dialogue about issues of immediate significance with the benefit of examining material in other historically specific contexts.

The course on philosophical literature that I developed for young col-lege students effected consequences of unimaginable magnitude when I taught it in the prison college program. We used the idea of the cave to mine the mysterious depths of mind, soul, and being. Our larger inquiry was: What are the multifarious uses of the cave in literature that refer-ence human experience, sensory and spiritual, and how and why does the cave come to represent such divergent themes of enlightenment, freedom, power, sense perception, love, and language? To the prison students, the cave was not an abstract concept; it was neither a thought-experiment nor purely a literary idea. For them, the question of the cave as it relates to human experience was a lived reality. I could write extensively here about student responses to all readings, from Friedrich Nietzsche's *Thus Spoke*

Zarasthustra (1883) to Josh Trank's thriller *Chronicle* (2012), but a focus on two texts will suffice, one that opened their eyes to an important idea and the other that opened my eyes to a fascinating new interpretation.

In "Eurydice," a poem by Carol Ann Duffy, students encountered a radical retelling of the Orpheus myth from the perspective of Eurydice. Eurydice, no longer the passive prize of Orpheus, emerges a feminist emphatically submerged: her verse, addressed to women, is a truth telling of her resistance to resurrection. Having read Ovid's mournful tale and Rainer Maria Rilke's elegiac rendition earlier in the semester, students found this new telling difficult to swallow. Their initial reaction to this poem betrayed their entrenched narrow-minded masculinity, wherein Eurydice is deemed ungrateful, a snooty woman who cannot appreciate Orpheus's unyielding love. Because of their prior careful reading of verse, however, students were able to hold their accusations; they realized that we have always been told these stories only from the male perspective. That realization rattled them. They began to think back to all texts they ever read, even to all interactions they ever had, and realized how narrow their views have been on matters where the female perspective was conveniently forgotten, drowned out, or replaced. As the students began to see the violence of androcentricism, they found solidarity with feminism.

On the first page of Franz Kafka's novella *Metamorphosis*, Gregor Samsa wakes up a creature writhing on its armored back, bemused, before it a flurry of wriggling legs. It is less Samsa's inexplicably sudden transformation from ordinary man to extraordinary creature than the gradual tragic consequence of this transformation that emblematizes Kafka's story as modernist fiction in response to bureaucratic capitalism: Samsa can no longer work and is rendered useless. When I brought this story into the prison classroom—a story that has more interpretations than Samsa has wriggling legs—I did not expect to encounter a radical new reading. The students unanimously understood Samsa's condition as equivalent to the prisoner's. They extended the allegory across Samsa's confinement to his room, his unintelligible screeching voice, and the insufferable relationship he endures with the external world. They argued that once placed behind bars, a prisoner wakes up, like Samsa, transformed into a monster, an unforgivable pariah. Even upon a prisoner's release, his voice will be unintelligible, his relationships will have worn thin, and he will struggle to find work, food to eat, a place to live, and a place to call home. According to much Kafka scholarship, Samsa's tragic uselessness to a world of commerce is an appropriate critique of twentieth-century modern bureaucracy. But the enduring stigma of his creatureliness, which prevents him from any kind of socialization, is, for these particular students, the real tragedy, and they see the story as a critique of systems, not only bureaucratic, that continue to fail them.

Writing from the Inside

The course "Writing from the Inside" drew upon traditions of nonviolence intersecting with rhetorical genius. Although it is perhaps cliché to work with the writings of Mahatma Gandhi, Martin Luther King Jr., and Anne Frank, I was insistent that revisiting popular cultural figures with a critical lens could rebuild students' frameworks of engagement with them. I wanted students to interrogate cultural heroes. What literature did these figures produce that made them heroes? How did they come to represent or secure revolutions for marginalized groups? How integral to these heroes' discourse was critical thinking through writing? In what ways do we, can we, should we challenge these heroes' infallibility? Intended to inspire emulation and critique at once, these questions informed our written engagement with Gandhi's famous speeches, King's "Letter from Birmingham City Jail," and Anne Frank's *The Diary of a Young Girl*.

I intentionally saved our reading of *The Diary of a Young Girl* for the end of our course. No student in this course had read it before, nor were they excited to read it now. Although this diary of a young girl initially posed a noteworthy trial to this group of adult men, it compelled them to follow how this girl's maturation into womanhood paralleled her maturation as a writer. As a result, students began to draw inspiration from an unlikely source. A text that at first glance promised at best to be a reductive account of the atrocities of World War II became a strange mirror to their own plight of marginalization. The empathy that students had for Anne in her annex was remarkable, precisely because that empathy was drawn through the appreciation of her writing.

At first, Anne's writing is unsophisticated and unequivocally judgmental, but as her living quarters close in upon her and as her options narrow, she becomes more discerning about her environment. She becomes an expert writer able to weave together turbulent developments within her body with domestic strife in the annex and the political nightmare in the Third Reich. Her diary becomes a testament to the doggedness of reflection through writing and to the critical development of ideas through the composition of words. Students thus began to fall into the world of Anne's confinement and to draw inspiration from her as a writer. Reading Anne's diary in such a way as to highlight her rhetorical genius changed their minds, on the one hand, about their mistaken assumptions regarding young female writers and, on the other hand, about their mistaken assumptions about themselves as writers.

Conclusion

As teachers in the prison setting, we encounter prisoners foremost as students. We teach them to see themselves as serving out more than their sentence. If we, as bell hooks would assert, *engage* our pedagogy with transparent and participatory methodologies, then we can better provide our students with the intellectual confidence to fight against oppression. In the collaborative environment, we also help them nurture a selfless fight against oppression where they learn to align themselves in solidarity with other oppressed groups. In this way, with freedom of thought inalienable, we remind them that they can change how they see themselves and their role in society and how instrumental critical inquiry can be a tool in that process of change.

References

Bell, Lee Anne. 2016. "Theoretical Foundations for Social Justice Education." In *Teaching for Diversity and Social Justice*, 3rd ed., edited by Maurianne Adams and Lee Anne Bell, 3–26. New York: Routledge.
Bell, Lee Anne, Michael S. Funk, Khyati Y. Joshi, and Marjorie Valdivia. 2016. "Racism and White Privilege." In *Teaching for Diversity and Social Justice*,

3rd ed., edited by Maurianne Adams and Lee Anne Bell, 133–82. New York: Routledge.

Davis, Lois M., Robert Bozick, Jennifer L. Steele, Jessica Saunders, and Jeremy N. V. Miles. 2013. *Evaluating the Effectiveness of Correctional Education*. Santa Monica, CA: RAND Corporation. At http://www.rand.org/pubs /research_reports/RR266.html.

Florence, Namulundah. 1998. *Bell Hooks' Engaged Pedagogy: A Transgressive Education for Critical Consciousness*. Westport, CT: Praeger.

hooks, bell. 1990. *Yearning: Race, Gender, and Cultural Politics*. Boston: Consortium.

Kittler, Friedrich A. 1990. *Discourse Networks 1800/1900*. Stanford, CA: Stanford Univ. Press.

Kittler, Friedrich A., and John Johnston. 1997. "There Is No Software." In *Literature, Media, Information Systems: Essays*, 147–55. Amsterdam: GB Arts International.

McPeck, John E. 1990. *Teaching Critical Thinking: Dialogue and Dialectic*. New York: Routledge.

"Measuring the Power of a Prison Education." 2016. NPR, July 31. At http://www .npr.org/sections/ed/2015/07/31/427741914/measuring-the-power-of-a-prison -education.

Moule, R. K., Jr., D. C. Pyrooz, and S. H. Decker. 2013. "From 'What the F#@% Is a Facebook?' to 'Who Doesn't Use Facebook?': The Role of Criminal Lifestyles in the Adoption and Use of the Internet." *Social Science Research* 42, no. 6: 1411–-21.

Public Safety Performance Project. 2011. *State of Recidivism: The Revolving Door of America's Prisons*. Washington, DC: Pew Charitable Trusts. At http://www .pewcenteronthestates.org/uploadedFiles/Pew_State_of_Recidivism.pdf.

Roose, Kevin, and Pendarvis Harshaw. 2015a. "After Years behind Bars, Can Prisoners Re-enter a Digital Society?" *Fusion*, Feb. 4. At http://fusion.net/story /42775/after-years-behind-bars-can-prisoners-re-enter-a-digital-world/.

———. 2015b. "Inside the Prison System's Illicit Digital World." *Fusion*, Feb. 3. At http://fusion.net/story/41931/inside-the-prison-systems-illicit-digital-world/.

Wellbery, David E. 1990. Foreword to Friedrich A. Kittler, *Discourse Networks 1800/1900*, vii–xxxiii. Stanford, CA: Stanford Univ. Press.

5

Something Other Than Progress

Indigenous Methodologies
and Higher Education in Prison

ANNA PLEMONS

> We may believe in the doctrine of Progress or we may not, but in
> either case it is a matter of interest to examine the origins and trace
> the history of what is now . . . the animating and controlling idea of
> western civilization.
>
> —J. B. Bury, *The Idea of Progress* (1920)

In their essay "Respect, Writing, and Community," Sara Guest, Hanna
Neuschwander, and Robyn Steely tell a story of a formerly incarcerated
person who stopped by directly upon his release from prison to pick up a
copy of an anthology that included work he had written seven years earlier
while in jail. The authors note that the writer ended up "burying that copy
of the anthology with his mother after she had passed" (2012, 53). This
haunting story highlights the role of writing in the complicated interplay
between life inside and outside the prison. It reaffirms the importance of
seeing writing in places such as prison as deeply relational, often reciprocal,
and always about respect. It also resonates with the way Marty Williams describes the writing workshops at California State Prison–Sacramento (otherwise known as New Folsom), where he was both student and teacher
in the California Arts in Corrections (AIC) program.[1] When I began

1. Information about Arts in Corrections is available in the Arts-in-Corrections Records, Record Series 721, University of California at Los Angeles Archive, and in the

teaching at New Folsom in 2009, I was a guest teacher in Williams's class, which afforded us many opportunities to talk about prison pedagogy. In those conversations, he often reminded me that incarcerated students do not need fixing or saving but rather teachers willing to show up, show respect, bring their own best work, and teach what they know.

Yet the impulse to fix and save incarcerated students is strong, in large part because prison education has been swept up in the same frenzied distribution of resources based on data-driven, evidence-based program models that we see happening across institutions of higher education. In this climate, teachers who build respect, relationality, and reciprocity into their pedagogy must grapple with the tension between producing the data that validate their work and creating ethical, humanizing educational spaces inside near-totalizing US prisons. Such data-oriented classroom models often sacrifice dialectical, responsive classroom pedagogy in an effort to meet the demands of what political theorist Wendy Brown describes as a governing neoliberal logic that extends "a specific formulation of economic values, practices, and metrics to every dimension of human life" (2015, 30). This economic logic is pervasive and dominates the first paragraph of the RAND Corporation report on prison education, which makes the case for using "taxpayer dollars judiciously to support programs that are backed by evidence of their effectiveness—especially during difficult budgetary times" and for "investing in evidence-based programming, investigating promising practices, and making science a priority" (Davis et al. 2014, iii). In the context of higher education in prison, there is a real danger that an economic logic (perhaps the same one that drove prison expansion in the first place) and its attendant discourses further commodify and dehumanize incarcerated people and whittle the shape of educational opportunity down to the few forms that can demonstrate direct progress toward individual economic rehabilitation—namely, job training.

---

following publications: Bernstein 2010; Brewster 1983, 2010; P. Brown 2017; Cleveland 1994, 2000, 2003; Lockard and Rankins-Robertson 2011; Plemons 2013; Tannenbaum 2000; Tannenbaum and Jackson 2010; Wenzer 2011.

One of the many factors that complicate the fusing of prison educational opportunities with individual economic value is sentencing. Many of the AIC students at New Folsom are serving life-without-the-possibility-of-parole (LWOP) sentences, which means that they will leave prison in body bags—either by violence or by illness or by old age. A LWOP sentence complicates the already illusive economic benefit of a college degree. Furthermore, LWOP status could be used to exclude some otherwise qualified and eager students by means of evidence-based program models that measure the value of non-credit-bearing courses based on their ability to encourage enrollment in GED programs or reduce recidivism. Played all the way out, such a scenario suggests that the primary value of non-credit-bearing work is its expediency in encouraging credit-bearing work.

This logic also jeopardizes the hard-won and already precarious existence of programs such as Arts in Corrections. I offer this predicament not as a basis for a binary argument but as an illustration of the complicated and fraught relationship between data collection on education and respectful, relational, and reciprocal prison classroom pedagogy. Moving beyond an economic, zero-sum logic for the conversation about higher education in prison requires taking a closer look at the cultural values, rhetorics, and discourses that animate the options that seem to be presently available. And critically considering what seems to be available is crucial because "present actions are like layers of snow added to a snowball—the shape of the present outer layer determines the future shape of the whole" (Cordova 2007, 175).

Critical prison educators can and are pushing back against economic logics and helping shape the conversation about what empirically counts as "progress" for incarcerated students (Alexander 2010; Hartnett 2010; Jacobi 2011; Plemons 2013; Pollack and Eldridge 2015). These efforts broadly align with the call in composition studies for decolonial work that does more than pivot from the center. Specifically, Ellen Cushman has critiqued emancipatory projects in composition, noting that they often "fall short of their social justice goals because they critique a content or place of practice without revealing and altering their own structuring tenets" (2016, 239). In this chapter, I suggest that the project of altering the structural tenets that sustain prison education requires both a critique of the economic logics ubiquitous in the field and a methodology that can account for and respond to the protracted and relational work incarcerated students are already doing inside and outside the classroom.

In taking up Cushman's call for "decolonial possibilities through research and teaching that are dedicated to leveling the social, epistemic, semiotic, and linguistic hierarchies that (de)humanize us all" (2016, 235), I turn to Indigenous scholars. The scholars invoked in this chapter inform the design of classroom pedagogies that seek to be respectful and responsive to the articulated needs and relationships incarcerated students bring to class. These same methodologies suggest alternative measurements for evaluating programmatic value—measurements that challenge a neoliberal obsession with progress and its attendant value on expediency.[2]

Western Obsession with Progress

Part of the scholarly critique of prison education programming, in particular writing-based programming, is that such programming often keeps the focus on the individual and not on the systemic issues of incarceration (Jacobi and Johnston 2012). This attention to the individual is maintained in large part by explicit and implicit encouragement of salvation narratives, or tales of linear progress from a negative past to a positive future (Meiners 2007). Walter Mignolo notes a similar obsession with rhetorics of salvation, pointing out how antiquated terms such as *conversion* have been subtly replaced with a modern discourse of linear "development" (2011, xxiv). In resonance, Indigenous scholar V. F. Cordova's comments on Western notions of *progress* and *change* illuminate the linear nature of such thinking. She writes, "In the West, the notion of directed motion is called 'progress.' 'Change' is understood as a necessary marker for the

2. Although there are also Western schools of thought that have noted that humans exist in complex, often elusive networks that complicate the binaries of modernism (actor-network theory, post-structuralism, ecocriticism, etc.), I choose to use Indigenous theory here as part of an overt move to highlight scholars whose work "interrupt[s] a pre-existing, ongoing conversation" premised in Western ideology and does something other than "weld Indigenous methods to existing bodies of Western knowledge" (Kovach 2009, 36).

arrival of (or at least, approach toward) the definitive, the unchanging" (2007, 70). As Cordova points out, a linear and fused relationship between the concepts of progress and change foreclose attention to other ideological orientations.

This understanding of why individual, short-term, linear data-collection measures are insufficient if not injurious is informed by comments from Jack, a white AIC student who is featured in a particularly intense scene in Michel Wenzer's acclaimed documentary *At Night I Fly* (2011). In the scene, likely filmed in 2003, Jack admits that although the classroom camaraderie and mutual respect that he has built with his AIC classmates are deeply important to him, he is as yet unwilling to acknowledge his cross-racial friendships in class when he is on the yard because of the yard's rigid and often bloody racialized codes. A heated conversation erupts as Jack's classmates challenge his choice to privilege his own bodily safety and political position with white gang members over a public respect and recognition of his Black, Latino, and Asian classmates.

I met Jack in an intensive journaling class seven years later. In that class, he wrote about an event where inmates ate with visiting community members. Real food was served—sandwiches with lunchmeat, mayo, fresh lettuce and tomato. Jack wrote about a moment in which he takes the last sandwich, only to have a Black inmate ask him to split it. He draws the reader into his very real and serious dilemma. In the piece, Jack ponders the consequences of this one act. In the end, he splits the sandwich. When he finished reading the piece in class, another writer in the group, Eugene, admitted that he was the man with whom Jack shared the sandwich. Eugene told Jack how important that moment was for him and marked it as significant in his own process of building cross-racial trust. They stood to hug.

As I witnessed the event, I did not understand that Jack had been weighing the choice to publicly out himself as a wavering white supremacist for the better part of a decade and that his choice to split the sandwich was deeply informed by his experiences with his classmates. And when I realized how long it took Jack to make the choice to share the sandwich and then eventually write about it, I also realized that the expedited, individual transformational processes we foist upon incarcerated writers are at best a sham and at worst an act of violence.

A reading of this story *could* focus on Jack's alleged individual transformation. But a reader could instead consider how over the course of ten years Jack used his classroom opportunities to join a community in deeper and deeper ways. It cannot be empirically proven that Jack was transformed; he was transferred to another prison shortly after the sandwich incident. But it can be stated that over the course of a decade Jack grappled in very real ways with issues of relationality and accountability and did end up building relationships of consequence that propelled him to critically conscious, creative action. His protracted relational experience within AIC classrooms affirms the argument that the types of measurements we can take in six- or twelve-week courses are not likely to capture the deepest relational work students are doing.

Furthermore, such measurements might actively preclude slower, deeper work because the types of evidence that short-term projects *can* demonstrate will drive the types of claims educators are able to make on future resources and in turn narrow the eligibility requirements for students. As Cordova points out, current shapes determine future forms. If the current shape of prison higher education is being molded by "a governing rationality that disseminates market values and metrics to every sphere of life" (W. Brown 2015, 176), then one can expect that this calculus will leave many prospective students even farther outside systems of privilege, which have been stubbornly out of their reach often from their birth.

Evidence of the way economic logic permeates the discourse on prison higher education abounds. One example is an often cited study that looks at whether arts programs "may motivate those with long sentences to pursue educational degrees" (Halperin, Kessler, and Braunschweiger 2012, 6). Although one may appreciate that the study's intention is to support such programs and find ways to situate their value in the evidence-based discourse of the age, the authors' justification for the study is deeply troubling. Ronnie Halperin, Suzanne Kessler, and Dana Braunschweiger suggest that a "skeptical researcher, prison administrator, or politician could claim that most evidence for the efficacy of prison arts programs is weak because there is no way to determine that it is the specific enrichment program that actually creates positive change in the participants" (2012, 8). This explanation of why existing evidence is weak exemplifies Wendy

Brown's claim that "the market value of knowledge—its income-enhancing prospects for individuals and industry alike—is now understood as both its driving purpose and leading line of defense" (2015, 187).

The blinding effects of a hyperfocus on efficacy are most pronounced in the next sentence, where Halperin, Kessler, and Braunschweiger continue to explain why studies of arts programs have thus far been ineffective in demonstrating value: "It is just as likely, they [the skeptical researcher, prison administrator, and politician] could argue, that a special kind of inmate—one predisposed to succeed in prison and post-release—elects to participate in these kinds of voluntary programs" (2012, 8). Suggesting that a study eschew attention to the "predisposition" of some incarcerated people to seek out positive avenues of expression and self-efficacy behaviors both undervalues the fortitude of such individuals and papers over attention to the economic, racialized contexts that contribute to incarceration. Second, a hyperfocus on individualized intervention strips incarcerated people of their agency and their ability to write and tell their own story of how they got into (and possibly out of) prison. It also falsely disconnects incarcerated people from the relational circles inside and outside the prison that inform and inspire the choices they may make in regard to education. To suggest that scholars look for studies that can strip out the variable of a predisposition to "succeed in prison and post-release" is to have missed the rehabilitative forest for the trees.

Furthermore, although the Halperin, Kessler, and Braunschweiger study has been important to policy makers working to capture more funding for prison arts programming, the linear and casual relationship it suggests between non-credit- and credit-bearing programs subsumes one type of program in the service of another, again making use of a Western logic of progress. The assumptions built into this type of study work against a respect for incarcerated students and the complicated constellation of relationships they carry with them. These same assumptions also wear out the integral connections between teacherly intention and ethical practice. In response to such a dilemma, some starting points for bringing intention and practice into closer alignment through Indigenous methodologies are discussed in the following section.

Relational Methodologies for the Prison Classroom

A strong body of work by Indigenous scholars exists that justifies and de-scribes decolonial options (to use Mignolo's term) in academic design. My purpose in invoking Indigenous scholars here is to acknowledge that this body of work has been unequivocally significant to my understand-ing of both how things are and how they might be. As a non-Indigenous scholar, I come to this work as an outsider, so I am cautious about the dangers of appropriation. Because of my positionality, in this chapter I do not want to speak for or over Indigenous scholars, so I have not attempted any comprehensive survey of the literature. Rather, my intention is to story the disconnection between education's emancipatory aims and colonial mechanisms in my own local context and to point other scholar-teachers grappling with this tension to scholarship that has helped me (re)imagine what might be possible in the prison classroom.

In contrast to a Western ideology of individual progress, Indigenous critical theory (Cordova 2007; Deloria 1999) does not privilege the indi-vidual as the primary focus of inquiry or unit of value. By moving away from a hyperfocus on the individual, Indigenous critical theory makes space for prison educators to acknowledge the complicated relationships that already exist between students, teachers, administrators, and the host of advocates (familial and otherwise) that support incarcerated students. These relationships are, many times, part of the motivation for and experi-ence of education and cannot be easily abstracted from that experience. Likewise, by challenging individual evaluations and expedited timetables, Indigenous critical theory provides frames for building more integrated, holistic methods of program evaluation.

A cornerstone of much of this body of work is recognition of the re-latedness of things (Cordova 2007; Deloria 1999). This "always already" relationality leads scholars to see that the goal of research is not so much to build better relationships but rather to recognize that people and things are already related (Cordova 2007; Deloria 1999). Brian Yazzie Burkhart adds that "in American Indian philosophy we must maintain our con-nectedness, we must maintain our relations, and never abandon them in search of understanding, but rather find understanding through them" (2004, 25). To further articulate his point, he makes this comparison: "The cogito, ergo sum tells us, 'I think therefore I am.' But Native philosophy tells us, 'We are, therefore I am.' A Native philosophical understanding must include all experience, not simply my own" (25). Therefore, a relational research orientation informed by Indigenous philosophy requires something other than an individualized, linear metaphor for understanding the reasons for and construction of research methodologies.

Many Indigeneous scholars have made contributions that texturize the theoretical articulation of relationality. These scholars make specific, ethical suggestions regarding ways to measure and evaluate the value of a program without the colonial hyperfocus on individual transformation (Arola 2014; Atkinson 2001; Haas 2007, 2012; Hampton 1995; King, Gubele, and Anderson 2015; Kovach 2009; Maracle 1990; Mihesuah and Wilson 2004; Smith 2012; Weber-Pillwax 1999; Wilson 2008). These scholars ask questions about what is real and how we know it to be such. They also ask scholars to consider their complicity (relatedness) in historical and contemporary colonialism (Haas 2007).

In her work on slow composition, Kristin Arola (2014) questions the purpose and value of speed and efficacy in writing pedagogy and leads writers to be mindful of their relationship to the materials they are using. Lisa King, Rose Gubele, and Joyce Rain Anderson (2015) describe an ethical, relational landscape for the study of Indigenous rhetorics in the classroom. Each of these contributions, along with the ones not mentioned by name, make some space for a theoretically robust consideration of something other than the individual. The way they describe both the goals and implementation of research projects can help prison educators represent the values and successes of their programs with something other than short-term representations of individual progress.

In constructing a relational methodology for the writing class at New Folsom, Shawn Wilson's work has been particularly useful. He suggests circular instead of linear paradigms for thinking about the goals and methods of research projects. He calls for research methodologies "whose purpose is the strengthening of relationships and/or the bridging of distance" (2008, 11). By replacing the line with the circle, Wilson's metaphor challenges scholars to develop methodologies that disrupt a scholarly hyperfocus on the individual and attend, rather, to the community and the relationships that exist therein.

Prison education projects that demonstrate the strengthening of community and the bridging of distance set out to do and measure different kinds of things, and many programs already exist that make the community rather than the individual the primary unit of value. The SpeakOut! program, run through the Community Literacy Center at Colorado State University, and the Prison Creative Arts Project (PCAP), housed at the University of Michigan's Residential College, are two such examples. On its homepage, PCAP announces that its mission is to "collaborate with incarcerated adults, incarcerated youth, urban youth and the formerly incarcerated to strengthen our community through creative expression" (PCAP n.d.). Both SpeakOut! and PCAP have a reciprocal, relational ethic built into the program model, and this ethic helps each program in turn stay attuned to the connections between community work inside and outside the prison as well as to the particular borderlands in between.

A third example comes from the Education Justice Project (EJP) at the University of Illinois. EJP runs a broad host of credit-bearing and non-credit-bearing programs, including an English as a Second Language (ESL) program called Language Partners. Language Partners offers training by Illinois faculty to incarcerated "teaching partners," who in turn "provide language instruction to men from the general population at the prison" (Language Partners n.d.). This program invites incarcerated people to participate as both teachers and students, thus disrupting a deficit model that presumes that knowledge bearers and educational practitioners must come from outside the prison. Andrea Olinger and her colleagues note that the program's "gains are uniquely reciprocal: volunteer teachers—novices in a prison classroom—have learned to become resources, not experts, [and] teachers—attuned to learners' needs but newer to TESL—are developing expertise in the field" (2012, 68). By securing awards and publishing scholarly articles, Language Partners offers an alternative form of political currency that programs can use in lieu of individual narratives of transformation. ·

In my own work, a community-oriented, relational ethic has been a source of much institutional tension, but it has also afforded opportunities that were not imaginable without a reorientation of my scholarly gaze from the individual to the community. Reading Shawn Wilson's text *Research Is Ceremony* (2008) at a colleague's suggestion required a close look at how the ideological assumptions in the research study I had been conducting at New Folsom were at odds with the project's relational intention. In the end, it was concluded that the study was unsalvageable. But while in the process of sitting with that academic failure, I received an email from Carol Hinds, the parent of a student in a writing workshop I was teaching at the prison. Panicked by the possible breach of protocol regarding overfamiliarity, I hurriedly phoned my institutional contact, but my relationship with this mother was ultimately sanctioned because of her official role on the Inmate Family Council at New Folsom. Having authorized contact with a family member of an incarcerated student—something I did not imagine was possible—brought Wilson's call for projects that bridge distance into sharp focus. It also bolstered motivation to imagine what else might be tactically possible in the near-totalizing US prison when scholars design pedagogy, research, and advocacy work focused on strengthening the connections between incarcerated students and their families and advocates.

Hinds and I have had a few opportunities to present together at regional and national venues, and she has been invited to our university as part of campus-wide programming on issues of incarceration. Her most recent presentation included pictures of her son in the visiting room early in his incarceration and more recently since he has been enrolled in AIC classes. In her talk, she also told the story of another incarcerated student named Jacob, who saw the inside of the visiting room for the first time (almost two decades into his life sentence) when he went there to perform as part of a classical guitar class. As she tells it, being in the visiting room gave Jacob the courage to make contact with his own family, some of whom believed him to be dead.

As she worked through her talk, the students in attendance sat in rapt silence, save for the few who were quietly crying. Such a scene would be hard to evaluate in economic terms. The efficacy of a mother's comments to the audience or the return on investment for stakeholders responsible with building a career-oriented undergraduate experience would be very hard to calculate. It would be equally hard to quantify how her public-speaking opportunities—before undergraduates, California legislators, and so on—contribute, as she says they do, to her own healing process or to the healing process of the many people who stop her in the hall to share their own stories of incarcerated loved ones. And then there are her son and the relational intersections between her experiences speaking and his experiences in the classroom. She says that since he has started working with AIC, she feels that she has gotten her son back. He still is not present at the Thanksgiving table, but she once again has a relationship with the son she raised.

There ought to be room in an evaluation of the efficacy of prison education programs for stories like that of this mother and son. There ought also to be room for the deeply relational outcomes present in a story like that of Jacob, who made it to the visiting room after seventeen years and was inspired to send a letter to his family. Such an evaluation, though not impossible, will require a broad and creative calculus.

Circling Back: The Relationship between Theory and Story

Considering the deeply problematic nature of amassing data to gain purchase in a conversation dominated by a discourse obsessed with economic value, one may wonder again if the "master's house" can indeed be "dismantle[d] with the "master's tools" (Lorde 2007). In response to this critical question, it is important to understand that a bourgeoning prison system and the wake of its destruction cannot be made any smaller or less invasive by educational justice work without close attention to the way an obsession with progress still animates the projects we undertake and circumscribes the types of evidence used to justify such projects. Of course, scholars with their "eyes on the ought to be" (Branch 2007) can also be pragmatic in the ways they engage a system that is not likely to slow its drive toward "progress" long enough to consider where the road it is building actually leads. It is in that tension—between giving in and giving up—that prison scholars and teachers "make the road by walking" (Horton and Freire 1990, 6).

Yet continuing to make the road does not require the use of the same worn-out tools. The body of Indigenous scholarship that legitimates the measuring of something other than rapid, individual acts of transformation is encouraging. It suggests that teacher-scholars in the US prison system can build decolonial projects that strengthen communities and bridge distances and can find ways to validate that work. Indigenous scholarship also validates the role of story in theory making and suggests that the cleaving apart of words that "prove" from words that "show" is a futile exercise that unnaturally separates parts of a whole (Maracle 1990). Reclaiming the scholarly and economic value of story is not a fool's errand, as has been evident in the policy-making process that afforded AIC a comeback in 2013. When the California legislature was considering whether to reinstitute a version of AIC or not, both Carol Hinds and the former director of AIC, Jim Carlson, spoke before a joint legislative subcommittee. Hinds spoke of her relationship with her son and other incarcerated students. Carlson brought a poem, written on a paper lunch bag, that an incarcerated artist in lockdown at San Quentin had given him twenty-eight years earlier.

Carlson referenced the poem and its suggestion that if creative, educational opportunities were made available to incarcerated people, they would be taken. By serendipity, the poem's author, having been paroled, was also at the meeting. Carlson was able to publically return the poem to its writer before prominent members of both legislative houses. Later that year, when the inspector general of California called a public meeting, Carlson was also able to invite Raymond Vincent, the son of a former AIC student, to speak. Vincent talked about how his father's participation in AIC's guitar-building program kindled his own love for music and gave them something to talk about in the visiting room. The son, now grown, has become an accomplished iconographer and is contracted to teach his craft for AIC at New Folsom (P. Brown 2017). Stories like these bring shape to the claim that a holistic conversation about prison education cannot be built or sustained solely by data collected about individuals. These stories and the way that they are directly connected to AIC's reinstatement also suggest that the families and loved ones of incarcerated students provide important evidence that can sustain (or revive) a program during even the most challenging budgetary times.

In my own work, an attention to respect, reciprocity, and relationality as articulated by Indigenous scholars has driven a new project at New Folsom. The project offers incarcerated students a non-credit-bearing course on various aspects of literary practice and provides them with the curricular materials and postage needed for them then, in turn, to legitimize their role as literacy mentors in their own circles of influence by teaching those same practices to their loved ones outside the prison. The project also makes provision for participants, from both inside and outside, to participate in a series of formal poetry readings in the visiting room and have their work published in an anthology.

What is distinctive about this project is that its goal of strengthening ties with loved ones considers the community rather than the individual as the primary focus and articulates the value of that focus by situating itself as a response to a policy priority coming from the California Governor's Office. The project does not require individual narratives of transformation or need to make an economic claim. Rather, the attendant research study asks incarcerated participants to describe the rate and quality of contact between themselves and their writing partners before, during, and after the program. This study is a direct attempt to enact the type of work that Cushman calls for—work that levels the dehumanizing effects of colonial thinking by presupposing that incarcerated students are already (or are ready to be) literacy mentors in their own circles of influence. The project presumes that incarcerated participants do not require an external, behavioral intervention but rather the opportunity and infrastructure to engage in meaningful activities with their respective communities inside and outside the prison.

Whereas the methodology for the AIC project comes from Indigenous theory, its inspiration is a story Carlson tells about the direct connection between classroom work and the visiting room. As Carlson tells it, after he started the juggling program at San Quentin in the 1980s, a class participant reported two significant things that happened for him as a result of the program. After the juggling class began, he heard real laughter on the Upper Yard for the first time. And, more personally, he and his sons made juggling balls out of crumpled paper during a visit. It was the first time since his incarceration that he had been able to teach his sons anything. The image of this father, creating juggling materials in the visiting room and smiling as he passes on his skill to his two young sons, speaks of the need to look for ways to join work that is respectful, relational, and reciprocal and to demand that the value of such work be measured in more expansive and inclusive ways.

References

Alexander, William. 2010. *Is William Martinez Not Our Brother? Twenty Years of the Prison Creative Arts Project*. Ann Arbor: Univ. of Michigan Press.

Arola, Kristin L. 2014. "Slow Composition: An Indigenous Approach to Digital Making." Paper presented at the Digital Discussions in the Humanities and Social Sciences Colloquia Series, Virginia Polytechnic Institute and State University, Blacksburg, Sept. 5.

Atkinson, Judy. 2001. "Privileging Indigenous Research Methodologies." Paper presented at the Indigenous Voices Conference, Cairns, Australia.

Bernstein, Lee. 2010. *America Is the Prison: Arts and Politics in Prison in the 1970's*. Chapel Hill: Univ. of North Carolina Press.

Branch, Kirk. 2007. *Eyes on the Ought to Be: What We Teach When We Teach about Literacy*. New York: Hampton Press.

Brewster, Larry. 1983. *An Evaluation of the Arts-in-Corrections Program of the California Department of Corrections*. Santa Cruz, CA: William James Association. At http://www.williamjamesassociation.org/reports/Brewster_report_full.pdf.

———. 2010. "The California Arts-in-Corrections Music Programme: A Qualitative Study." *International Journal of Community Music* 3, no. 1: 33–46.

Brown, Patricia. 2017. "No License Plates Here: Using Art to Transcend Prison Walls." *New York Times*, Apr. 3.

Brown, Wendy. 2015. *Undoing the Demos: Neoliberalism's Stealth Revolution*. New York: Zone Books.

Burkhart, Brian Yazzie. 2004. "What Coyote and Thales Can Teach Us: An Outline of American Indian Epistemology." In *American Indian Thought*, edited by Anne Waters, 15–26. Malden, MA: Blackwell.

Bury, J. B. 1920. *The Idea of Progress: An Inquiry into Its Origin and Growth*. London: MacMillan.

Cleveland, William. 1994. "California's Arts-in-Corrections: Discipline, Imagination, and Opportunity." In *Higher Education in Prison: A Contradiction in Terms?* edited by Miriam Williford, 54–62. Phoenix: Oryx Press.

———. 2000. *Art in Other Places: Artists at Work in America's Community and Social Institutions.* Westport, CT: Praeger.

———. 2003. "Common Sense and Common Ground: Survival Skills for Artists Working in Correctional Institutions." In *Teaching the Arts behind Bars,* edited by Rachel Marie-Crane Williams, 28–39. Boston: Northeastern Univ. Press.

Cordova, V. F. 2007. *How It Is: The Native American Philosophy of V. F. Cordova.* Edited by Kathleen Dean Moore, Kurt Peters, Ted Jojola, and Amber Lacy. Tucson: Univ. of Arizona Press.

Cushman, Ellen. 2016. "Translingual and Decolonial Approaches to Meaning Making." *College English* 78, no. 3: 234–42.

Davis, Lois M., Jennifer L. Steele, Robert Bozick, Malcolm Williams, Susan Turner, Jeremy N. V. Miles, Jessica Saunders, and Paul S. Steinberg. 2014. *How Effective Is Correctional Education, and Where Do We Go from Here? The Results of a Comprehensive Evaluation.* Santa Monica, CA: RAND Corporation.

Deloria, Vine, Jr. 1999. *The Vine Deloria, Jr., Reader.* Edited by Barbara Deloria, Kristen Foehner, and Sam Scinta. Golden, CO: Fulcrum.

Guest, Sara, Hanna Neuschwander, and Robyn Steely. 2012. "Respect, Writing, and Community." In *Circulating Communities: The Tactics and Strategies of Community Building,* edited by Paula Mathieu, Steve Parks, and Tiffany Rousculp, 49–70. Lanham, MD: Lexington Books.

Haas, Angela M. 2007. "Wampum as Hypertext: An American Indian Intellectual Tradition of Multimedia Theory and Practice." *Studies in American Indian Literatures* 19, no. 4: 77–100.

———. 2012. "Race, Rhetoric, and Technology: A Case Study of Decolonial Technical Communication Theory, Methodology, and Pedagogy." *Journal of Business and Technical Communication* 26:277--310.

Halperin, Ronnie, Suzanne Kessler, and Dana Braunschweiger. 2012. "Rehabilitation through the Arts: Impact on Participants' Engagement in Educational Programs." *Journal of Correctional Education* 63, no. 1: 6–23.

Hampton, Eber. 1995. "Memory Comes before Knowledge: Research May Improve If Researchers Remember Their Motives." *Canadian Journal of Native Education* 21:46–54.

Hartnett, Stephen, ed. 2010. *Challenging the Prison–Industrial Complex: Activism, Arts, and Educational Alternatives*. Urbana: Univ. of Illinois Press.

Horton, Myles, and Paulo Freire. 1990. *We Make the Road by Walking: Conversations on Education and Social Change*. Edited by Brenda Bell, John Gaventa, and John Peters. Philadelphia: Temple Univ. Press.

Jacobi, Tobi. 2011. "Speaking Out for Social Justice: The Problems and Possibilities of US Women's Prison and Jail Writing Workshops." *Critical Survey* 23, no. 3: 40–54.

Jacobi, Tobi, and Elliot Johnston. 2012. "Writers Speaking Out: The Challenges of Community Publishing from Spaces of Confinement." In *Circulating Communities: The Tactics and Strategies of Community Publishing*, edited by Paula Mathieu, Steve Parks, and Tiffany Rousculp, 173–200. Lanham, MD: Lexington Books.

King, Lisa, Rose Gubele, and Joyce Rain Anderson, eds. 2015. *Survivance, Sovereignty, and Story: Teaching American Indian Rhetorics*. Logan: Utah State Univ. Press.

Kovach, Margaret. 2009. *Indigenous Methodologies: Characteristics, Conversations, and Contexts*. Toronto: Univ. of Toronto Press.

Language Partners. n.d. Education Justice Project, Univ. of Illinois. At http://www.educationjustice.net/home/programs/language-partners/. Accessed Aug. 4, 2016.

Lockard, Joe, and Sherry Rankins-Robertson. 2011. "The Right to Education, Prison–University Partnerships, and Online Writing Pedagogy in the US." *Critical Survey* 23, no. 3: 23–39.

Lorde, Audre. 2007. "The Master's Tools Will Never Dismantle the Master's House." In *Sister Outsider: Essays and Speeches*, 110–14. Berkeley, CA: Crossing Press.

Maracle, Lee. 1990. *Oratory: Coming to Theory*. Vancouver: Gallerie.

Meiners, Erica R. 2007. *Right to Be Hostile: Schools, Prisons, and the Making of Public Enemies*. New York: Routledge.

Mignolo, Walter. 2011. *The Darker Side of Western Modernity: Global Futures, Decolonial Options*. Durham, NC: Duke Univ. Press.

Mihesuah, Devon Abbott, and Angela Cavender Wilson, eds. 2004. *Indigenizing the Academy: Transforming Scholarship and Empowering Communities*. Lincoln: Univ. of Nebraska Press.

Olinger, Andrea, Hugh Bishop, Jose R. Cabrales, Rebecca Ginsburg, Joseph L. Mapp, Orlando Mayorga, Erick Nava, et al. 2012. "Prisoners Teaching ESL:

A Learning Community among Language Partners." *Teaching English in the Two-Year College* 40, no. 1: 68--83.

Plemons, Anna. 2013. "Literacy as an Act of Creative Resistance: Joining the Work of Incarcerated Teaching Artists at a Maximum-Security Prison." *Community Literacy Journal* 7, no. 2: 39–52.

Pollack, Shoshana, and Tiina Eldridge. 2015. "Complicity and Redemption: Beyond the Insider/Outsider Research Dichotomy." *Social Justice* 42, no. 2: 132–45.

Prison Creative Arts Project (PCAP). n.d. Univ. of Michigan. At http://www.lsa .umich.edu/pcap/. Accessed Aug. 4, 2016.

Smith, Linda Tuhiwai. 2012. *Decolonizing Methodologies.* 2nd ed. London: Zed Books.

Tannenbaum, Judith. 2000. *Disguised as a Poem: My Years Teaching at San Quentin.* Boston: Northeastern Univ. Press.

Tannenbaum, Judith, and Spoon Jackson. 2010. *By Heart: Poetry, Prison, and Two Lives.* Oakland, CA: New Village Press.

Weber-Pillwax, Cora. 1999. "Indigenous Research Methodology: Exploratory Discussion of an Elusive Subject." *Journal on Educational Thought* 33, no. 1: 31–45.

Wenzer, Michel. 2011. *At Night I Fly* (documentary). Story, AB.

Wilson, Shawn. 2008. *Research Is Ceremony.* Halifax, Canada: Fernwood.

Part Two

Jail and Juvenile Hall Writing

6

Curating Counternarratives beyond Bars

Speaking Out with Writers at a County Jail

TOBI JACOBI

> As teachers of life writing, as purveyors of stories, we are in an
> extraordinary position to interrupt—even for just a semester, even for
> just a day—the larger narratives that threaten to isolate our students,
> to keep them from the often messy and self-implicating practice of
> learning to listen to each other.
> > —Stephanie Guedet, "Feeling Human Again: Toward
> > a Pedagogy of Radical Empathy" (2016)

> I write because of your reactions.
> > —Brandee Frickin' Sue, "Why I Write" (2016)

Since 2005, I have been directing a university community literacy center and working with confined youth and adults in northern Colorado
through SpeakOut! writing groups. In weekly creative and expository writing workshops, we work to document and share the life experiences of
those who occupy the edges of public imagination. We enter with three
or four writing prompts and a will to explore language and the reaches
of our collective curiosity. We leave with stories and memories that writers often desperately want to engage with larger audiences. They want to
mentor younger generations, including their own families and communities. They want to counter the fiction of contemporary television and film.
They want to change the trajectory of their lives—and writing is helping
them to imagine something new. Writing by itself, however, cannot affect

meaningful change without accompanying plans for publication, dissemination, and circulation.

In their recent edited collection on "pedagogies of public memory," Jane Greer and Laurie Grobman (2015) call for increased attention to spaces for production of public memory. In this chapter, I am interested in discussing how such attention might be deepened when partnered with the simultaneous call for public rhetorical engagement by writers and teachers of writing.[1] Curating writing as a tactical rhetorical practice of (counter)public memory offers incarcerated people opportunities for engagement that can result in personal and social change. Specifically, I highlight several collaborations that move the SpeakOut! writers beyond site-specific weekly workshops and into dialogue with new publics. Situating prison writing pedagogies as rhetorical public-memory work can shift perceptions of incarcerated people, a necessary move if we are to create and embrace more humane systems of justice and reparation in the United States. I offer the SpeakOut! writing workshop model as one way that confined writers might take up the call to participate in the shaping of public memory and record.

The SpeakOut! program has been sponsoring writing spaces for confined youth and adults in Larimer County, Colorado, since 2005, growing from one weekly workshop with incarcerated women to six weekly workshops with men, women, and youth writers. In the centuries-old tradition of prison writing and alongside contemporary teacher-activists such as David Coogan (2015), Simone Davis and Barbara Roswell (2013), Stephen Hartnett (2011), Laura Rogers (2009), Ann Folwell Stanford (2005), Tobi Jacobi and Ann Stanford (2014), and Megan Sweeney (2012), we facilitate the workshops as a means of offering literacy as an active and dynamic tool for self-expression, reflection, communication, and social change. In collaboration with volunteer facilitators, writers gather for twelve weeks each spring and fall to write, discuss, and revise creative and expository work.

1. Extensive scholarship in public rhetoric and community writing has emerged from such scholars as Paula Mathieu, Shannon Carter, Stephen Parks, Eli Goldblatt, and Deborah Mutnick.

Each sixty- to ninety-minute weekly session offers writers opportunities to experiment with language, read and respond to published work, revise and craft their writing, and seek feedback from peers and facilitators on written and visual drafts. The *SpeakOut! Journal* is published in May and December and includes work from all six workshop groups (two youth, four adult). It typically features two hundred or more pages of poetry, prose, and artwork submitted by workshop participants. Copies of it are distributed free of charge to writers within our community and across the country. This dissemination is where the greatest opportunity for public engagement lies as various publics consume narratives that challenge the images of prison cemented by soundbite news reporting and pop-culture representations such as *Orange Is the New Black* and the seemingly end-less loop of *Law & Order*.

In their essay on rhetorical education in the dissent press, Diana George and Paula Mathieu bring Michael Warner's work with public/ counterpublics to literacy studies, arguing that "counterpublics engage in alternative rhetorical strategies while seeking to effect change in a more-dominant public sphere. . . . A publication can create a counterpublic space only if readers pay attention and if they seek to respond, speak back, or write letters to the editor: in other words, when the discourse reflexively circulates" (2010, 253). Such reflexivity can be difficult to document for publications that circulate across carceral and community sites. Seven to nine hundred copies of the *SpeakOut! Journal* are distributed annually, most of them regionally in northern Colorado, where many of our writers and their support networks live. We aim for reflexive circulation by includ-ing feedback postcards and informational bookmarks with each journal copy. These invitations for engagement—learning more about our pro-gram (bookmarks), listening to writers' words (journals), and engaging in dialogue (feedback to writers on postcards)—encourage readers to produce responses to narratives that counter many of the culturally available mes-sages about criminality.[2]

---

2. To date, we have had mixed results with this tactical approach to social change. These varied outcomes are largely owing to the transient nature of working with both

An alternative way of charting the reflexivity of the work of SpeakOut! is to consider the writers themselves as the counterpublic rather than focusing only on the text that represents their work. We have increasingly been encouraging writers in the program to consider this role through opportunities for engagement that move beyond the traditional activities within the workshop. Several special projects demonstrate the possibility of curating change through public engagement, and I highlight them here: a university–jail collaboration, a special workshop with local makers, and a counternarrative exercise featuring archival remixing.

Curating Civility through a University–Jail Writing Exchange

The university–jail writing exchange offers advanced undergraduate students with opportunities to engage with what is for most a very new public: writers behind bars. In the spring of 2015, writers from the mixed Speak-Out! women's workshop began collaborating with Colorado State University students enrolled in "Rhetoric and Civility," a course focused on exploring and understanding civility from a range of perspectives. The collaboration included three exchanges and was repeated in the fall of 2015 and the spring of 2016. Writers in both locations began by grappling with the idea of civility and incivility and aiming to understanding one another by writing and exchanging poems and prose. Some university students then visited the jail workshop and participated in producing collaborative texts. In the spring of 2015, after writing and exchanging a series of "I am" and "We are" poems,[3] participants made comments such as: "I think our initial consensus was that we were much different than any of the people who would be responding to our poem. However, that notion went out the window very quickly after receiving the replies and the SpeakOut writers'

---

college-age volunteers and writers within a county jail or rehabilitation center. It is also a challenge to assess impact given a paucity of human and financial resources; most energy and funding go to the program rather than to postworkshop and publication activity. That said, we do continue to adapt and encourage engagement.

3. To read the original collaborative poems, see "LCDC & CSU Collaboration" 2015.

version of the same poem," and "We all felt like we were able to be heard, even just a little." In subsequent versions of the exchange in the fall of 2015 and the spring of 2016, we continued to nuance the exchange by offering the writers different ways to open their collaboration (e.g., writing based on a brief excerpt from Nelson Mandela or writing about a decision they felt good about). In each case, writers did some reflecting upon their own lives, wrote, and then responded to each other (often using pseudonyms). University students sometimes have strong affective responses to the col-laboration, including shock, discomfort, relief, and surprise. There is often palpable discomfort when I visit their classroom as a guest speaker. Some have been victims of crime. Some have a firm belief in the justice system or seem to find it distasteful to be asked to think beyond the comfort of mainstream free America. Others are curious about jail, about the people who live and work there. Our brief time together closes with their receipt of a copy of the journal and an invitation to visit the jail. As an excerpt from a student email message indicates, the sequence of the course often encourages university students to reset their understanding of incarcer-ated people, perhaps embodying the kind of reflexivity that the circulating journal can (but might not always) produce.

From: [student@gmail.com]
Sent: Tuesday, April 5, 2016 10:07 p.m.
To: Dr. G
Subject: Writing exchange

Hello Dr. G,

This is [student's name] from your Rhetoric and Civility course. I told you today that I was really impressed by the writing exchange that we did for class. I know we are doing a writing reflection on the exchange as part of the assignment, but I wanted to share my feelings about it with you while they are still fresh.

As I said after class, I was completely blown away by the quality of the writing that I received. Even the handwriting was far better than mine. But what left the greatest impression [on] me was not just this. I had a feeling I recognized the name of the writer whose piece

I received, so I revisited the *Speakout* book Tobi gave us, and sure enough two of his other poems were featured there.

What is interesting is that in my first glance through the book I went through and dog-eared the pages with the poems that I felt had the greatest impact or that I wanted to revisit. And one of those poems was authored by the individual I exchanged writing with.

It is hard to explain, but there is such a difference between reading the poems published in the book and reading a poem written in pencil on lined paper. Reading the poems in the book, there was this sense that these writers could be *anybody*: me or you or my friends or family, and yet, despite that, somehow they are living very differently [*sic*] lives. That is a very powerful lesson in and of itself, but reading the actual handwriting left the impression the person on the other side was *somebody*. An actual person, rather than a disembodied voice or abstract concept. . . .

After writing my piece I was embarrassed of it. I felt like I didn't get at the heart of the assignment, and that the rushed quality would come off as disrespectful to the person reading it. But the response I received (even if it was chugged out in only ten minutes) was so thoughtful and intelligent. The writer found underlying meaning that I thought would have been completely lost and pointed out aspects of my personality in my writing that I didn't realize were even there. It was honest while still being encouraging. I have had my writing critiqued what feels like hundreds of times in my life and I have never received a wonderfully holistic response like the one that I got through this exchange. After turning in my writing I was so done with it, and I never wanted to see it again. But the response that I received is the kind that makes me want to add more to the piece: to revisit and revise. The quality of the response made me feel like my writing was worth-while [*sic*].

I was skeptical of this exchange at first, but I am now so thankful that I had the opportunity to participate in something like this. There is really no way to understand without experiencing it for yourself. For how little work I had to put in, I got so much reward from it. I never would have thought I would enjoy this as much as I did. . . .

Please send my thanks to Tobi and her staff for making this experience possible. And thank you as well for including this in your curriculum. I don't know if I would have ever been able to do something like this if you hadn't.

—[student's name]

This student's active reflection upon her own engagement and sense of understanding as it emerged from textual response reveal a few intriguing possibilities about the future of such work. She was surprised to get thoughtful and smart feedback from her reader in the jail and to relate to the narrative he told. The exchange stirred deep ties within her own history as a writer and suggested a regular need for this kind of opportunity to learn across the borders of the traditional campus. She also felt enjoyment in the process and inspired to "revisit and revise" her own work. Perhaps most important was this student's recognition of her incarcerated partner's humanity and lived experiences. I point to her reflections not as universal outcomes but rather as emergent opportunities for changing how we might regard and relate to one another. The pedagogy guiding this collaboration channels the spirit of critical democratic education and reciprocal service learning by design. We did not ask participants to reveal details about themselves in a biographical or geographical way (as a letter-writing exchange might do), nor did we ask members of either group to defend their history, experiences, or subject positioning. Rather, each group was invited to respond to a shared text, in this case writing on a decision each felt positively about. The result was a diverse set of specific narratives on choices that made large and small impacts on the writers, which influenced how they came to know one another. Our collaboration ended with the groups writing responses to this phrase: "what we want our words to do." One student wrote in response:

My Words

I want my words to not only inspire,
but also spark something from deep within,
set a fire.
Have you chase everything your heart desires.

I want my words to explode in the air,
And also tell my story.
I want my words to make you think. And re-think.
To enlighten, to be a song of experience.
To be heard and understood.
I want my words to make people wander, but not get lost.
I want my words to make you shut up and listen.
I want my words to be witty, maybe a phrase that'll make you change
    your ways.
My words are my revenue, my words are priceless.
My words are eternal.
My words will take you places you never thought you wanted to go.
I want my words to comfort and to bring bliss.
My words are my therapy; they always take care of me.
I want my words to work.

The last line particularly resonates with the spirit of this collaboration. Although the rise of service-learning programs and pedagogies has certainly provided ample opportunities to develop ethical practice, the work done in the SpeakOut! project aims to engage writers in deep reciprocity by both making their own words work and working with the words of people in a different subject position. Further, when we publish the textual product of such work, we curate opportunities for others to shatter fixed notions of difference and to confront the material realities that people behind bars face (e.g., writing with stubby pencils, risking confiscation of written work). When participants—behind and beyond bars—are invited and encouraged to engage with each other, we open opportunities for counternarration and collaboration that move beyond the shock value of writing from different locations.

Engaging with Local Communities
through an Antique Letterpress

In the SpeakOut! program, we also pursue collaborations with local art and literary groups to offer participants opportunities to see the arts and humanities at work in the world. Our youth program invites residents re-manded to two local rehabilitation centers to write on campus each week with SpeakOut! facilitators in an effort to encourage them to see campus as a space where they are welcome and can imagine future study. In the spring of 2016, the two youth writing groups partnered with Wolverine Farm Letterpress & Publick House (www.wolverinefarm.org) to create prints of their work using wooden and metal type blocks and an antique letterpress. Teens moved off campus and joined a letterpress artist to de-sign two broadside posters featuring images and their collaborative poetry, which were displayed at our spring reading and journal launch. Each of the writers received copies to distribute; other copies were disseminated throughout the local community and among potential program support-ers as a tangible by-product of the teen writing group's work together. One of the poems is shown in figure 3.

The project was not without challenges. Working with tiny metal type is an exercise in patience (as is setting type backward!), and the writers had to take turns carefully designing each line before printing. The opportu-nity to experience an active hub of literary activity within our community, however, made up for the potential tedium of typesetting. The teens com-posed their collective poem in the bright workspace of the café and later returned to give their reading at the close of the spring workshop series.

This kind of experience moved the writers outside of their known en-vironments (a rehab center) and the expectations of the weekly SpeakOut! session (a college classroom with its familiar pattern of writing and shar-ing). The popularity of making and makers' communities offered Speak-Out! participants a chance to engage in several ways:

- Writers participated in an active local arts community.
- Writers created a collaborative poem based on individual and shared experiences.
- Writers experimented with design and layout using a historic letterpress.
- Writers experienced serious literacy work outside the conventions of traditional school.

Actions speak louder than words,
or so they say.
You see, words are unicorns. Unicorns are abstract.
But they're cool, unique. They bring a sense of innocence.
Words are not always unicorns. Words are fake.
They can be used unnecessarily.
Words are juxtaposing
They can bring joy to people but also hate,
can heal people but also hurt.
Words can only do so much.

The mouth doesn't just speak. Also, eyes speak for us.

Actions speak louder than words,
or so they say.
Words are atomic bombs. Atomic bombs are fake.
They can be used unnecessarily.
Words are someone slamming a chair on someone's head,
leaving a nasty bruise.
They are taunting jabs you feel in the hallway.

Words can be helpful, lifting someone in a time of need.
Words are crutches to those who can't hold themselves up,
or the warm feeling of coming inside on a warm day
Words start as gibberish, when we're babies and end on a breath.

Watch what you say.

Even though words can cause damage, they can also change the world
for the better.

—Spring SpeakOut! 2016—
printed at Wolverine Farm Letterpress & Publick House

3. A poem written, typeset, and printed as a poster by SpeakOut! students for the *SpeakOut! Journal*, Spring 2016, edited by Tobi Jacobi. Image provided by Tobi Jacobi.

This work aligns well with the situated literacy practices that have emerged across community literacy projects (such as those discussed in Barton, Hamilton, and Ivanic 2000; Flower 2008; Goldblatt 2007; Hull and Schultz 2001; Parks 2010) and that are particularly well suited for carceral literacy work. The opportunity to move beyond school-based literacy and even special programming such as the SpeakOut! workshops provides youth participants with ways to envision writing as an affective and functional means of shaping and making public their emerging sense of identity. Although it may be difficult to replicate this field experience for writers within jails and prisons, there are ways to invite engagement with unique historical materials and artifacts, as I highlight in my final example.

Remixing Experience through Archival Prison Artifacts

Writers in the SpeakOut! program also have had the opportunity to work with some historical documents from the New York Training School for Girls of the 1920s. The Training School operated from 1904 to 1975 in Hudson, New York, as a residential campus for girls between twelve and sixteen years old. Girls were remanded to the "school" for offenses ranging from truancy and petty theft to headier issues such as "immoral behavior" and "incorrigibility." A familiar undertone of poverty, domestic violence, abandonment, and racism lay just below the surface in social reports, physical exams, and school curricula and practices. We focused our time on reproductions of materials found at a garage sale in Hudson by a local business owner. We began with a micro-pop-up museum displaying a range of artifacts, from old snapshots and institutional records to letters and court documents. Participants learned about the history of the institution, discussed and wrote about selected archival photographs and documents, and eventually created collage responses to the contemporary US prison industry. The resulting collages (see figures 4–7) demonstrate a keen understanding of the social and political inequality embodied by current carceral practices, their makers working to divert the Foucauldian gaze and reclaim some power by assuming more control over the production of visual and textual narratives of confinement and identity.

Population Under Control of the U.S. Corrections System, 1980 and 2013

TRENDS IN U.S. CORRECTIONS

Prison   Jail   Parole   Probation

International Rate of Incarceration, per 100,000, 2013

State Expenditures in Corrections in Billions, 2013

YOUTH COMMITMENTS AND ARRESTS

YOUTH

Number of Women in State and Federal Prisons, 1980-2014

U.S. State and Federal Prison Population, 1925-2014

LIFE SENTENCES   MASS INCARCERATION

Rate of Youth in Residential Placement per 100,000, by Race and Ethnicity, 2013

Number of People Serving Life Without Parole Sentences, 1992-2012

AMERICAN INDIAN COMMITMENT DISPARITIES, 2013

Number of Youth Committed to Juvenile Facilities, 1997, 2013

Highest and Lowest State Incarceration Rates (per 100,000), 2014

Number of Youth Held in Jails and State Prisons, 1985-2014

Should I Still be incarcerated?

And history is replete with acts of mistaken repetition.

Youth in adult jails

Youth in adult prisons

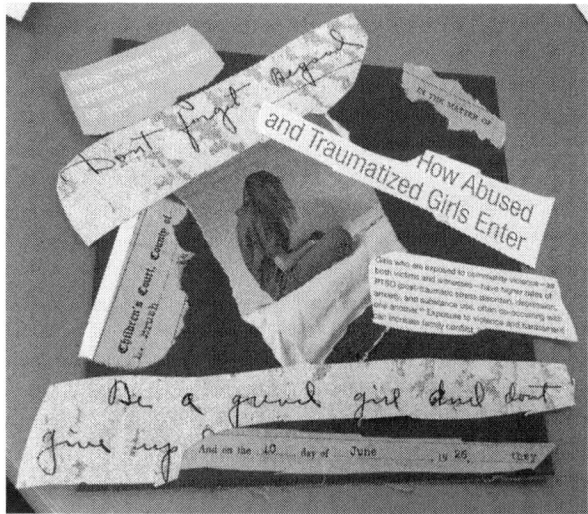

4–7. Collages by anonymous makers,
Larimer County Jail, spring 2016.

These opportunities offer writers a chance to move beyond their own circumstances by contemplating the long view of imprisonment and justice in the United States. Remixing current narratives of incarceration with those constructed nearly a century ago in a different geographical and social landscape invites writers to see commonalities and to understand long-held perspectives on who gets locked up and why. In the introduction to their collected volume *Telling Stories to Change the World*, Rickie Solinger, Madeline Fox, and Kayhan Irani argue that counternarration sometimes involves "unearthing and airing toxic histories . . . giving birth to a new language that can tell a new story in the interests of community and justice" (2008, 9). In jail, this process manifests as the contrast between, on the one hand, dingy cinderblock walls, muffled intercom codes, and glinting razor wire and, on the other, stories that explode into a hundred colors and sounds as pens begin moving in the workshop room. Participants in our archival writing and collage project demonstrated the power of unearthing the stories of incarcerated girls long gone and the relevance of their experience in the face of contemporary sentencing practices and policies on crime. This kind of reflexive narrative remixing opens the possibility of imagining meaningful change by shifting the institutional narratives that have a strong hold on how incarcerated people are portrayed and thus consumed by the general public.

Conclusion: Pursuing Change in Spaces of Confinement

> We caught her. She had six pieces of pizza in her pants.
> —jail staff person to SpeakOut! advocate

Sometimes writers put pizza down their pants. Even when they are warned repeatedly, sometimes the desire is too strong. *Was this a challenge to authority? Was it a physical need for salty, cheesy triangles of dough that overwhelmed their sense of logic and self-preservation? Or was it indeed self-preservation to say, "To hell with consequences!" and walk tall from a special event toward their housing unit with pizza packed against their hips, knowing that when they are caught, they will claim democracy, the need to share with those left behind? Maybe it was the need for the structure that would come with code violations and program restrictions. Or perhaps the Mountain Dew clouded judgment, a fizzy high that hadn't been felt in five months.*

These explanations raced through my mind as we cleaned up and offered the last few cupcakes and oranges from our *SpeakOut! Journal* launch and celebration to the officers and staff at the front desk of the jail. I worried a fair amount about how this act of defiance might be read by the volunteer coordinator, by the programs staff, by my fellow workshop facilitators. *Would it undermine our program? Would we lose support? Would we need more training?* The women who ratted on the pizza snatcher were desperate to protect their program and watched me tell a staff person, who then phoned up to the pod, where the women were searched upon entry. No oranges were smuggled in to make jailhouse hooch. No candy canes were hidden to become contraband threats. Just a hip load of cold pizza.

This anecdote provides a stark reminder that the varied opportunities for literacy engagement highlighted here cannot replace or erase the material reality of living behind bars. Incarcerated people—whether confined teens or jailed adults—are often hungry for engagement that moves beyond what is sponsored institutionally or delivered by the many religious volunteers flooding our prisons and jails. Sometimes they are ready to write stunning political critiques or deeply personal prose poems. Sometimes they just want extra pizza.

It is important not to read too much into that singular moment. It is not the moment to remember from an evening when thirty writers stood before their peers and strangers and to speak poems, essays, and microfictions written in their SpeakOut! workshops, demanding what Stephanie Guedet calls "radical empathy" (2016, 2). It is not the moment to remember from an event that closed with writers risking violations for being late because they were consumed with signing each other's journals like yearbooks on the last day of high school. That moment is not the most important outcome, yet it is the one that reminds me how fragile the entire system is, how a snack taken for granted by thousands represents freedom, choice, inequality, and a defiant middle finger to institutions such as jails and the university programs they allow in.

On the same night, a writer with the pen name LyriCalled brought down the (jail)house with his poem:

'Merica (excerpt)

Like talk-show topics satisfying our craving for contention,
"United we stand." Yeah, in the filth of our own degradation.
Talk shows without talking, just fighting and screaming,
Who's the baby-daddy? My brother-cousin. Which one? Same person.
"Trans-species marriages up next. But first a word from our sponsors."
Then show an ad for a topical cream relieving genital soars.
There's a pill EVERYTHING say doctors prescribing unnecessarily,
Filling prescriptions mean pharmaceutical money, which buys their
     loyalty.
'Merica!
Pop song, soda pop, pop nation, ditchin' cops,
Mad-props, bass-drops, fast food eatin' feeding troughs.
Lethargic nation built on empires of drive-thru services,
Instantaneous gratification to feed the impatient masses.
Hot dog eating competitions awarding obesity,
3rd world countries suffer starvation while we exceed with plenty.
'Merica

◼

Don't just eat the shit that they feed you,
Listen, read, write, paint, create to defy the norm! Be what you want to!
Wake up 'Merica! The line in the sand is drawn,
Stand up in rebellion before all our freedoms are gone,
So raise your voice to be heard!
No change can be made 'til it's born of your word.
Your life is more than ephemeral inconsequence,
So live for an ideal that defines your essential existence
'Merica!
              (LyriCalled 2015, 51–52, 55)

Advocates of prison writing and education programs encourage teachers,
activists, and scholars to develop increased and sustained access to programs that make space for incarcerated people in order to imagine local
and global change. Michelle Alexander admonishes us as a nation: "We
have all been complicit in the emergence of mass incarceration in the

United States. . . . [W]e must break that silence and awaken to the human rights nightmare that is occurring on our watch" (2001, A21). *Will stolen pizza radically transform the world? Will LyriCalled's social critique successfully fuel a desire for both personal and political change?*

In her critical examination of the Community Writing Center she founded and ran for ten years, Tiffany Rousculp notes that "writers may assert agency and make choices, but if they wish to vibrate the web of a discursive environment, they must acknowledge and respond to the norm. Still, acclimating to the norm for too long and in too many ways subsumes agency and choice into the web—and change stops" (2014, 152). To keep change movements alive and engaged, to realize the transformation that Angela Davis (2003) and the prison-abolition movement have envisioned, prison educators are obligated to the ongoing curation of counternarratives and spaces such as those described in this essay. Advancing prison writing as an active way to build community and public countermemories offers teachers and activists an approach for imagining and curating the programing and spaces required for meaningful public engagement that will radically transform the ways we think about justice in America.

References

Alexander, Michelle. 2001. "The New Jim Crow." *American Prospect* 22, no. 1: A19–A21.

Barton, David, Mary Hamilton, and Roz Ivanic, eds. 2000. *Situated Literacies: Theorising Reading and Writing in Context.* London: Routledge.

Brandee Frickin' Sue. 2016. "Why I Write." *SpeakOut! Journal Retrospective,* back cover.

Coogan, David. 2015. *Writing Our Way Out: Memoirs from Jail.* Richmond, VA: Brandylane.

Davis, Angela. 2003. *Are Prisons Obsolete?* New York: Seven Stories Press.

Davis, Simone, and Barbara Roswell. 2013. *Turning Teaching Inside Out: A Pedagogy of Transformation for Community-Based Education.* New York: Palgrave Macmillan.

Flower, Linda. 2008. *Community Literacy and the Rhetoric of Public Engagement.* Carbondale: Southern Illinois Univ. Press.

George, Diana, and Paula Mathieu. 2010. "A Place for the Dissident Press in Rhetorical Education." In *The Public Work of Rhetoric*, edited by John Ackerman and David Coogan, 247–66. Columbia: Univ. of South Carolina Press.

Goldblatt, Eli. 2007. *Because We Live Here: Sponsoring Literacy beyond the College Curriculum*. New York: Hampton Press.

Greer, Jane, and Laurie Grobman. 2015. *Pedagogies of Public Memory: Teaching Writing and Rhetoric at Museums, Memorials, and Archives*. New York: Routledge.

Guedet, Stephanie. 2016. "Feeling Human Again: Toward a Pedagogy of Radical Empathy." *Assay* 2, no. 2 (Spring): 1–24. At http://www.assayjournal.com/22-guedet.html.

Hartnett, Stephen, ed. 2011. *Challenging the Prison–Industrial Complex: Activism, Arts, and Educational Alternatives*. Urbana: Univ. of Illinois Press.

Hull, Glynda, and Katherine Schultz, eds. 2001. *School's Out! Bridging Out-of-School Literacies with Classroom Practice*. New York: Teachers College Press.

Jacobi, Tobi, and Ann Folwell Stanford. 2014. *Women, Writing, and Prison: Activists, Scholars, and Writers Speak Out*. Lanham, MD: Rowman and Littlefield.

"LCDC & CSU Collaboration." 2015. *SpeakOut! Journal*, Spring, 105–14.

LyriCalled. 2015. "'Merica." *SpeakOut! Journal*, Spring, 51–55.

Parks, Stephen. 2010. *Gravyland: Writing beyond the Curriculum in the City of Brotherly Love*. Syracuse, NY: Syracuse Univ. Press.

Rogers, Laura. 2009. "Diving In to Prison Teaching: Mina Shaughnessy, Teacher Development, and the Realities of Prison Teaching." *Reflections* 8, no. 3: 99–121.

Rousculp, Tiffany. 2014. *Rhetoric of Respect: Recognizing Change at a Community Writing Center*. Urbana, IL: Conference on College Composition and Communication of the National Council of Teachers of English.

Solinger, Rickie, Madeline Fox, and Kayhan Irani. 2008. Introduction to *Telling Stories to Change the World: Global Voices on the Power of Narrative to Build Community and Make Social Justice Claims*, edited by Rickie Solinger, Madeline Fox, and Kayhan Irani, 1–15. New York: Routledge.

Stanford, Ann Folwell. 2005. "Where Love Flies Free: Women, Home, and Writing in Cook County Jail." *Journal of Prevention and Intervention in the Community* 30, nos. 1–2: 49–56.

Sweeney, Megan. 2012. *The Story within Us: Women Prisoners Reflect on Reading*. Urbana: Univ. of Illinois Press.

7

Writing with Incarcerated Teen Women

Trauma-Informed Pedagogy, Health, and Gender Equity

TASHA GOLDEN

I'm in a gym at a juvenile detention facility in Ohio, trying to calm seven teenage writers. It's the last day of a five-day workshop, and we've been setting up for the closing program, during which they're supposed to read their poetry.

And they're refusing.

One young woman's "I'm too scared" had sparked several others, and now I'm reminding them that their work deserves to be heard. I show them how to adjust the height of the mic, encourage them to breathe. "We'll practice," I say. "I'll stand at the mic with you, if you want."

Later, with dinner served and an audience waiting, the young women line up to read. They're visibly nervous, still asking to skip the whole thing. But one suddenly steps up to the mic. She reads in a near whisper, and the audience erupts in applause. Another young woman follows her, and another. As the remaining writers share their work, the first two slip over to ask me, "Can we read another poem?"

Those two form a new line, and the others join it. And then the line just forms and reforms like this. They're reading poems they haven't even shared with each other yet, poems addressed to family or staff who are right here in the audience. Some cry while reading, and they keep going. They stand with each other by the microphone, sometimes an arm around a shoulder. And the audience is leaning in. Listening. Learning.

■

I first led a writing workshop for young incarcerated women[1] in 2012, when I was invited to be the writer-in-residence at an Ohio juvenile detention facility. Although delighted by the participants' enthusiasm for the workshop, I was unprepared for how often their writing indicated adverse childhood experiences: domestic violence, loss of a family member, parental incarceration, poverty, parental divorce or separation, mental illness in the home, and so on ("Infographic" 2013). It quickly became clear that effective creative-writing pedagogy with this population would require trauma-informed practices based on research regarding vulnerable youth populations and gender inequities in the juvenile justice system.

Studies indicate that a "history of physical or sexual victimization is one of the most common characteristics of girls in the justice system," and young women are more likely than young men to have mental illnesses or learning disabilities (Sherman 2005, 21). Unfortunately, most detention facilities fail to address these concerns (Sherman 2005, 12). In fact, despite two decades of studies consistently indicating significant differences between males and females in the justice system and significant inequality in their treatment, juvenile detention facilities are still designed and operated with males in mind. Young females remain an underfunded, understudied, and underserved afterthought (Banks, Kuhn, and Blackford 2015, 1–2; Hodgdon 2014). In addition, the link between a young woman's experience of sexual abuse and her involvement in the juvenile justice system is so significant that it has been termed the "sexual abuse to prison pipeline" (Saar et al. 2015), and incarceration has been shown to exacerbate

1. This chapter refers to females in the juvenile justice system as "young women," a choice made not without hesitation. Most of the writers I have worked with over the years refer to themselves as "girls" and explicitly prefer the term *girls* over *young women*. Out of respect for them, I am inclined to use the term *girls*. But the literature in criminal justice and sociology often uses that term in a way that seems less a conscientious uptake of girls' own identifier and more a diminutive reference to them as young and needy. For that reason and because many readers may find the term *girls* to be similarly demeaning, I use *young women*.

the trauma associated with abuse: "For girls who see women in society as less powerful than men, who have seen their mothers victimized in abusive relationships, and who have been victimized themselves, developing a sense of mastery and control is particularly important. Detention, however, makes girls feel powerless" (Sherman 2005, 25). Nevertheless, there remains a lack of gender-specific, trauma-informed programming for incarcerated young women (Banks, Kuhn, and Blackford 2015, 2).

Writing workshops would seem to offer such programming via accessible opportunities for expression, education, and group collaboration. However, these benefits are often impeded by the detention environment itself, misguided staff intervention, over- or undermedication, emotional family visits and court appearances, and difficult group dynamics. In addition, young incarcerated women's voices are vulnerable to censorship practices that generally do not apply in adult prison. They typically are not allowed to use curse words or to write about drugs, and detention officers (DOs) sometimes "suggest" edits that alter a writer's meaning or intention.[2] Such censorship precludes the open expression that leads to improved health and social outcomes, and it further silences a population that is already muted. Indeed, although the literature about young women involved in the juvenile justice system has grown in recent years, it rarely includes their actual words or narratives. The discourse surrounding incarcerated young women is dominated by criminal

---

2. I recently heard a DO tell a young writer that she shouldn't "write about her own mother that way." Although the DO likely did not intend to do harm, such criticism affects a writer's sense of freedom of expression. Officers differ in their level of interest, curiosity, and involvement in writing workshops. For example, some DOs circle the room and ask to read participants' work, which can be either caring or intrusive, depending on their relationship with the participant. Other DOs sit and write with the group and share their writing aloud, which tends to be positive unless they dominate the conversation or overinfluence the participants. Because workshop participants see their DOs daily and often develop strong relationships with them, they regularly invite DOs to read their work, and this exchange seems positive. In general, workshop facilitators should feel free to suggest the level of involvement from staff that they feel is appropriate: either inviting (a specific type of) participation or suggesting that direct participation be limited to the incarcerated population.

justice journals, sociologists, judges, probation officers, health experts, and educators—figures whose knowledges, in the Foucauldian sense, register as more "qualified." For example, the "Girls Study Group published seven in-depth analyses from 2008–2013; not one includes a quote from a young woman served by the juvenile justice system. Similarly, a meta-analysis of studies regarding 'Detention Reform and Girls' from the Annie E. Casey Foundation offers only one short quote from a young woman potentially impacted by such reform; ironically, it describes the way in which 'they [the juvenile justice system] take your voice away' (Sherman, 21)" (Golden 2017, 165).

Taken together, these factors reveal that responsible writing pedagogy in workshops for young incarcerated women must be trauma informed, readily adaptable, and responsive to research regarding gender disparities among detained youth. It must also resist censorship, foster reciprocity, and actively seek participant input. Finally, it must include active circulation of young women's voices among those whose decisions affect their lives. By investing in these practices, writing workshops for young incarcerated women will challenge not only the lack of gender-responsive programming in detention but also the lack of young women's input in juvenile justice discourse.

The observations in this chapter derive from research-based writing workshops that I have conducted in Ohio, Indiana, and Kentucky since 2012. Part one discusses the theoretical foundation for writing workshops for this population, drawing connections between trauma, creative writing, and health. Part two provides recommendations and details regarding logistics and implementation. I argue throughout for *performance* and *publication* as crucial workshop components not only for their impact on participants' health but also for their roles in the amplification and circulation of young women's narratives.

Part One: Theory, a Strengths-Based Approach

Although an understanding of the difficulties faced by young justice-involved women is crucial, a *focus* on these difficulties in writing workshops risks pathologizing young women or engendering pity for them. Successful workshops are founded on young women's profound strengths, even while remaining sensitive to potentially painful histories. As Meda Chesney-Lind and Katherine Irwin have written, "Girls who enter this system . . . are able to articulate their problems and are clear about needing to find spaces to rebuild lives that were often shredded by forces over which they had no control" (2008, 182). Young women know their stories and needs; indeed, although arts programs in juvenile justice facilities often purport to "give youth a voice," youth already have a voice. The issue is whether anyone is *listening*. Thus, the role of workshop facilitator may be most productively seen as that of space holder, question asker, disseminator, and amplifier. When given the opportunity, young women bring their own shared wisdom to bear in processing, articulating, and revising their narratives, creative works, and political statements. Significantly, these practices result in health benefits.

Beginning in the 1980s, psychologist James Pennebaker conducted studies indicating that "not talking about a trauma . . . placed people at even higher risk for major and minor illness" than trauma alone (Pennebaker and Evans 2014, 5). His work revealed that stigma, silence, and repression exacerbate trauma. In response to these findings, researchers over the past three decades have studied the role of "expressive writing"—the articulation and narration of difficult experiences—in mitigating trauma symptoms and their health consequences. More than three hundred studies[3] have now confirmed that "writing about traumatic experiences for as little as twenty minutes a day for three or four days can produce measurable changes in people's physical and mental health" (Pennebaker and Evans 2014, 3), including improved immune function, improved grade-point average, decreased pain, reduced depressive symptoms, reduced

3. Naíran Ramirez-Esparza and James Pennebaker wrote in 2007, "There have now been over 200 articles published by labs around the world using the writing method to influence health, biological activity, emotions, and behaviors" (2007, 212). Eight years later the number had increased by a large percentage: "at least 300 studies about the benefits of expressive writing have been published" (Pennebaker and Evans 2014, 9).

anxiety, and more (Frattaroli 2006, 823–24). Applying these studies to writing workshops in juvenile detention, one can postulate that young women who do not talk about the difficulty of their histories or current circumstances may physically and mentally suffer more than those who do; similarly, opportunities for directed writing in a detention facility should result in improvements in participants' mental and physical health.

So what did these hundreds of "expressive-writing" studies ask of their participants, resulting in so many health benefits? Here is the standard prompt, developed by Pennebaker:

> For the next [x number of] days, I would like for you to write about your very deepest thoughts and feelings about any difficult or emotionally disturbing events you are experiencing in your life right now. You may also tie your topic in with any past stressful or traumatic experiences you've had. In your writing, I'd like you to really let go and explore your very deepest emotions and thoughts. You might link your topic to your relationships with others, including parents, lovers, friends, or relatives. You may also want to link your experience to your past, your present, or your future, or to who you have been, who you would like to be, or who you are now. You may write about the same general issues or experiences in all days of writing, or on different experiences each day. Don't worry about grammar or spelling—that is not important. All of your writing will be completely confidential. (Gortner, Rude, and Pennebaker 2006, 297)

This prompt may at first appear unsettling; it invites significant disclosure, which may be triggering for those with trauma histories. But participants in expressive-writing studies, including "grade-school children and nursing home residents, arthritis sufferers, medical school students, maximum security prisoners, new mothers, and rape victims" (Pennebaker and Evans 2014, 40), have overwhelmingly appreciated the opportunity to articulate their experiences. In Pennebaker's studies, participants wrote at great length about "terrible divorce stories, rape, physical abuse in the family, suicide attempts, and . . . quirky things that could never be categorized" (Pennebaker and Evans 2014, 7). Even when volunteers had emotional difficulty while writing,[4] they "reported that the . . . experience had been profoundly important for them" (Pennebaker and Evans 2014, 7). This is a reminder to workshop facilitators that emotional discomfort in writing is not always detrimental and that emotional comfort may not signal health. Participants should always be free to decline writing to this prompt, and it is *always* wise to consider whether writing prompts are too intrusive or daunting, particularly when working with vulnerable populations. But expressive-writing studies show that Pennebaker's prompt—despite being intrusive and daunting—is consistently welcome and beneficial.

Given these findings, facilitators of writing workshops for young incarcerated women may consider drawing on Pennebaker's prompt while experimenting with modifications. For example, participants may read and watch poetry, songs, and stories that exemplify the type of disclosure Pennebaker's prompt invites and then imitate these examples via creative prompts. By doing so, they may approach their own difficult experiences from new and potentially productive angles. Such writing may also lead to improvements in what the juvenile justice system calls "prosocial behaviors"[5] because "writing seem[s] to make people more socially comfortable—better listeners, talkers, indeed better friends and partners" (Pennebaker and Evans 2014, 12). As a result, young women may experience additional health benefits via improved interactions with peers, facility staff, family, and others.

---

4. James Pennebaker and John Frank Evans note that many study participants felt a bit worse—("sad, even weepy")—immediately after writing. They attributed this effect to having spent time thinking about traumatic experiences, and the feeling dissipated "within an hour or two" (2014, 11). In fact, participants were keen to continue participating, and "the long term effects" left them "happier and less negative," with drops in "depressive symptoms, rumination, and general anxiety" in the following weeks and months (11).

5. "Prosocial behaviors include helping, sharing, and cooperation, while antisocial behaviors include different forms of oppositional and aggressive behavior. The development of empathy, guilt feelings, social cognition, and moral reasoning are generally considered important emotional and cognitive correlates of social development" (McCord, Widom, and Crowell 2001, 66).

In addition to Pennebaker's research on the health benefits of expressive writing, Ivor Goodson and Scherto Gill argue that constructing personal *narratives* helps writers gain both a sense of control over their stories and an awareness of "the kind of social institutional cultures, political systems and economic models that result in people being disempowered" (2014, 28). Through this awareness, writers can more critically locate their experiences and relationships within history, politics, and institutions. This greater awareness is significant because a young woman's recognition or affirmation that her circumstances may not have resulted strictly from her own choices can ameliorate the shame and self-blame that accompany many trauma experiences. This recognition is additionally significant because the justice system's emphasis on individual responsibility and personal resilience often fails to acknowledge the role of systemic inequities that ultimately influence involvement in the justice system, which disproportionately affects poor young people and young people of color.[6]

In addition, critically engaging with their personal narratives allows writers "to adapt, modify, and shift their stories" (Goodson and Gill 2014, 32). In the process, they deconstruct the ancestral, institutional, and cultural storylines that prevent the development of new stories and values (Goodson and Gill 2014, 128, 133).[7] The need for deconstruction is readily apparent in workshops with young incarcerated women, who often write about being told they are worthless or that they will end up just like their (imprisoned) mother, sister, or other family member. The shame and fear generated by such storylines are unmistakable.

Clearly, mental health benefits result not only from writing one's difficult personal narrative but also from thinking critically about the backstories, contexts, and external messages that may have generated them. Writing workshops should include time and guidance for this kind of

---

6. For extensive research regarding the "school-to-confinement pathways" that disproportionately affect young black women, see Morris 2016.

7. Similar benefits of narrative have also been explored at length in the fields of narrative medicine (Charon 2008) and life writing (Couser 2011; Smith and Watson 1996; Wright 2004).

critical thinking and for the revisions that it may lead to. Narrative revision can thus become a powerful act of autonomy and resistance.

Although the health outcomes detailed by expressive-writing studies have resulted from unstructured, reflective freewriting, guided *creative* writing such as poems or structured narratives can offer additional benefits. For example, writer and former therapist Sophie Nicholls argues that creative writing provides distance from one's feelings, making it easier to articulate difficult experiences. A writer gets "some initial release from writing her feelings out onto the page, and then moves on to begin to *shape* her material, learning to *craft* and *redraft* it, ultimately developing a new relationship with aspects of her self-experience" (2009, 174, my emphasis). To be sure, both freewriting and structured works are productive for personal exploration and offer health benefits. But, says Nicholls, "by looking beyond the 'expressive' phase, we can exploit the full potential of writing for health and well-being" (2009, 174).

Creative writing is also beneficial in group settings because even when it is personal, it is often easier to share than freewritten journal entries. In my experience, when workshop participants write poems, they regularly share their work with the group—even if just a line or two. But when they write letters or freewrite in their journals, they are more reluctant to share the work; doing so seems to feel riskier. Thus, creative writing generates a collection of shared work among participants, and sharing it aloud nurtures group discussions.

Such sharing also contributes to self-esteem, self-efficacy, and positive group dynamics. Genevieve Chandler, Susan Jo Roberts, and Lisa Chiodo demonstrate that "the sharing of writing through reading aloud and receiving positive feedback provided students with a different way of knowing each other, a new way of interacting," and that "students reported an increased sense of wellbeing [*sic*] from hearing about the lived experience of their peers" (1999, 77). Although it is not necessary to share one's work in order to experience the mental and physical health benefits of expressive writing, in-group sharing—particularly in conjunction with group agreements about confidentiality and support—provides a safe way to practice freely chosen disclosure, skillful responses to others' vulnerability, and the felt sense of having been heard. Such experiences are

beneficial for participants while in detention; ideally, they also provide
ongoing models for the experience of being both respected and respectful
among peers—informing future choices regarding social expectations and
behaviors.[8]

Creative writing also lends itself to group goals such as performance
and publication, which significantly improve group dynamics among
participants. As noted earlier, writing itself improves prosocial behaviors;
when it is combined with a common goal, such as a closing program for
an audience, participants often become even more supportive and trust-
ing of one another. For example, the study of a performing arts program
designed for incarcerated adult women found that participants "improved
skills in conflict resolution, bonding, trust, and intimacy"; there was also
"an increase in group collaboration" (Gardner, Hager, and Hillman 2014,
20–21). Improving group dynamics not only reduces altercations among
women while in detention (thus helping reduce disciplinary action) and
allows facilities to readily observe the value of this type of programming
for young women.

Including performance in writing workshops provides an additional
means of addressing trauma symptoms among participants: body movement. Bessel van der Kolk has long argued that healing from post-traumatic
stress disorder requires victims to verbalize their trauma; however, such
verbalization may remain impossible until victims have *"physical* experiences that directly contradict the helplessness, rage, and collapse that are

8. To clarify, the focus here is less on teaching young women to "be respectful" than
on providing opportunities to experience how it feels to be respected and to celebrate
their abilities to genuinely support other women. The hope is that the memory of this
experience will encourage them to build, engage in, and rely on networks of supportive
women. This distinction is necessary because juvenile justice environments often focus
on "teaching kids to be respectful," particularly of authority, without acknowledging that
many young women have been victimized by someone whose position of authority gave
him or her power and occasion to take advantage of them. As a result, behavior that juvenile justice staff perceive as disrespectful may be a learned method of self-protection
that is less revealing of disrespect than of the limited means some young women have to
advocate for their safety and dignity.

part of trauma" (2015, 4, my emphasis). Therefore, van der Kolk suggests forms of movement, such as theater/drama, music, dance, or all three; for those with histories of trauma, these embodied activities can alter the body's habitual movements and trauma responses (2015, 296–358).

Of course, such art forms may be beyond the resources or expertise of a typical writing-workshop facilitator; however, a number of their re-habilitative benefits can be accessed simply through the staging of a pro-fessional closing program during which young women read their poetry for an audience. After all, "acting" need not be about following a script, as in traditional drama; it can instead be about deliberately embodying and projecting chosen personalities and characteristics. Participants can be encouraged to experiment with embodiment during performances by focusing on breath control, voice projection, body posture, and the pace at which they read. Van der Kolk confirms the benefits of these experiments, noting that "our sense of agency . . . is defined by our relationship with our bodies and its rhythms. . . . In order to find our voice, we have to be *in* our bodies. . . . Acting is an experience of using your body to take your place in life" (2015, 331).

Participants can also take their place in their lives by helping organize the closing program. In this way, they not only take ownership of the pro-gram but also gain the opportunity to imagine and take up various roles or even characters: planner, decorator, server, greeter, emcee, performer, or a combination of them. Just as poetry provides a safe "container" in which to try new thoughts and articulations, a closing program provides a container in which to try new bodily movements and emotional expres-sions. This is significant because "traumatized people are terrified to feel deeply. They are afraid to experience their emotions, because emotions lead to loss of control. In contrast, theater is about embodying emotions, giving voice to them . . . taking on and embodying different roles" (van der Kolk 2015, 335).

Closing programs may not be full theatrical productions, but they *can* provide significant opportunities for young women to experiment with in-habiting unfamiliar roles, voicing their poems as an actor would or safely representing themselves and their stories before a respectful audience. And, as van der Kolk argues, young people who share their stories "learn that if they can embody their experiences well enough, other people will listen. They will learn to feel what they feel and know what they know" (2015, 341). Such learning is crucial both for healing from trauma and for mitigating the severe toll that detention can take on self-esteem.

Building on part one's theoretical foundation for writing workshops, part two provides recommendations for implementation, including scheduling and participation, lesson planning, pedagogical stance, and dissemination.

Part Two: Praxis

Writing workshops in adult prisons are often provided once a week for eight to twelve weeks for prisoners who have met the facility's participation requirements. In contrast, workshops for detained young women typically include all of the females in the facility because the overall number of young women in each facility is relatively low. In addition, the ideal workshop runs daily—perhaps for a total of five days—because juveniles in detention facilities have short and uncertain stays that render once-weekly workshops inadequate for producing individual or group benefits. Even in a five-day workshop, the group changes every day, with participants being released and others coming in. By including all the young women in an intensive week-long experience, daily workshops help participants get to know one another, focus clearly on a few consistent ideas or themes, and cocreate a safe expressive space while in a destabilizing situation.

At the same time, the demands of such a schedule raise important questions about sustainability. Until incarceration alternatives are more regularly sought by the juvenile justice system, sustainable, trauma-informed programming for incarcerated women may ultimately require partnerships with several organizations that can alternate weeks of programming. For example, evidence-based restorative justice, mentorship, meditation or yoga, and arts programs could be offered in alternating five-day workshops. It is also useful to develop partnerships with university departments and local government agencies. For example, creative-writing and English departments might offer community-engagement courses that train undergraduates and graduates to facilitate workshops in juvenile facilities. Such courses might also cross-list with departments such as psychology, women's and gender studies, sociology, criminal justice, public health, and more.

Lesson Plans

Every facilitator should work to develop a program that combines her unique perspectives and approaches with an understanding of trauma-informed pedagogy and of the women with whom she will be writing. However, as a beginning, five general components are significant and reliable: laughter, safe space, specificity and familiarity, visuals, and imitation.[9]

1. *Elicit laughter.* As with any group, it is wise to begin with introductions and icebreakers. The first writing prompt can then function as an additional icebreaker: for example, participants can be invited to write silly and simple pieces that describe themselves using wild and absurd metaphors. This writing encourages laughter and establishes that writing in the workshop space will not be a high-stakes scenario—that the point is not to be "good at it." By beginning with silly or open-ended writing prompts, facilitators affirm that there is neither judgment nor a grade for the workshop; instead, the workshop is about participants taking time for themselves, being honest, having fun, and experimenting. Similar fun writing activities can then be included throughout the week, offering planned breaks for levity and sharing.

2. *Provide a safe space.* It is important on the first day to invite participants to discuss what will make them feel safe and respected while they are writing with the group. This invitation can be especially productive when combined with a conversation about what makes them feel *unsafe* or *dis*respected in detention and in group settings more generally. After brainstorming, participants may want to write up their own group

9. Facilitators should also note that literacy levels vary widely in juvenile facilities. In situations in which a participant is unable to read or write, detention staff are often willing to act as scribes; however, this approach might affect a young woman's sense of expressive freedom. It is useful to ask your facility contact about participants' reading skills before beginning, and perhaps bring a covolunteer who can act as a scribe as necessary.

guidelines for the week. They may write such "rules" as "What gets shared in here stays in here," "No making fun," and "Applaud after every poem, even if you didn't like it!" The guidelines can be fun, but they should also genuinely help establish a safe atmosphere.

3. *Be specific and use the familiar.* Most young women in detention facilities are beginning writers who are often uncertain where to begin when faced with a blank page. Using very specific prompts and familiar forms—such as letter writing—helps get pens moving. You may also find it useful to avoid calling the writing "poetry," at least when beginning. Even when participants imitate poems or write within particular poetic structures, describing their work as "poetry writing" often seems to make writers feel alienated or daunted by the process. This alienation might be addressed through a quick redefinition of what poetry is, but, given time constraints, it may be just as productive to focus on writing without iden- tifying a genre.

4. *Incorporate great visuals.* Visual cues are a great way to generate initial ideas and descriptive language, particularly for beginning writers and those who aren't sure how to get started. For example, projecting sev- eral photos of different landscapes—beautiful, haunting, intimidating, bright, dark, peaceful, stormy, and so on—can help set up one of the fol- lowing prompts: "Which landscape are you? Why? Are you more than one? When are you one or the other?" Or, "When in your life has your landscape changed? What changed it?" Photos offer participants a way in: writers can begin by describing the landscape they chose or by com- bining or contrasting photos. Given the benefits of experiencing multiple artistic genres, I also incorporate a visual arts project whenever possible, even if it involves simply bringing in magazines and inviting participants to create collages in their journals. Visual arts increase expressive oppor- tunities and encourage participation from young women who may be less interested in writing. Such projects have also been shown to elevate writ- ers' mood and sense of well-being following expressive-writing sessions (Pizarro 2004, 10–11).

5. *Read and imitate women's poetry.* As a process, imitation is very approachable, and it consistently generates fresh and imaginative work. Imitation provides a structure and logic that writers can "fill in" with their

ideas, helping them get started. Perhaps more importantly, it verifies for incarcerated young women that other women have experienced hardships like their own and that many of them have chosen to *write about* their experiences. Poems from writers such as Adrienne Rich, Audre Lorde, Kitty Tsui, Emily Dickinson, Kelly Norman Ellis, Claudia Rankine, and others provide models of brave disclosure and creative storytelling. Discussing such poetry and the courage it may have required to write it can lead to insightful group conversations about loneliness and stigma or about how meaningful it can be to hear someone else articulate our feelings. The combination of reading women's works, imitating them, and then discussing the whole process reduces the isolation of both trauma and detention.

Reading and discussing published poems can also initiate generative critical analyses of workshop participants' own storylines. For example, workshop participants may read a published poem and then discuss what they feel is good or bad about how a character is treated; they might also try to reimagine the "story" or circumstances, sharing what they wish would have happened differently. If participants are then invited to apply this same supportive objectivity to their own writing, they can re-view and revise their words or storylines or relationships or circumstances.

Finally, reading and imitating published poetry helps young women begin thinking about how their *own* words might influence or help someone else. In fact, this may become its own writing prompt: "Who may need to hear that she's not alone?" Or "How might your story help another person?"

Pedagogical Stance: Modeling Disclosure

Adopting Paolo Freire's concept of a "teacher-student"[10] in juvenile detention facilities requires power sharing through invited input about discussions, goals, group guidelines, and prompts. It also requires that, when

10. "Through dialogue, the teacher-of-the-students and the students-of-the-teacher cease to exist and a new term emerges: teacher-student with students-teachers. The teacher is no longer merely the-one-who-teaches, but one who is himself taught in dialogue with the students, who in turn while being taught also teach. They become jointly responsible for a process in which all grow" (Freire 2005, 80).

possible, we facilitators avoid asking of participants what we remain un-willing to contribute ourselves. For example, expecting vulnerability and openness from young writers without modeling it for them will likely re-sult in silence or a lack of trust or both. My approach to modeling disclo-sure has been to share my own story and to perform a song or two that is in some way vulnerable. Over the years, participants have kept me at arm's length until I share something of myself in this way; the difference in trust before and after is remarkable. In an authoritarian, hierarchical institution where leadership is often distant, powerful, and impervious, offering one's own vulnerability—through storytelling, performance, or conversation—carries great weight. Just as published poems model disclosure for young writers, sharing one's *own* story models intelligent trust, narrative control, and healthy disclosure. It also enacts mutuality and reciprocation, which are necessary for safety and dignity yet conspicuously absent in detention.

Dissemination

As noted earlier, a professional closing program can help participants "learn to feel what they feel and know what they know" (van der Kolk 2015, 341). Performance and publication are also valuable in that they amplify young women's voices, providing opportunities for these voices to influence circumstances, relationships, and even policy. For example, when facility staff, probation officers, and juvenile judges are invited to closing programs, young women have the opportunity to tell their stories *as they wish to tell them*: to provide context, to be recognized as more and other than troubled youth in scrubs. Young women regularly state that this opportunity is significant to them, regardless of how they personally feel about the invited guests.

In addition, although judges, staff, and probation officers have direct impacts on participants' lived experiences, they may know little about these experiences beyond personal observations and interactions. Because juvenile justice literature rarely includes young women's voices, even those officers and staff who follow juvenile justice studies and reports are unlikely to have read firsthand accounts. A performance or closing pro-gram therefore expands the audience's knowledge of incarcerated young women and may influence perception and treatment. In the best situations, probation officers and detention staff participate in the program by performing or by reading their own poetry; in this way, closing programs may also foster mutual listening and learning.

When security allows, workshop facilitators should consider working with the facility's administration to invite participants' guardians, community leaders, workshop funders (if applicable), and one or two local poets and journalists to a performance or closing program.[11] As the opening story indicates, young women often share work *for* or *about* individuals in attendance. When guardians are present, this sharing can generate necessary conversations, helping bridge relational divides. Community leaders may be invited because their decisions—particularly regarding education, community youth activities, and juvenile justice—can and should be influenced by a personal knowledge of young women's experiences. When women writers attend, they not only offer encouragement to young writers but may also (with permission) take young women's poems back to their writing classrooms, poetry workshops, and readings—further amplifying young women's voices. Finally, when a local journalist attends, a subsequent article may raise awareness of the conditions of young women in detention and further disseminate their words. In short, a closing program can reach both the immediate audience and, through it, a larger community. Ultimately, the goal is to amplify and circulate young women's voices so that young women (1) are recognized and appreciated for the art and knowledge they offer, (2) can challenge stereotypes regarding female juvenile justice involvement, and (3) are provided a means to influence actions and policies that affect their lives.

Similarly, if funds allow, printed books of their poetry are highly valued by workshop participants, and they can be distributed to facility administration, government officials, teachers, potential funders, scholars, and others whose knowledge and decisions in some way shape the writers'

---

11. A list of invitees should be run by the participants for their approval; in my experience, no participant has turned down the opportunity to invite an individual or organization, but asking the participants reflects respect for their opinions and privacy.

worlds. Such books allow young women's words to reach far beyond the detention center's walls.[12]

Writer's Autonomy

For any closing program or book, it is important to ensure that young women are not forced to share work they prefer to keep private. If a workshop facilitator senses that a participant's hesitancy to share—whether in the group or at the closing program—is owing more to nerves than to privacy concerns, it is appropriate to encourage and cheerlead, to help her practice, or to ask if she would like a friend to read her work aloud for her. But to *force* sharing is a violation of young women's privacy and could be damaging. Facilitators might instead include opportunities to write light-hearted poems, which tend to be easier to share if writers need to protect their more personal work. If a young woman remains unwilling to share written work, she could be invited to share artwork instead, to photograph the closing event (with the facility's camera and permission), or to read a published poem. There are always ways to include her.

Some detention staff may be inclined to force young women to "participate" in the workshop by sharing their work aloud. Facilitators can counter this demand by making expectations clear to staff before beginning a workshop or program (via a meeting or even a program brochure); it is also helpful to remind participants daily that they are *not* required to share something they don't wish to share.

It is also important to give young women final say regarding which of their writings are included in any book that is printed and to provide choices regarding how their work is identified. Although participants often ask that both their first and last names be used, the books typically identify the

12. Before leaving the workshop, be sure to obtain permission from writers to include their work in a workshop book. I often type out and print their work for them and ask, "What do you definitely NOT want included in the book?" In addition, be sure the book is approved by the facility before it goes to print. Each facility will have different policies regarding how the book should be presented, how to identify the facility, and how to refer to the writers.

poems as having been written in a juvenile detention facility, making the use of full names a violation of juveniles' rights to privacy according to the law. However, facilitators *can* provide several other options—nicknames, initials, pseudonyms, and so on—that allow for some choice of identification.

Closing

Writing workshops with young incarcerated women suggest connections among trauma, storytelling, circulation, and health. They confirm that access to writing and the arts is a public health imperative. These workshops also underscore the need for further research at the intersections of writing pedagogy, health equity, and public policy. Young women's written works have much to teach scholars, educators, and the juvenile justice community about youth identities, methods of survival, risk factors for involvement in the criminal justice system, and desires for belonging and meaningful change. Because of what such writing can do, our work as facilitators and instructors is to create safe spaces for dialogue and expression, to listen deeply, and to amplify and circulate the words and wisdom of young women. In this way, we provide opportunities for participants' improved health while revealing to our communities and to the juvenile justice system itself the value of firsthand knowledge and participatory research. Modeling a learning posture as the teacher-students of young writers, we may create important pathways for improved advocacy, scholarship, and policy.

■

i am a road

in the middle of nowhere
i have cracks but can still get you
where you needa go.
i am also a meadow
calm & beautiful
and i just keep on going.
i have a lot of room for you.

(T. 2014)

References

Banks, Breanna, Tarah Kuhn, and Jennifer Urbano Blackford. 2015. "Modifying Dialectical Behavior Therapy for Incarcerated Female Youth: A Pilot Study." *OJJDP Journal of Juvenile Justice* 4, no. 1: 1–17.

Chandler, Genevieve E. 1999. "A Creative Writing Program to Enhance Self-Esteem and Self-Efficacy in Adolescents." *Journal of Child and Adolescent Psychiatric Nursing* 12, no. 3: 70–78.

Charon, Rita. 2008. *Narrative Medicine: Honoring the Stories of Illness.* New York: Oxford Univ. Press.

Chesney-Lind, Meda, and Katherine Irwin. 2008. *Beyond Bad Girls: Gender, Violence, and Hype.* New York: Routledge.

Couser, G. Thomas. 2011. *Memoir: An Introduction.* New York: Oxford Univ. Press.

Frattaroli, Joanne. 2006. "Experimental Disclosure and Its Moderators: A Meta-analysis." *Psychological Bulletin* 132, no. 6: 823–65.

Freire, Paulo. 2005. *Pedagogy of the Oppressed.* New York: Continuum.

Gardner, Amanda, Lori L. Hager, and Grady Hillman. 2014. *The Prison Arts Resource Project: An Annotated Bibliography.* Working paper. Washington, DC: National Endowment for the Arts.

Golden, Tasha. 2017. "Subalternity and Juvenile Justice: Gendered Oppression and the Rhetoric of Reform." *Reflections* 17, no. 1: 156–88.

Goodson, Ivor, and Scherto Gill. 2014. *Critical Narrative as Pedagogy.* New York: Bloomsbury.

Gortner, Eva-Maria, Stephanie S. Rude, and James W. Pennebaker. 2006. "Benefits of Expressive Writing in Lowering Rumination and Depressive Symptoms." *Behavior Therapy* 37, no. 3: 292–303.

Hodgdon, Hillary. 2014. *Girls and Boys in the Juvenile Justice System: Are There Differences That Warrant Policy Changes in the Juvenile Justice System?* Future of Children. Princeton, NJ: Princeton Univ.; Washington, DC: Brookings Institution. Adapted from Elizabeth Cauffman "Understanding the Female Offender," and Thomas Grisso, "Adolescent Offenders with Mental Disorders," *Juvenile Justice* 18, no. 2 (Fall 2008): 119–42, 143–64, and Melissa Sickmund, *OJJDP Fact Sheet: Delinquency Cases in Juvenile Court 2005* (Washington, DC: Office of Juvenile Justice and Delinquency Prevention, June 2009), at http://futureofchildren.org/futureofchildren/publications/highlights/18_02_Highlights_08.pdf.

"Infographic: The Truth about ACEs." 2013. Robert Wood Johnson Foundation. At http://www.rwjf.org/en/library/infographics/the-truth-about-aces.html.

McCord, Joan, Cathy Spatz Widom, and Nancy A. Crowell. 2001. *Juvenile Crime, Juvenile Justice*. Washington, DC: National Academy Press.

Morris, Monique W. 2016. *Pushout: The Criminalization of Black Girls in Schools*. New York: New Press.

Nicholls, Sophie. 2009. "Beyond Expressive Writing: Evolving Models of Developmental Creative Writing." *Journal of Health Psychology* 14, no. 2: 171–80.

Pennebaker, James W., and John Frank Evans. 2014. *Expressive Writing: Words That Heal*. Enumclaw, WA: Idyll Arbor.

Pizarro, Judith. 2004. "The Efficacy of Art and Writing Therapy: Increasing Positive Mental Health Outcomes and Participant Retention after Exposure to Traumatic Experience." *Art Therapy* 21, no. 1: 5–12.

Ramirez-Esparza, Naíran, and James W. Pennebaker. 2007. "Do Good Stories Produce Good Health?" In *Narrative State of the Art*, edited by Michael Bamberg, 211–19. Amsterdam: John Benjamins.

Saar, Malika, Rebecca Epstein, Lindsay Rosenthal, and Yasmin Vafa. 2015. "Sexual Abuse to Prison Pipeline: The Girls' Story." Human Rights Project for Girls, June 1. At http://rights4girls.org/wp-content/uploads/r4g/2015/02/2015_COP_sexual-abuse_layout_web-1.pdf.

Sherman, Francine T. 2005. *Detention Reform and Girls: Challenges and Solutions*. Pathways to Juvenile Detention Reform. Baltimore: Annie E. Casey Foundation.

Smith, Sidonie, and Julia Watson. 1996. *Getting a Life: Everyday Uses of Autobiography*. Minneapolis: Univ. of Minnesota Press.

T. 2014. "i am a road." In *Know Me: A Compilation of Poetry and Art by the Young Women at the Miami Valley Juvenile Rehabilitation Center*, 74. Springfield, OH: Project Jericho.

Van der Kolk, Bessel A. 2015. *The Body Keeps the Score: Brain, Mind, and Body in the Healing of Trauma*. New York: Viking.

Wright, Jeannie K. 2004. "The Passion of Science, the Precision of Poetry: Therapeutic Writing—a Review of the Literature." In *Writing Cures: Introductory Handbook of Writing in Counseling and Therapy*, edited by Gillie Bolton and Stephanie Howlett, 7–17. New York: Routledge.

8

"Can a Poem Stop a Jail from Being Built?"

On Fugitive Counter-Ethics as Prison Pedagogy

MEGHAN G. MCDOWELL AND ALISON REED

In 2016, we began facilitating a reading group at the Norfolk City Jail. Once a week during the semester, we met with six to eight men who qualified for "program privileges" and thus were given the option by jail staff to participate in the reading group. Each week we gathered to discuss the day's reading in what passed for a classroom inside the jail: a noisy corridor that connected two cellblocks. Against one wall there were four white picnic tables, bolted down to the floor, stacked one after the other. Though those accommodations were better suited for cafeteria-style dining than collective study, we did our best to position our bodies so as to bend sharp angles into a passable circle.

A guard station was located at one end of the corridor, ostensibly for our protection. On any given day, one to three guards milled about the station—busying themselves with mundane tasks, checking social media, or making small talk with one another. At best, the guards ignored us; at worst, they exercised what can be described as a form of authoritarian arbitrariness. More days than not, we arrived to find more than half the jailed students missing. The guards were responsible for escorting students to the "classroom," yet they often claimed to forget about our reading group, despite the fact that it was scheduled for the same day and time every week. Moreover, students were consistently left off the escort list or prevented from coming to class owing to unspecified violations.

To counter the guards' presence, we gathered around the tables placed farthest from their station. This choice felt like our unspoken and modest effort to reappropriate the space for our own purposes, to use the relative distance, noise, and heat emanating from the cellblocks to buffer our conversations. In a space of hypervisibility, our group desired to keep something for ourselves. Of course, we also knew that the conduct of the guards, the positioning of the "classroom," the sensory disregulation induced by erratic temperatures, sounds, and a lack of natural light were specifically engineered to make teaching and group study nearly impossible. Yet despite or perhaps because of this terrain of (im)possibility, we came together to read, reflect, exchange ideas—to plan, plot, and make sense of ourselves.

Our aim in this chapter is to critically examine the coming together of two white, queer, prison abolitionists employed as faculty members at a nearby university and a small group of jailed students who were almost exclusively modestly educated black men in the prime of their lives[1] for its *generative possibilities*.[2] Through a shared reading and study of texts

1. The demographics of our reading group reflect nationwide trends, in which modestly educated black men in the prime of their lives from low-wealth neighborhoods are disproportionately policed, arrested, and incarcerated (Gilmore 2007; Wolfers, Leonhardt, and Quealy 2015).

2. We want to emphasize this point. Our focus in this chapter is to amplify jailed students' theorizations of the carceral state. We are attempting to put this critical analysis in conversation with the logics that govern the neoliberal university in order not only to underscore the symbiotic relationship between the jail and the university but also to highlight contradictions in this relationship that allow for the growth of alternative ways of knowing and being in the world. Our focus here, then, is not on a nuanced reading of the ways in which we all internalize the carceral state—replicating its logics and practices in our daily lives. Although this important work must continue to be done, in this chapter we offer an abolitionist reading of the knowledge produced during our study group meetings and emphasize the political possibilities for building inside/outside alliances that account for vastly different material experiences with incarceration. We thus recognize the fragility yet urgency of a coalitional "we" that describes a shared commitment across social locations. However, real institutional restraints sometimes impeded our earnest desire for collective study with jailed students. For example, we did not obtain approval

ranging from *The Hunger Games* (Collins 2008) to *Between the World and Me* (Coates 2015), our group posed questions about racial capitalism, white supremacy, insurgent knowledge production, history, and resistance. Whereas the national debate on mass incarceration focuses largely on federal and state prisons, jail—with roughly 731,000 people locked up on any given day and nearly 12 million *new admissions* in an average year—is arguably mass incarceration's "front door" (Vera Institute of Justice 2015). Given this fact, jails are increasingly urgent yet often overlooked sites to consider questions about power, pedagogy, and justice.

Specifically, we argue that jailed students have theorized a set of obligations, what we term "fugitive counter-ethics," that not only serves as an indictment of the harmful and harm-inducing logics that govern the neoliberal university but also suggests ways to build alternative pedagogical praxes guided by improvisation, self-determined action, and what Michael Hames-García (2004) calls "relational freedom"—the core principles of fugitive counter-ethics.

In this spirit, we have chosen to frame our chapter around four pedagogical imperatives that stem directly from and remain in conversation with fugitive counter-ethics. We begin with the concept of "false teaching" theorized by a jailed student in our class. The term *false teaching* describes the deliberate, systemic omission of social identities and movement legacies that pose a challenge to the dominant order of the US educational apparatus. Next, we unpack how jailed students theorize the fugitive counter-ethics of improvisation and self-directed action through a critical reading of *The Hunger Games*. We connect this theory to Stefano Harney and Fred Moten's (2013) concept of "study" as a method to make visible and to disarticulate the forms of antirelationality that implicitly guide teaching expectations in the neoliberal university. We close

---

from the Institutional Review Board prior to conducting our reading group because we did not and do not conceive of our time at the jail as a "study." We were then legally prohibited from including direct in-text quotations of writing by anonymous students. The only allowable workaround was to paraphrase, thereby ghosting the specific characterizations and turns of phrase that animate the heart of this analysis.

by taking up the last principle of fugitive counter-ethics, "relational freedom." We draw from the black radical tradition's theorization and practice of revolutionary love to argue that relational freedom is a call to action that challenges the neoliberal university's positioning of prison education programs as a humanitarian project divorced from social movements and structural change.

False Teaching and the "Humanizing" Rhetoric of Prison Programs

A close reading of Ta-Nehisi Coates's book *Between the World and Me* generated a serious discussion about the ways educational projects often occlude histories of struggle. During a back-and-forth conversation, students began to theorize the idea of "false teaching," which guides this section. False teaching, to paraphrase students, means pedagogy delimited by what power wants you to know. Neoliberal education programs of false teaching, including those that take place in prison, serve the interests of the state rather than those of radical political projects. Following student theorists, we offer a critique of how so-called humanizing rhetoric writ large dominates the way prisons and the people in them become legible to policy makers and universities. Both the university and the jail cleave to a limited vision of education as preparation for assimilation into the oppressive status quo, while those deemed unassimilable become props for other people's morality and invulnerability. A fictitious concept of the prisoner gets figured as a fungible, captive audience for reconciling demands of tough-on-crime yet soft-hearted security. In other words, prison expansion works hand in hand with so-called humanitarian efforts to cage prisoners less brutally. The racialized figure of the prisoner, as an abstract receptacle for white fears of violence and fantasies of saviorism, centralizes the pitfalls of prison programs marked by education for assimilation.

Destructive political aims—to reaffirm the status quo as a benevolent good—underwrite the prison program's humanizing rhetoric. In addition to softening the image of the jail, this rhetoric presumes to index incarcerated people with more "human" faces, but for radical pedagogues in prison and jail settings it is the inhumanity of *cages* and of the people who champion them that sparks abolitionist action. Such institutional rebrandings evoke the specter of race, but only in its containment and rehabilitation to fit safely into the racial order's expectation of its capitalist production. The humanizing rhetoric of jails acts as a vehicle through which the language of cultural pathology flows between the jail and the university in the guise of justice. The university constantly pushes this humanizing rhetoric, which obscures the ongoing operations of an institution never designed for radical study.

The notion of "false teaching" makes visible the masks education wears to defang radical study through its safe containment. Indeed, the relationship between social justice and the neoliberal university is rife with contradiction. Public education, as one of the collective goods in the process of rapid privatization, has become a key site of struggle amid current austerity politics and ongoing post–civil rights backlash. The neoliberal trifecta of austerity, precarity, and contingency works to gut tenure lines, compound student debt, and dismantle disciplinary formations, in particular those with explicit social justice missions. Ethnic studies programs emerged out of midcentury student-of-color-led activism and today strive to remain accountable to these legacies despite institutional attempts to erase or sanitize racial justice movements. Although organizers in the 1960s and 1970s fought for diversification of university curricula and hallways, their victories were also defeats, as the culture wars of the 1980s made way for two warring threads, paradoxically strengthened by each other: one, white rage against the presence of liberatory praxes emerging out of social identities and movements not aligned with the presumed Eurocentric basis for knowledge consumption at the university; and, two, the co-optation of the language and strategies originally deployed by decolonization movements. Multiculturalist logics of diversity management, inclusivity, and comfort sanitize and tokenize race while absenting the critique of institutional racism, a critique that has the power to radicalize people across racial lines.

To champion the language of race while absenting discussions of racism satisfies an institutional need for antiracist subjects divorced from praxis,[3] replacing a real commitment to the eradication of injustice through community organizing with celebrated forms of "service and volunteerism"—the neoliberal replication of colonialist logics of the White Man's Burden (Harkins and Meiners 2014). The uncritical celebration of community-outreach programs eviscerates notions of the collective good, replacing it with individual acts of benevolent charity. Although educational institutions should certainly have a relationship with adjacent communities, strategic "outreach" without meaningful exchange incorporates the language of community into the neutralization of a power imbalance. In other words, the mere existence of justice-oriented programming in universities and prisons does not demonstrate a genuine investment in social transformation but rather often a hierarchical relationship of care between community and university wherein the university gets falsely lionized as public servant. In the case of education-in-prison programs specifically, the neoliberal university capitalizes on the strategies of prison abolition but does not pursue the broader vision of a holistic transformation of society that builds social relations and concepts of justice not dependent on violent masquerades of crime and punishment.

We stand at a crossroads where white students rage against the sanitized pledge to social justice in higher education, and yet that commitment has already been co-opted to serve the interests of the neoliberal university. (One might imagine a hoard of hunters taking aim at a menacing polar bear, but that bear was taxidermied long ago by those same hunters.) Given the redoubling of backlash, what does it mean to be in the university but not of the university, to use Harney and Moten's generative formulation? How might we extend that question to think through prison pedagogy that is in the jail but not of the jail? As Harney, Moten, and others have argued, a commitment to prison abolition requires a radical

3. We are grateful for ongoing conversations with Felice Blake, organizer of Anti-racism, Inc. We also thank a member of that collective, Daniel Silber-Baker, for inspiring our essay title through his deep exploration of how radical acts of the imagination contest prison expansion.

rebuilding of the university anew, and the transformation of education requires an abolitionist commitment to the impossibility of "humanizing" cages.[4]

Education in the university by design prepares students to become good consumer-citizen-subjects (hence the reviling of disciplines that at least in theory reject normative terms of racial capitalist existence). Under the guise of decreasing recidivism, the carceral institution selectively champions programs that prepare formerly incarcerated people for reentry into a world where they will properly abide by rather than disrupt the social order's rules of capital—a paradox when one considers that the existing social order depends on the criminalization of those very bodies as capital.[5] Jailed students are acutely aware of these contradictions. To paraphrase an observation made by several of the students we have studied with: "Forget jail. It looks like a jail out there." A student recording broadcast on the *Inside Prison Podcast* offers a similar analysis: "My living conditions—where education is limited by visions of recidivism haunting my re-entry like the shadows of barbed wire fences" (Rose 2016).

The neoliberal university, then, molds education into a repackaged commodity with a waning market value and in so doing exploits the language and labor of justice movements while absenting people invested in those very movements from its classrooms. Without recognizing its role in reproducing hierarchy, the university situates prison education programs in the fray of absented activists and a Teach for America brand of hardship tourism that does little to structurally address and redress the school-to-prison pipeline, a two-tiered public K–12 system, segregation, and other educational injustices (Tomlinson and Lipsitz 2013, 12–16). This Teach

4. As Harney and Moten write, "The slogan on the Left, then, *universities, not jails*, marks a choice that may not be possible. In other words, perhaps more universities promote more jails. Perhaps it is necessary finally to see that the university contains incarceration as the product of its negligence" (2013, 113, italics in the original). See also Kelley 2016.

5. One example of this paradox would be how neoliberal distance-learning programs at prisons and universities understand students as income generators (Lewen 2008, 695).

for America–style incorporation of the community good finds an easy outlet in the popular framing of prison programs as "humanizing" incarceration—often against the program facilitators' stated aims and political proclivities.

What remains most troubling about the university's anxious repetition of the insidious refrain "people, not prisoners" is its categorical denial of humanity to incarcerated people not brought into the fold of service or volunteer projects administered by the university. Cloaking prisoners in the language of dehumanization ignores how they theorize their own lives, offer transformative solutions, as well as incite and mobilize organizers on the outside with their active struggle on the inside. In addition to not minimizing the very real restrictions that antiblack, anti-Latinx, anti-indigenous, and antipoor carceral regimes enact on individuals, hegemony sees the creative vitality of people refusing oppressive ways of organizing social life as a danger to its perpetuity. Prisons exist not only as a simple solution to complex economic and social problems but also as a political tool of maintaining dominance—incarcerating challenges to power. The proliferation of political prisoners in the wake of black liberation movements makes this claim clear (Camp 2016).

The disenfranchisement and "dehumanization" of radicalized prisoners achieves the political end of absenting their voices from the struggle, but it would be highly presumptive at best to assume prisoners allow the inhumane weapons of the state or legal status to wholly crush their personhood. As Cedric Robinson reminds us in *Forgeries of Memory and Meaning* (2007), the messiness of power disallows its desired seamless hold on subjects. Much scholarly attention has necessarily been focused on social debt and what Orlando Patterson (1982) describes (in the context of slavery's reduction of enslaved people to the legal status of nonpersonhood) as "social death."[6] But it is incarcerated social *life*, precisely, that exists

---

6. In a landmark study of blackness as a condition of ontological impossibility, Patterson defines "social death" as slavery's denial of legal rights to personhood to enslaved Africans and their descendants, reducing the slave to a "social nonperson" in the eyes of the law (1982, 5). Many ethnic studies scholars have mobilized and extended Patterson's influential "social death" thesis to the afterlives of slavery. Abdul JanMohamed (2005),

as the precondition for its annihilation. Ultimately, we must understand the rhetoric of dehumanization in jails and prisons to be part of the same mechanism that facilitates the humanization of jails and prisons through the civilizing mission of the neoliberal university's production of "good" (i.e., capitalist-conforming) subjects. Fugitive counter-ethics, in its insistence on incarcerated social life over and against state-sanctioned death economies, instead looks to how prisoners theorize their own lives, write their own narratives, and activate—through their artistry and activism—abolitionist visions of a world without cages.

Trojan Horse Tactics: Study and *The Hunger Games*

In 2016, we began our spring semester by reading *The Hunger Games* (2008–10), the best-selling dystopian trilogy by Suzanne Collins set in a futuristic world destroyed by human-induced climate change. Through the eyes of the novel's sixteen-year-old heroine, Katniss Everdeen, the series examines dynamics of social control, capitalism, (in)justice, solidarity, and resistance. According to our field notes, the third week of class began in a typical fashion, which is to say there was no clear beginning. Unlike on the outside, the form and rituals that typically inaugurate the start of class were unavailable to us at the jail. There was no classroom to enter, let alone to stand authoritatively in front of, nor were we temporally bound by a class period. On this particular day in the jail, half the class was missing, leaving just four students. Yet among those who were present, the conversation was lively. We flowed in and out of discussions about musical tastes, professional sports, and the poor selection of books at the jail library and learned the names of other prisoners who were interested in joining our reading group.

Dylan Rodríguez (2008), and Lisa Marie Cacho (2012), for example, examine how the operation of racial power—from the prison–industrial complex to immigration policy—constrains people's material circumstances and psychic lives. The daily violence of racial regimes means that some subjects are "formed, from infancy on, by the imminent and ubiquitous threat of death" (JanMohamed 2005, 2).

After roughly thirty minutes had passed, we teachers began to eye one another. *Should we begin? Is it worth starting if half the class is missing? Which one of us should issue the call to begin? Then again, has class already begun?* In their groundbreaking text *The Undercommons: Fugitive Planning and Black Study* (2013), Harney and Moten describe that moment when teachers begin class, perhaps with a hearty "Good afternoon!" or by clearing their throats and saying, "Let's get started" (126). In that instance, they argue, instructors act "as an instrument of governance" by calling the class to order. What instructors "presuppose is that there is no study happening before [they] got there, no planning happening. [They] call class to order and *then* something can happen—then knowledge can be produced" (126, emphasis in original).

Ironically, the organized disorder of the jail made it easier for us to see "what new kinds of things might emerge out of the capacity to refuse to issue the call to order" (Harney and Moten 2013, 126). In so doing, we found that abandoning the call facilitated something closer to what Harney and Moten define as "study—a mode of thinking with others separate from the thinking that the institution requires of you"—to take place (2013, 11). For example, we eventually found our way to *The Hunger Games* and began to take turns reading aloud from a pivotal passage that describes Katniss mourning the loss of a fellow tribute, Rue. During our collective reading, we paused to consider why Rue's death, in particular the choice to grieve her passing, proves to be a turning point for Katniss. Students suggested that Rue's death changes the conditions of the "game," enabling Katniss to think outside the box, including radically reevaluating why she is playing in the first place. Students theorized that Rue's death has not, as the Capitol hopes, demoralized Katniss to the point of giving up but instead has politicized her. She has come to the games with one goal: to make it back home. Now, students surmised, Katniss recognizes that the only way to avenge Rue's death and protect her own loved ones is by overthrowing the Capitol. To paraphrase one student's conclusion, it is the love that Katniss has for her family and Rue that ignites her revolutionary consciousness.

As this synopsis makes evident, the similarities between the Hunger Games and jail were not lost on the students. Therefore, they recognized that Rue's death is a catalyst for Katniss, enabling her to make life in the arena by deciding to overthrow the Capitol on her terms. By escaping the games without having to kill, Katniss and her fellow tribute turned accomplice Peeta not only expose but also refuse the logics of the Capitol. To paraphrase another student, Katniss refuses to be a pawn in the Capitol's death match. Rather than do what is expected of her—kill or be killed—Katniss does the unexpected and becomes illegible to the game itself by creating her own moves. After all, the student commented, the Capitol can never fully own the hearts and minds of tributes.

This analysis also illuminates the core elements of what we term fugitive counter-ethics. As articulated here, fugitive counter-ethics gestures toward a commitment to improvisation (doing the unexpected), self-determined action (making her own moves), and what Hames-García identifies as "relational freedom"—the belief in a "collectivist self and the impossibility of freedom while others are unfree" (2004, 230). Moreover, the fugitive counter-ethics theorized here demonstrates jailed students' astute capacity to find and make life "where death and destruction dominate" (Gordon 2008, 654)—in other words, to remember there is love out there, too.

Fugitive counter-ethics grates against the educational status quo of training students to be better capitalists by emphasizing study over and against instruction. As opposed to a neoliberal education, critically conscious study proposes another mode of thinking about justice-oriented pedagogy that is collective, collaborative, and nonhierarchical.[7] In elaborating this concept of study, Harney and Moten emphasize one of its meanings "as a sketch in preparation," which turns on the "unfinished or the unready or the unfit" (2013, 173). Those deemed "unfit" for existing institutions, such as the jailed students we studied with, often offer the most transformative epistemologies for social change.

---

7. We are grateful for a lively discussion with Eli Meyerhoff in which he elaborated his concept of "modes of study" from his forthcoming book *We Are the Crisis: Study against the Romance of Education.* See also Dyke and Meyerhoff 2013.

Therefore, we argue that study must inform our pedagogical practices in a way that might be deemed *criminal*, especially in the intellectually hyperpoliced spaces of the jail and the university. Our use of the word *criminal* here signals an embrace of Moten and Harney's argument that the only ethical relationship we can have with the university is necessarily a criminal one: "To abuse [the university's] hospitality, to spite its mission, to join its refugee colony, its gypsy encampment, to be in but not of—this is the path of the subversive intellectual in the modern university" (2013, 101). Intentionally taking on the mantle of criminality exposes and undermines entrenched expectations of who and what constitutes both crime and education in the popular imaginary.

Fugitive counter-ethics as pedagogy deploys Trojan Horse tactics to exchange radical ideas—such as using Suzanne Collins's *The Hunger Games* as the platform for discussing key concepts from Cedric Robinson's work *Black Marxism* (1983). In so doing, we could critique state-sponsored brutality through coded language: for example, when the guards loomed over our shoulders during our class, as they were apt to do, especially when conversation seemed particularly lively, we called (out) the police by their ironic name in Collins's dystopian world, *peacekeepers*, which we would signal to humorous effect using air quotes;[8] referred to the US government as "the Capitol," the seat of power in the text; and elaborated histories of slavery with reference to District 11, the segregated agricultural unit of production in *The Hunger Games*, rather than directly invoke plantation capitalism in the antebellum South. What we call "Trojan horse tactics" suggest possibilities for the symbolic, evocative language of fiction, which can do work for us both to strategically hide and to reveal radical critique, particularly as necessary in spaces of confinement.

Practicing study as an expression of fugitive counter-ethics in the classroom puts an emphasis on creating spaces of mutual transformation and

---

8. Humor, in fact, serves as a Trojan horse tactic. Shared laughter enables horizontal sociality around a mutual distrust of prison guards, for example, by making visible who we stand with and for.

deep teaching against hollow forms of "diversity" or "representation" that replace analysis of entrenched realities of racism with myths of its heroic defeat. Study, after all, should be about ego-shattering exposure to history rather than complacent comfortability and genocidal erasure. As Coates recollects during his time at what he calls "Mecca," Howard University, "It began to strike me that the point of my education was a kind of discomfort, was the process that would not award me my own special Dream but would break all the dreams, all the comforting myths of Africa, of America, and everywhere, and would leave me only with humanity in all its terribleness" (2015, 52).

Whereas teaching at the jail might function like neoliberal education in that it divorces learning from social justice movements and their radical pedagogies, using fugitive counter-ethics to guide our pedagogical practices demands a commitment to exposing how and why the neoliberal carceral state scapegoats certain groups of people for what are in effect complex social, political, and economic problems (Gilmore 2007). Study must also expose students to black freedom dreams and movement legacies—to survival amid suffering and to a deeply politicized love in the face of immense violence.

In short, fugitive counter-ethics in the classroom requires study, capacious visions of personal freedom and collective social life, as well as nonauthoritarian teaching for the transformation of—not assimilation into—existing institutions.[9] Refusing the call to order therefore serves as an inaugurating act that shares as kin one student's urging not to be a pawn in authority's game. Although risky and fraught with myriad forms of neoliberal entrapment, devising pedagogical practices that center study—a mode of being "with and for"—remains an ethical imperative if we are to work against the limited vision, shared by universities and jails alike, of education as preparation for assimilation into a society predicated on racially gendered premature death.

---

9. The phrase "teaching for transformation, not assimilation," guides Ninth Ward organizer and teacher Kalamu ya Salaam's activism in New Orleans, especially with Students at the Center. For more information, see http://www.sacnola.com/.

Writing Relational Freedom

This section considers one student's call for fugitive counter-ethics not only to disinvest in death economies but also to invest in community-based alternatives to jails and prisons. This investment in collective social life makes necessary the space of art as a vessel for bringing abolitionist imaginaries into existence. At the end of the semester, one student produced a creative piece that contrasted the physical and psychic conditions of the jail to the conditions of a world where imagination becomes reality. Although this world may read at first glance like wishful thinking or cliché, the student's writing advanced an argument in the black radical tradition about materializing visions of a transformed social world through art and activism. This juxtaposition of harsh material realities against the possibilities of other worlds-within-worlds powerfully demonstrates the abolitionist ethos of fugitive counter-ethics. Thus, we suggest that we must wrest love back from its institutional incorporation to promote humanization projects dependent on and ultimately bolstering the inhumane apparatus of the state. Our students reminded us of the urgency of revolutionary love in the fugitive planning of life economies.

Much understandable resistance exists to the assertion of sociality and love as galvanizing forces, which is steeped in the bleeding-heart liberal discourse this chapter seeks to oppose, but in the black radical tradition love has always meant something more than compassion or romance, something more than the false hope of salvific community or human relationality that inevitably reverts to a dialogue of transcending rather than transforming unlivable social conditions. As James Baldwin prophesizes in a letter to his nephew on the one hundredth anniversary of Emancipation, "There is no reason for you to try to become like white people and there is no basis whatever for their impertinent assumption that *they* must accept *you*. The really terrible thing, old buddy, is that *you* must accept *them*. And I mean that very seriously. You must accept them and accept them with love" ([1963] 1993, 8). The revolutionary call of (and to) love is not about selective humanization but about mutual recognition that we must abolish the structures that differentially order the conceptual trap of the "human" as such. Baldwin's point, which jailed students took seriously, is to contest the inhumanity of power's abstraction of the human—not to seek recognition within its existing racial schema. If we understand the interconnected web of survival, love, and activism as an assertion of preexisting humanity, not as a claim to it, we can think more critically about the false generosity of the neoliberal university and its pedagogies of de/humanization.

In a writing project we worked on at the end of the semester, students wrote letters to real or imagined loved ones after the model of Baldwin and Coates. They testified to feelings of aloneness without a safety net of love and care and to the intense vulnerability and unsafety of getting positioned as a threat to society. Despite loss, students urged others toward self-determination in the ethos of relational freedom: "See I'm telling you guys these things because I don't want y'all to lose faith, because when you lose faith you lose self. I remember a time when I lost myself." Students in our class imagined futures where unfreedom wasn't one's birthright: "As Ta-Nehisi Coates stated, 'And I am now ashamed of the thought, ashamed of my fear, of the generational chains I tried to clasp onto your wrists.' Instead of clasp the generational chains upon your wrists, let's break the chain." The chain represents both a systematic cycle of injustice and literal, physical restraint. After all, in an era during which we have seen a steady decrease in violent crimes, we have also seen an unprecedented increase in incarceration.[10] College-in-prison programs can, with minimal cost to the university, erect a smooth facade over larger patterns of

10. As Ruth Wilson Gilmore points out, the "California state prisoner population grew nearly 500 percent between 1982 and 2000, even though the crime rate peaked in 1980 and declined, unevenly but decisively, thereafter" (2007, 7). Amid an economic crisis, unchecked spending on the death economies of prisons, detention centers, and jails drastically reduces funds for life economies. In the name of reducing government regulation and so-called public safety, economic policies and mass incarceration severely cut public expenditure for basic social services such as education and health care—proving that profits take precedence over people. The university follows the same logics of rapid privatization and austerity measures—endemic to neoliberalism—that actively disinvest in public education, holistic health care, youth development, and other community programs and at the same time invest in the carceral state's expansion. Simultaneously, however, the university touts rhetorics of service in which prison programs figure increasingly, despite a slash in funding during the Clinton era.

redirecting funds from justice initiatives led by students and faculty of color to prison-building projects.

Although the benevolent incorporation of social justice rhetoric exposes some uneasy pedagogical congruities between the educational and carceral state, we also want to reflect on one of the most jarring differences between each site: the visibility of white supremacy. Whereas in university classrooms white supremacy must be unveiled precisely by reckoning with its enforced invisibility, in the jail whiteness remains relentless and repetitive. White supremacy and class privilege can be seen, heard, felt, and understood through the bodies cycling in and out of captivity as well as the edifice of cages that unevenly contains them: indeed, our incarcerated students understood white supremacy as structure. Their resistance to discussing white supremacy in class was not, as we initially guessed, the popular and reactionary refusal to discuss race so endemic to our times— but something else. Over the course of our time studying *Between the World and Me*, it became apparent that this book was a student favorite[11] precisely because of its examination of systemic racism. However, students were most interested in Coates's intracommunal analysis of race and racism. White supremacy was the stale air of the jail, the redundant and repetitive voices outside the block, and the cold metallic bars of their cages. Even the one white student in the class had a complex analysis of how his whiteness functioned as property within racialized space and how a critical conversation about whiteness implicated but did not exile him. Therefore, to overemphasize whiteness seemed an affront to the realities of life inside.

This affective pooling of testimony, urgency, and energy around a conversation on Ta-Nehisi Coates at the jail contrasted starkly with teaching James Baldwin's *The Fire Next Time* on campus. Yet *Between the World and Me* clearly echoes *The Fire Next Time*'s epistolary form and central concerns around criminal white "innocents" (for Coates, the Dreamers), violence and history, and a deeply politicized love born out of struggle. Just as Coates describes how fictions of race attempt to obfuscate white brutality in an era of mass incarceration, the figure of the prisoner acts as foil to white

---

11. Confirmed in our end-of-semester surveys.

"innocence" and immunity. Baldwin's text asks white students to unpack how their freedom depends on the unfreedom of so-called others in order to generate a new basis for identity formation not predicated on subordination.

Discussion of Baldwin's work in the college classroom outside prison typically necessitates diagramming the burning house about which Baldwin famously writes—"Do I really *want* to be integrated into a burning house?" ([1963] 1993, 94)—to bring to light the routinely invisible whiteness of its foundations. In the fifty-year gap between Baldwin's and Coates's publications, from 1963 to 2013, at the bicentennial of the Emancipation Proclamation, exists that slow-burning flame: the omnipresence of whiteness whose interests both the jail and the neoliberal university protect. Pairing Baldwin and Coates offers vital classroom conversation at both the university and the jail on how to disrupt the insidious people/prisoners binary. Moreover, as one student reminded us, writing projects that hinge on the relational freedom central to fugitive counter-ethics juxtapose the pains and pleasures of living to imagine an otherwise and otherwhere free from mass incarceration's replacement of communal care with cages.

Abolitionist Time Zones

Creative production cannot directly stop a jail from being built, but it can shift the political landscape that rationalizes prison-expansion projects. During our study of Coates's *Between the World and Me*, we kept returning to the question of what it means to lose one's body. In so doing, students developed the concept of "time zones" to characterize the jail. Changing landscapes and experiences make possible the recognition of time's passing, but the warped temporality of the jail transforms moving time into still time, wherein repetition and monotony produce anger and listlessness. In this way, students reflected, the class allowed them to take hold of time. This active reclamation defies state restraints on time, as students wear reminders of their court or release date printed on their ID wristbands. Amid the jail's suspended time, abolitionist imaginaries can come into existence through the moving time of growth and study. The abolitionist orientation of fugitive counter-ethics does not wait for a messianic upturning of global racial capital but exists in transformative zones of social encounter—the messy work of living out activist imaginaries through collective praxis.

Fugitive counter-ethics urges us to consider how we can act as accomplices to former, current, and future students inside jail struggling to get free in the long run and how we can alleviate their suffering in the short term. One possible route is to forge alliances between inside students and outside students that are defined not by paternalistic notions of service, community, or democratic engagement but by fugitive counter-ethics: improvisation, self-determined action, and relational freedom—theorized here as the revolutionary call to remember that, as one student said, there is love out there, too. Although no modest task, networking our teaching into ongoing social justice movements will undoubtedly open up "other sites of intervention, build [unforeseen] allegiances, and create new modes of communication" (Harkins and Meiners 2014).[12] With that, we improvise; we study; we account for and are accountable to the queer, black, brown, indigenous, poor, and rebellious bodies ghosted by the state; we turn to fugitive thought for insurgent practices of safety, justice, and freedom; we employ haunting as an experiential mode to devise new pedagogical practices that are disloyal to the project of the neoliberal university itself. As we inhabit the structures that inhibit and incite our subtle social transformations, we must listen carefully to visions of a just world that jailed students call into being.

References

Baldwin, James. [1963] 1993. *The Fire Next Time*. New York: Vintage.
Cacho, Lisa Marie. 2012. *Social Death: Racialized Rightlessness and the Criminalization of the Unprotected*. New York: New York Univ. Press.

12. Following our initial reading group, we cofounded Humanities Behind Bars, a prison education program committed to abolitionist praxis. Codirected by Kendrick McCray, a formerly incarcerated student, Humanities Behind Bars also formed Humanity Without Bars, a grassroots community organization devoted to collective study and critique of the carceral state as part of its coalitional efforts to join local antiprison activist struggles. For more information, see http://humanitiesbehindbars.org/.

Camp, Jordan T. 2016. *Incarcerating the Crisis: Freedom Struggles and the Rise of the Neoliberal State*. Berkeley: Univ. of California Press.

Coates, Ta-Nehisi. 2015. *Between the World and Me*. New York: Spiegel & Grau.

Collins, Suzanne. 2008. *The Hunger Games*. New York: Scholastic.

Dyke, Erin, and Eli Meyerhoff. 2013. "An Experiment in 'Radical' Pedagogy and Study: On the Subtle Infiltrations of 'Normal' Education." *Journal of Curriculum Theorizing* 29, no. 2: 267–80.

Gilmore, Ruth Wilson. 2007. *Golden Gulag: Prisons, Surplus, Crisis, and Opposition in Globalizing California*. Berkeley: Univ. of California Press.

Gordon, Avery F. 2008. "Methodologies of Imprisonment." *PMLA* 123, no. 3: 651–57.

Hames-García, Michael. 2004. *Fugitive Thought: Prisons, Movements, and the Meaning of Justice*. Minneapolis: Univ. of Minnesota Press.

Harkins, Gillian, and Erica Meiners. 2014. "Beyond Crisis: College in Prison through the Abolition Undercommons." *Lateral* 3 (Spring). At http://csa lateral.org/issue3/theory/harkins-meiners.

Harney, Stefano, and Fred Moten. 2013. *The Undercommons: Fugitive Planning and Black Study*. New York: Automedia.

JanMohamed, Abdul R. 2005. *The Death-Bound Subject: Richard Wright's Archaeology of Death*. Durham, NC: Duke Univ. Press.

Kelley, Robin D. G. 2016. "Black Study, Black Struggle." *Boston Review*, Mar. 7. At https://bostonreview.net/forum/robin-d-g-kelley-black-study-black-struggle.

Lewen, Jody. 2008. "Academics Belong in Prison: On Creating a University at San Quentin." *PMLA* 123, no. 3 (May): 689–96.

Meyerhoff, Eli. Forthcoming. *We Are the Crisis: Study against the Romance of Education*. Minneapolis: Univ. of Minnesota Press.

Patterson, Orlando. 1982. *Slavery and Social Death: A Comparative Study*. Cambridge, MA: Harvard Univ. Press.

Robinson, Cedric J. 1983. *Black Marxism: The Making of the Black Radical Tradition*. Chapel Hill: Univ. of North Carolina Press.

———. 2007. *Forgeries of Memory and Meaning: Blacks and the Regimes of Race in American Theater and Film before World War II*. Chapel Hill: Univ. of North Carolina Press.

Rodríguez, Dylan. 2008. "'I Would Wish Death on You . . .': Race, Gender, and Immigration in the Globality of the U.S. Prison Regime." *The Scholar & Feminist Online* 6, no. 3 (Summer 2008): 1–9.

Rose, Avion. 2016. "Jail Bird." *Inside Prison Podcast*, May 2. At https://www.youtube .com/watch?v=EInfptM8RlQ.

Tomlinson, Barbara, and George Lipsitz. 2013. "Insubordinate Spaces for Intemperate Times: Countering the Pedagogies of Neoliberalism." *Review of Education, Pedagogy, and Cultural Studies* 35, no. 1: 3–26.

Vera Institute of Justice. 2015. "Incarceration's Front Door: The Misuse of Jails in America." Feb. At http://www.vera.org/sites/default/files/resources/down loads/incarcerations-front-door-report.pdf.

Wolfers, Justin, David Leonhardt, and Kevin Quealy. 2015. "1.5 Million Missing Black Men." *New York Times*, Apr. 20. At http://www.nytimes.com/inter active/2015/04/20/upshot/missing-black-men.html?_r=0.

Part Three

Organized Prison Writing

9

Writing, Bodies, and Performance

Cultural Resistance behind Prison Walls

JULIE RADA AND RIVKA ROCCHIO

Mass incarceration in the United States demands a response. As citizens, as teachers, and as theater artists, we are called to intervene on this unjust, broken system. We recognize the limitations of our response. Nonetheless, some of the intrinsic characteristics of the theater are valuable in constructing a response to the system of mass incarceration. Dani Snyder-Young phrases the charge thus: "Artists and activists must identify whether *theatre* is the intervention their circumstances and goals require. Sometimes, its liveness, its balance between intimacy and distance, its poeticism, and its playful collaboration are *just* the things a project needs. And sometimes they are not" (2013, 3, emphasis in original). We respond emphatically yes, that in the case of incarceration in the United States these characteristics of theater Snyder-Young enumerates are precisely, though not exclusively, what the crisis needs. We lean on Snyder-Young's taxonomy here, putting liveness, intimacy/distance, poeticism, and playful collaboration in the context of prison theater workshops, using our respective projects as case studies, to examine how these four attributes of theatrical projects function as interventions on the prison system at large.

In the prison theater workshop, the presence of an outside artist as a facilitator and arts practitioner and, eventually, the presence of an audience at the performance event manifest in liveness, the immediacy of real humans connecting in the same time and in the same space. The presence of an audience witnessing a performance event brings out a dynamic interplay of intimacy and distance and perhaps serves as an antidote to the invisibility and isolation that constitute the prison experience. Poeticism, which can be described more broadly as aesthetics, functions in a liberational manner in places of proscription and confinement. It connects workshop participants to their own sensorial and embodied experiences and makes space for creative impulses to thrive. Playful collaboration serves to undermine the alienation of prison and positions an individual within a collective experience and a temporary community. Recognizing that our power as individual facilitators is extraordinarily limited, we endeavored with the Collective Crossroads project and the *Free Drama* script as cultural interventions to bring about small but meaningful effects in the "general historical evolution of wider social and political realities" (Kershaw 1992, 10) of a world in which so many are incarcerated. As such, the very idea of theater in prison, with the four attendant properties named earlier, challenges the given order as it revolves around ordinary people and their stories (Landy and Montgomery 2012, 130).

Philosophy and Practice of the Collective Crossroads and *Free Drama* Projects

The Collective Crossroads project took place in the spring of 2014, with Rada facilitating a thirteen-week workshop at Eyman State Prison, attended by approximately twenty male prisoners. The project resulted in an original performance entitled *Grounded: It's Breathtaking* performed for an audience of about fifty incarcerated men, Arizona State University (ASU) faculty, and Arizona Department of Corrections staff in April 2014. In the workshop, the voluntary participants discussed aesthetics and creative practices, learned specific performance-building techniques such as the Viewpoints, developed characters, engaged in physical improvisations, and composed original texts, individually and collectively.[1] Rada directed

---

1. The Viewpoints, developed by Mary Overlie and adapted for theater-making practices by Anne Bogart and Tina Landau, is a movement methodology that provides a vocabulary for developing physical moments.

the participants in this work, with the explicit goal, shared by the prisoners, of developing a performance ensemble. Using the image of a crossroads as a metaphor, we can envision individuals who retain a sense of their separate selves pausing momentarily at an intersection: a meeting place where an experience, such as a performance and its preparation, may be shared. These prisoners came from different histories and faced different futures, but they passed through the same crossing, sharing time in the prison theater workshop while continuing on their individual journeys. Mindful of not wanting to replicate hierarchies of power, the ensemble and Rada reflected as a group, recursively, on the role of leadership in ensemble, the need for consent to lead and teach, and continued emphasis on prisoners as agents of their own lives.

In the fall of 2015, Rocchio linked ASU theater undergraduate participants with prisoners at Eyman State Prison's Cook Unit, a medium-security facility holding a sex-offender population of about fourteen hundred men, to create an original play. The program allowed for three undergraduate participants and twelve prisoners to create a script, which eventually was entitled *Free Drama* and performed at Eyman on November 24, 2015, for an audience of ASU professors, Arizona Department of Corrections staff and administration, and Eyman prisoners. The university and prison participants did not meet in person until the day of the performance but communicated through writings. Rocchio's work focused on the process of cross-cultural collaborative theater making over the final end product, recognizing that the two are not separable. All ensemble members developed skills in ensemble building and collaborative storytelling by participating in theater exercises and activities to generate monologues, scenes, journal entries, and personal stories in the script development. Rocchio guided the ensemble through the process of identifying tone, purpose, and impact of each moment in the script so the group could sequence the play to their desired effect—creating a connection between the participants and the invited audience. Ultimately, *Free Drama* was a pastiche of monologues, spoken-word poetry, poems, and scenes that accomplished the artistic aim of using theater to build collective spaces of learning and creation across prison walls.

Because the two workshops took place at the same institution and in the same unit, two of the participants in Collective Crossroads had the opportunity to participate in *Free Drama* as well. These participants expressed feeling like veterans in the theater work and further articulated that their previous experience not only motivated a continued interest in theater but also compelled them to encourage others on the yard to participate. Their crossover allowed for some philosophical threads to run through both projects, so that the two workshops were in conversation with one another.

With both projects, the process of creating the script and the collective artistic collaboration of the participants both inside and outside prison were based on philosophical and pedagogical underpinnings that value collaboration and attempt to level hierarchies between learners and teachers. In the prison context in particular, we do not ascribe to the idea that prisoners require development in order to be "better" human beings, and we do not build the rehabilitative impulse into our pedagogy. From our limited anecdotal experience, it seems the conditions of incarceration may provide opportunities for positive self-growth should an individual wish to internalize them in such a way. Notably, it was with the workshop participants' expressed desire to learn and grow that we engaged, as opposed to imposing our own ideas of how to "develop" the participants in our own fashion.

Liveness: Performance as Visibility

Peggy Phelan asserts, "Performance honors the idea that a limited number of people in a specific time/space frame can have an experience of value which leaves no visible trace afterward" (1993, 149). The prison workshop is a pedagogical enterprise that makes space for collective artistic expression, with outcomes that can be measured in a tangible artifact—an original script—and illustrated through the less-tangible live-performance event. Though ephemeral, the performance makes temporarily visible the education at work. Claire Bishop writes that "art is given to be seen by others, while education has no image" (2012, 241). Staging a performance event for an audience opens up the possibility of cultural dialogue rather than framing the work as solely educational. Most models of education usually benefit only the student, the one who is educated. In a critical pedagogy that incorporates aesthetics, as the prison theater workshop does, students must test the communicability of their ideas and creative impulses in exchange with a live audience of spectators. Performances open the classroom walls and, in this work, the prison walls to allow participants to be seen. With no trace afterward, the prison performance dissolves into an experience of value—or, as one participant reported, "I felt like the performance touched other people and expressed things I needed to get out. Does it change my situation? No. I don't have a lot of good memories here. You've given me one. This is a good memory I will never forget."[2]

Liveness breaks the monotony and sameness of the daily life of prison for both prisoners and administrators. Another participant in Collective Crossroads described how the liveness and presence of an audience brought energy back into his life: "I've been locked up for twenty-two years; I think I was in shock. It was exhilarating. I felt alive for the first time."[3] Similarly, an ensemble member in *Free Drama* remarked that the performance gave him a chance to connect to others in a way he had not thought possible: "The performance, the entire experience, moved me in more ways than I could describe. I will remember it all forever."[4]

A performance captures and documents a moment in time in a particular, if temporary, community's story. Performance humanizes because it contains within it some of the complexity of the humanity of the people who have created it. The audience must contend with real people, performing in the same time and space, in and around them. They cannot be seen as generalized tropes but are necessarily individualized and made more dimensional, "implicat[ing] the real through the presence of living bodies" (Phelan 1993, 148). An audience has to contend with the reality of the prisoners, with the living, breathing, expressive body of each individual, as opposed to stereotypes of the imagined criminal "other."

2. Anonymous participant, Collective Crossroads, postworkshop discussion, Eyman State Prison, Apr. 16, 2014.

3. Ibid.

4. Anonymous participant, *Free Drama*, postworkshop survey, ASU, Dec. 17, 2015.

Balance of Intimacy and Distance

As an aesthetic form, theater offers a space that is neither too intimate nor too distant: "Too much intimacy can feel intrusive; too much distance can feel like nothing at all and can easily be disregarded" (Cohen-Cruz 2010, 11). Here we use the terms *distance* and *intimacy* as ways of describing both physical space (not too far, not too close) and emotional states (not too guarded, not too exposed). The liveness of the theatrical event and the presence of supportive witnesses fundamentally oppose the prison's function to separate and isolate. In our projects, audience and performers were close enough to sense each other's physical presence, hear each other's whispers, and see the small details and physical features that make each person unique. This kind of specificity, found only through physical closeness, transforms the abstracted "other" into someone real and individual. Prisoners moved into a conversational distance with members of the outside audience, though they never touched them. For those who have little contact with people who are incarcerated, this proximity may be threatening, though in the performance context the audience soon learns that they are relatively safe. For incarcerated performers with little contact with outsiders, the proximity to strangers may also seem intimidating. But in a performance context prisoners, too, learn that the audience is there to witness them and will not behave in any erratic or untoward way that will make them feel shy or put them at risk of institutional consequences. In essence, in the performances described here both groups learned that they could safely share physical space.

Live performance is an emotional experience, too. In Collective Cross-roads and *Free Drama*, both performers and witnesses visibly laughed, cried, and were demonstrably expressive in a range of ways often not expressed in social contexts, particularly in a prison setting. At least two participants in the Collective Crossroads project described in postproject assessments that they "felt seen" in the workshop and that this was "healing." After the performance, many of the men described feeling "understood."[5] A prison

5. Anonymous participants, Collective Crossroads, postperformance discussion with audience, Eyman State Prison, Apr. 11, 2014, and postperformance assessments distributed Apr. 11, 2016.

theater project does not render permanently visible those who remain un-witnessed, but it complicates the separation between those on the inside and those on the outside in practical and symbolic ways.

Paolo Freire writes, "Only through communication can human life hold meaning" (2000, 77). As humans, we need to be seen and heard; our identity is conferred through the expression of our voice. In both the Collective Crossroads and *Free Drama* projects, the individuals involved were represented in the script, through their writing, in their performances, through their bodies and voices, expressing and representing their experience. Perhaps it was not so much the content of the work but the fact of the performance act itself that most provided meaning to the participants. Engaged in performance, they held the audience's attention; they were fundamentally witnessed; they communicated and expressed themselves. Paul Woodruff writes,

> There is an art to watching and being watched, and that is one of the few arts on which all human living depends. If we are unwatched, we diminish and we cannot be entirely as we wish to be. If we never stop to watch, we know only how it feels to be us, never how it feels to be another. Watched too much or in the wrong way, we become frightened. Watching too much, we lose the capacity for action in our own lives. Watching well, together, and being watched well, with limits on both sides, we grow, and grow together. (2008, 10)

People who are incarcerated are unwatched by society, or they are watched too much and in the wrong way, becoming frightened or losing the capacity for action. Theater provides a space for supportive watching or witnessing because the space is neither too intimate nor too distant.

Intimacy and Distance in Writing

Collaborative creative practice is intimate work, and in the process of developing the *Free Drama* script the possibility of authentic connection existed within the workshop sessions. In particular, much of the writing was intimate in that the writers revealed themselves with vulnerability and, seemingly, without apology to readers. Even talking about intimacy, closeness, and truth can shut down a prison-based arts program before it gets started. At numerous volunteer and security trainings, the Department of Corrections emphasized the necessity of keeping discussions strictly on the subject matter, not giving personal details, and maintaining emotionally distant relationships with prisoners. Facilitating spaces in which connection and vulnerability can thrive is precarious work in any social context, but especially so in a prison.

Writing opens opportunities for understanding and connection with others in ways that discussion and other forms of pedagogical exchange may not. Jill Dolan describes the practice of writing creatively as a chance to "try on, try out, exchange with another site of anticipation, which is the moment of intersubjective relation between word and eye, between writer and reader, all based on the exchange of empathy, respect, and desire" (2005, 168). The engaged performance methodologies that created *Free Drama*, for example—collaborative-writing methods, dialogic theater-making practices, and the exchange of questions and responses—generate give and take between the prison and university communities. This exchange builds "actively committed relationship[s] to the people most affected by the subject matter" (Cohen-Cruz 2010, 9). In other words, the connective and close spaces created through the intimate practice of writing and performance can be created only through personal investment and a shift in expectations.

Shifting the power of who tells what story and how those stories are seen creates new spaces for understanding and empathetic connection. Although the monologues and scenes in *Free Drama* were grounded in personal stories, the writers did not perform them. In this manner, preexistent expectations and the assumption of knowledges become disrupted by learning, embodying, and reliving another's story. The casting for the performance disrupted expectations regarding age, gender, status of incarceration, and race, which served to dispel the limitations of performers retelling their stories and to fit in the pedagogical aim of creating cohesion between the inside participants and the outside participants. For example, a female university student performed a monologue written by an inside participant that described decades of drug abuse and the experience of becoming a father. Similarly, a middle-aged male incarcerated participant performed a monologue that captured the frustrations of fighting with a sister, the acceptance of a transgender identity, and judgment by strangers. This monologue, located in the opening moments of *Free Drama*, reads as a symbolic moment in which the possibilities for connection between the ensemble seem limitless.

The ability to try on other people's stories and to connect to others in an unfiltered way creates a powerful and intimate relationship. Many participants in *Free Drama* responded that their favorite moment was watching their own monologue performed by someone else. This speaks to the deep interpersonal experience that occurs in ensemble-based creation in an asset-based framework, in which participants feel supported, connected, and accomplished.[6] Rocchio recognized the success of the personal connection between inside and outside ensembles during the performance when she watched a writer cathartically cry as his monologue was performed by a university student actor. The performer wrote afterward about the emotional connection she felt between herself and the writer: "Even though we have rehearsed with the material separately prior to the actual performance day, I believe hearing and seeing their personal intimate words brought to the surface feelings they may not have known they were wrestling with. [He] approached me thanking me for the performance I had done. [He] felt I had respected his words."[7] In the performance of one another's stories, the two ensembles achieved collective intimacy through an emotional connection. This connection, built across distance and walls, traversed the physical distance that separated university and prison participants.

Poeticism: Aesthetic of Beauty in a Space of Scarcity

Spaces of containment are fundamentally aesthetically impoverished because they rely on separation and the reduction of complexity to sortable

---

6. Stephani Etheridge Woodson describes asset mapping as a model that "understands the diversity of capital assets" and begins with positive understandings of the resources and abilities of project participants (2015, 55).

7. Anonymous participant, *Free Drama*, postworkshop survey conducted at ASU, Dec. 17, 2015.

categories. In addition, because prisons operate on a principle of deprivation, sensory details such as visual, tactile, and gustatory complexity have been eliminated from the environment. The word *aesthetic* traces to Greek, is defined as being "sharp in the senses," and connects to intuition, observation, and experience. Sharpness in the senses creates meaning and synthesis in our lives (Lederach 2005, 69–70). To experience sensory deprivation is to experience a dampening in one of the modes by which we construct meaning in our lives and thus to create a sense of meaninglessness. In an anonymous preworkshop survey for Collective Crossroads asking why aesthetics is important, one participant wrote, "Because of the intrinsic joy of art and beauty."[8] Community-based theater practitioner James Thompson nods to Emma Goldman, lamenting that theater that proposes change to the social order is limited if it "forgets the radical potential of the freedom to enjoy *beautiful radiant things*," and he goes on to argue for centralizing the ephemeral by-products of "joy, fun, pleasure or beauty" (2009, 6, emphasis in original).

Prison is not a poetical place. Yet, in spite of the sensorial flatness of the prison environment, prisoners, like the rest of us, are sensual beings. In the Collective Crossroads project, Rada provided prompts to participants in which they were asked to share one sensual detail from their day or one experience that made them feel "sharp" in their senses. These individual sensorial tidbits accumulated in the script, so that in one scene the men describe the food from the prison cafeteria and the commissary they ate and compared it to other foods such as sushi, chai tea, and ripe fruit that they dreamed of eating. One character, fantasizing, exclaims, "I taste Hawaiian barbeque!" and his friend brings him back to the reality of prison: "Boiled chicken. Boiled chicken and watered-down barbeque sauce."[9] In this way, the performers shared their reality with a mixture of sadness and humor and created a sophisticated dialogue about the deprivation and

8. Anonymous participant, Collective Crossroads, preworkshop survey distributed Jan. 17, 2014, collected Jan. 22, 2014.
9. Eyman State Prison drama workshop participants, *Grounded: It's Breathtaking*, ed. and comp. Julie Rada (Mar. 2014).

cravings experienced in prison. Writing through the senses, sharing experiences that are both universal and specific, builds confidence because the senses are accessible to everyone. By using their five senses as source material, participants who were unaccustomed to writing and coming up with ideas on their own had the same intrinsic knowledge as anyone else. They were able to focus on what *was* available to them rather than to continue to dwell on resources or knowledges they lacked.

As practitioners, we have noted how the prisoners in both workshops demonstrated a high confusion threshold, particularly for untrained theater artists. In other words, the men's willingness to stick with something even when they did not entirely "get it" seemed relatively high compared to that of other collaborators with whom we have worked, though the prisoners made literal or aphoristic creative choices more commonly in their writing than in their physical work. Bishop asserts that "community arts today tends [*sic*] to self-censor out of fear that underprivileged collaborators will not be able to understand more disruptive modes of artistic production" (2012, 190). As artists, we prefer art that traffics in rupture, juxtaposition, and ambiguity (Bishop 2012, 192). Hoping not to impose our own artistic preferences on the workshop participants, we nonetheless discussed with them the aesthetics of nonlinear, abstract performance. In these conversations, we realized that rupture and the "unfinishedness" or "untidiness" of writing might be cultivated instead of avoided. In fact, rupture is perhaps an apt representation of prison life as well as more generally a representation of the human experience. In any theater workshop informed by critical pedagogy, the facilitator must acknowledge the dynamic in which the facilitator's artistic practice philosophically is "being with" the art of the participants, much like Freire's teacher learns *with* her students. In essence, our preferences mattered, and experimental, abstract theater-making methodologies should not be reserved for the cultural elite. If these methodologies inspire us as artists, they may inspire prisoner artists as well. Within every prison reside multitudes of skilled artists and writers, possessing greater or lesser degrees of aptitude, and countless cultural producers. Providing a range of art-making techniques from which to draw—from the basic to the most sophisticated—is essential in accessing the range of creative potential locked up in a prison.

Playful Collaboration

There is no such thing as a *neutral* educational process (Freire 2000, 34). In the practice of critical pedagogy, the practitioner makes power structures visible, names them, and intentionally works against hegemonic modes of instruction. In this way, she creates classrooms in which playful collaboration becomes the norm. Freire writes that "the teacher is no longer merely the-one-who-teaches, but one who is [her]self-taught in dialogue with the students, who in turn while being taught also teach" (2000, 80). Notably, other prison-based teaching artists acknowledge the prisoner-as-teacher dynamic as well. As Teya Sepinuck sums up regarding prisoners she taught, "They'd eaten, swallowed and digested questions that most of us barely take the time to acknowledge. They'd looked their demons in the eye and had found ways to live with what many would find unbearable. They would be my teachers" (2011, 165).

To practice this colearning dynamic demands attention to the arrangement of the space, thoughtful discussion prompts, and an appreciation of different ways of knowing. For example, as practitioners we facilitate work by standing or sitting in a circle with workshop participants, thus embodying a nonhierarchical relationship with them. Though our styles and histories are different, in our own ways we verbally articulate with participants how we aspire to work together as close to peers as circumstances allow, acknowledging the journey of learning together. Antonio Gramsci writes, "The intellectual's error consists in believing that one can know without understanding and even more without feeling and being impassioned" (1971, 418). Although we place emphasis on individual experience, transparency, and Gramsci's "understanding" in an attempt to correct the prioritization of academic knowledge over intrinsic ways of knowing, we realize that power never truly balances out. It is incumbent on the practitioner to recognize that the hierarchy can never be erased; yet although deliberately democratic spaces may be illusive inside prisons, the practitioner can leverage play to intentionally disrupt entrenched power structures.

Play is arguably one of the pillars of theatrical work. In both the Collective Crossroads and *Free Drama* workshops, we mindfully and strategically employed play as a tactic in our work, understanding play to be, as Bishop describes, a "non-alienating human activity available to all" (2012, 86). As the spirit of playfulness increased, so did the participants' trust in the work and willingness to explore other creative and emotional risks, embracing a range of experiences offered by the prison theater workshop. In places of high control, prescription, and supervision, such as prisons, play can feel and be disruptive and countercurrent to the status quo. Informed by liberatory praxis, the principal purpose of prison theater programs is to create, through play and other means, spaces of freedom and agency (Snyder-Young 2013, 62–63). These temporary spaces validate the expression of identity and humanness.

Friedrich von Schiller asserts that "man is only completely human when he plays" (1967, 15). The lack of usefulness in play and often in art is arguably their humanizing power, especially among incarcerated people. As Michel Foucault describes, where once a condemned man became the king's property, "now he will be rather the property of society, the object of a collective and useful appropriation" (1977, 109). In many cases, people who are incarcerated provide cheap and surplus labor for profit or are warehoused, deemed disposable, and made no longer necessary in the functioning of the global economy (Alexander 2012, 18). Particularly in the global economy focused on market production, play has a humanizing effect because it does *not* produce a product. Play cannot make a prisoner useful to society. Play produces temporary and intrinsic joy, and in play a prisoner's body and time cannot be appropriated for productive use.

We recall numerous examples of participants in both workshops throwing themselves into fun with abandon, demonstrating that their spirits were not broken by their conditions. Rada used the Hokey-Pokey as a vocal and physical warm-up but without naming it and with total solemnity, describing it as an advanced theatrical practice that integrates the entire expressive apparatus and calls on iconic, traditional, and cultural symbols. The men in the workshop were ready to dive into this as yet unnamed but seemingly serious practice. When they were surprised with "You put your right hand in," the levity in the room was palpable: all the men laughed and were totally engaged, moving through the entire Hokey-Pokey with full commitment and a bit of laughter.

Another example is from a rehearsal of *Free Drama* in which the men practiced the Viewpoints. In this particular composition, Rocchio invited the men to come in and out of the play space—allowing for a flexible negotiation between participant and observer to better develop an idea of what compels focus onstage. As one improvised moment came to a resolution, all of the men but one left the play space and went back to their seats. The lone man lay down in the space. A moment passed. Everyone waited. The seated men grew uncomfortable. The man was still on the floor. After an uncomfortably long time, the men began to snicker, and soon they all were laughing. The laughter reached a crescendo and then settled back to silence. After some time, it started up again. Eventually, after what might have been five minutes, another man joined the man lying on the floor, and the composition picked up again. When the group paused to discuss the moment, many things became clear—the men articulated the power of expectation, group response, and the importance of timing in humor on stage. When Rocchio pressed them about *why* what happened was funny, it was simply because they agreed it was funny. Laughter, humor, and joy are shared agreements that disappear almost as soon as they are recognized. Their ephemerality, however, does not negate their importance. Perhaps the spirit of play, manifested in a man lying down, in the ritual of the Hokey-Pokey, and in a number of other improvisations, possesses as much potential for resistance to the cruelty and isolation of prison as any radical form of protest.

Writing and Creating Collaboratively

Playful collaboration is illustrated most clearly in the process of developing the performance and composing an original script as an ensemble. Both workshops engaged in collective-writing processes to garner engagement and a sense of investment from all participants, regardless of writing ability, education level, or learning barriers. Even in collective writing, sometimes the participants' limitations and doubts get revealed—this is where the physical and embodied practices of theater intervene. When ensemble members were in the process of creating on their feet, Rocchio took on the role of scribe and jotted down notes, ideas, and phrases.

Although not a perfect system, this documentation allowed for the exploration and inclusion of those writers who struggled to put pen to page or to cross a language barrier or were otherwise blocked from written expression. Later, as the script took shape, the recollection of these moments of embodied text were referenced and incorporated into the text as meaningful contributions.

In Collective Crossroads, Rada facilitated a process called "bucketing."[10] In bucketing, participants are given a number of note cards and are encouraged to write a "creative unit" on each note card. A "creative unit" in the workshop is anything anyone says, does, reads, or sees at any time that is interesting, poetic, profound, funny, or insightful. These units can be collected from casual dialogue, structured activities, physical improvisations, or anything else. Over the process of several weeks, hundreds of note cards with "creative units" are generated. Because these units are tiny bits of information, they are not intimidating to write. The moments are, to some degree, taken out of context, later to be remixed into scenes, dialogues, imagery, and storylines. This is a simple and demystifying way to encourage a creative lens through which to filter one's experience of the world. Some participants generate a large volume of note cards, whereas others produce fewer, but every participant has something to contribute, and it is relatively easy to work these contributions into the larger final script. The note cards are anonymous, so it is difficult to privilege one voice over another or for a writer to stake a claim of ownership over a particular idea. The collaborative authorship of bucketing is a sloppy and tedious process, but it captures a group's collective intentions. Both inside prisons and in processes with creative professionals, Rada has experienced how the bucketing process allows a high level of investment on the part of all the artists in an ensemble and a sense of shared responsibility for the final product.

This process manifested in character discovery and development during a group composition exercise that spanned two workshop sessions.

10. Bucketing is a cocreation process designed by the LIDA Project and Brian Freeland, based loosely on Tristan Tzara's and later William Burroughs's cut-up method. Rada further adapted this process for collective script development.

The exercise prompt asked participants to complete the following sentence about what they believed: "The American Dream is. . . ." Then Rada asked them to consider a person, fictional or actual, who was very different from themselves who might hold this same belief. The characters they created were surprising and diverse. One man performed an eight-year-old girl from El Salvador with a disability; another performed a character who Rada assumed was an approximation of his mother; another performed a disillusioned retired soldier who had recently returned to Atlanta and discovered his home had changed. Rada also facilitated a "hot-seat" exercise in which the men embodied these characters, their physical and vocal idiosyncrasies, and engaged in extemporaneous dialogue with the other participants through a question-and-answer format. Meanwhile, the other participants were recording on their note cards snippets of text that were interesting or struck them as poetic. Rada later mixed up these characters into different scenarios, also suggested by participants, such as a TED Talk or a shared cab ride, so that the participants' characters rematerialized in the *Grounded: It's Breathtaking* script, as did much of the spoken text from the improvisation, sometimes in the mouths of other characters. In this way, many of the individual creations appeared alongside each other, and a multitude of voices was represented in the final performance. In their presentation of these characters, the participants became only partially transformed, and in their significant but not total transformation the sense of community in the working environment shifted. As men in the prison, they knew each other in daily interactions, but through performing they rediscovered one another through the performative act and formed new bonds.

During the creation of *Free Drama*, Rocchio invited participants to use a journal to best capture, generate, and source material. Naming the practice "journaling" seemed to free this writing from the expectation of polished or finished work. Participants did not associate journaling with the heady academic vocabulary of the university or with the specific requirements of texts such as poems, scenes, or monologues. In journal writing, participants focused on process and connection in their writing. The prison and university classes exchanged journal entries and highlighted sections of interest, wrote notes and questions in the margins, and requested what they wanted to read more about. Because the separate classes at the university and in the prison did not meet until the performance day, this method of working allowed the two ensembles to feel as if they were in the same room.

"The Artifacts of Ordinary Lives"

Everyone deserves access to art—to create and to consume art. In spite of—and maybe because of—the crimes that prisoners presumably committed, they should be allowed spaces for the possibility of something else—of imagining and performing alternate identities and ways of being. In a prison setting, this commitment to providing access to art and the context by which prisoners may explore their creativity oppose the institutional thinking that limits, confines, and attempts to squelch creative impulses. As citizens deeply troubled by the system of mass incarceration in the United States, we feel that the prison theater workshop and its accompanying performance are tactics in getting the human story of those inside "out." Arlene Goldbard writes, "A strong through-line [in this work] . . . has been to add human-scale information and meaning to the official record by sharing first-person testimonies and the artifacts of ordinary lives" (2006, 70). Research indicates that we generalize about cultures and develop prejudices about different people when we are unfamiliar with them; thus, getting the story out and bringing outsiders in may help make prison culture more familiar (Fiske 2010, 7). In the theater projects, humans and their ordinary, incarcerated lives are particularized, thus combating social stigma and negative cultural representations of the prisoner "other." Creative practice also may be used as a temporary tactic of survival, and the theater workshop may be used as a momentary space in which to practice resilience in the face of suffering. Alternative, nonhierarchical ways of being are imagined and valued. A theatrical work, with its liveness, intimacy and distance, poeticism, and playful collaboration, makes a space of possibility for meaning making and connection in a place designed for limitation and confinement. Though this theater space may seem more imaginary than tangible, we maintain hope that in it creative communities can build bridges between participants as well as between participants and the world at large, fostering understanding and eventually a change in the social order.

Creative space is a space for communion; performance presses the experience of being in the world out into the public. The men in the Eyman State Prison workshops created a sense of belonging to each other and a relationship to place—the place of the prison—that transcended their immediate limitations. Under the pretext of art making, the Creative Crossroads and the *Free Drama* projects allowed for a space of communion: a momentary coming together and making public of the humanity of a handful of men.

References

Alexander, Michelle. 2012. *The New Jim Crow: Mass Incarceration in the Age of Colorblindness*. New York: New Press.

Bishop, Claire. 2012. *Artificial Hells: Participatory Art and the Politics of Spectatorship*. London: Verso.

Cohen-Cruz, Jan. 2010. *Engaging Performance: Theatre as Call and Response*. New York: Routledge.

Dolan, Jill. 2005. *Utopia in Performance: Finding Hope at the Theater*. Ann Arbor: Univ. of Michigan Press.

Fiske, Susan T. 2010. "Are We Born Racist?" In *Are We Born Racist? New Insights from Neuroscience and Positive Psychology*, edited by Jason Marsh, Rodolfo Mendoza-Denton, and Jeremy Adam Smith, 7–16. Boston: Beacon.

Foucault, Michel. 1977. *Discipline and Punish: The Birth of the Prison*. New York: Pantheon.

Freire, Paulo. 2000. *Pedagogy of the Oppressed*. New York: Continuum.

Goldbard, Arlene. 2006. *New Creative Community: The Art of Cultural Development*. Oakland, CA: New Village.

Gramsci, Antonio. 1971. *Selections from the Prison Notebooks of Antonio Gramsci*. Edited and translated by Quintin Hoare and Geoffrey Nowell-Smith. New York: International.

Kershaw, Baz. 1992. *The Politics of Performance: Radical Theatre as Cultural Intervention*. London: Routledge.

Landy, Robert J., and David T. Montgomery. 2012. *Theatre for Change: Education, Social Action, and Therapy*. New York: Palgrave Macmillan.

Lederach, John Paul. 2005. *The Moral Imagination: The Art and Soul of Building Peace*. Oxford: Oxford Univ. Press.

Phelan, Peggy. 1993. *Unmarked: The Politics of Performance*. London: Routledge.

Schiller, Friedrich von. 1967. *On the Aesthetic Education of Man in a Series of Letters*. Translated by Elizabeth M. Wilkinson and L. A. Willoughby. Oxford: Oxford Univ. Press.

Sepinuck, Teya. 2011. "Living with Life: The Theatre of Witness as a Model of Healing and Redemption." In *Performing New Lives: Prison Theatre*, edited by Jonathan Shailor, 162–79. London: Jessica Kingsley.

Snyder-Young, Dani. 2013. *Theatre of Good Intentions: Challenges and Hopes for Theatre and Social Change*. New York: Palgrave Macmillan.

Thompson, James. 2009. *Performance Affects: Applied Theatre and the End of Effect*. Basingstoke, UK: Palgrave Macmillan.

Woodruff, Paul. 2008. *The Necessity of Theater: The Art of Watching and Being Watched*. Oxford: Oxford Univ. Press.

Woodson, Stephani Etheridge. 2015. *Theatre for Youth Third Space: Performance, Democracy, and Community Cultural Development*. Bristol, UK: Intellect.

10

The *Arthur Kill Alliance*

Prison Newspapers and Writing Education

LAURA ROGERS

Kirpal Gordon, currently a teacher, freelance writer, editor, and performance artist, was a language arts teacher at Arthur Kill Correctional Facility (AKCF), a medium-security men's prison in Staten Island, New York, and founder and editor of the *Arthur Kill Alliance* (AKA), the facility newspaper, from 1982 to 1989. During that same period, Gordon also established, produced, and edited *Empire!*, a journal of work by writers incarcerated throughout New York state. The newspaper incorporated the voices and concerns of the incarcerated writers into a publication that circulated within and beyond the prison and fostered dialogue throughout the facility, allowing the writers and editors to participate in public discourse. Gordon accomplished this through deep, daily immersion in the life of the prison, a commitment to honor the knowledge and home languages of the AKA writers and editors, and a dedication to creating a collaborative space in an institution that discouraged such collaborations.

Based on oral-history interviews with Gordon,[1] we can understand how Gordon drew together knowledge, activism, and writing in a collaborative space. The production of these publications operated in what Patrick Berry calls "the contextual now," a perspective that considers "the value of

---

1. Kirpal Gordon, oral-history interviews by Laura Rogers, Jan. 2014, New York City; all quotations by Gordon given in this chapter come from these interviews.

literacy in the present moment" and considers writing as "valuable in and of itself" (2014, 155) rather than as a way to reduce recidivism or increase chances of future employment. This history contributes to our knowledge of the genealogy of prison writing programs and the ways in which literacy can be achieved, sustained, and transformed in carceral environments, especially important today as we face simultaneously a growing prison population and a return to support for higher education in prison.

"Scribes to Their Tribe": The Power of Outsider Publishing

Although scholarship is emerging from prison literacy programs (Berry 2014; Jacobi and Stanford 2014), we have yet to investigate the histories of the individuals and programs, many of which were established in the 1970s and 1980s, that are foundational to such current prison literacy efforts as Tobi Jacobi's SpeakOut! workshops and numerous prison–university collaborations, including the Bard Prison Initiative and the Education Justice Project. In addition, although we have paid attention to the "literary" work of incarcerated writers in such anthologies as those edited by H. Bruce Franklin (1998), Bell Gale Chevigney (1998), and Jodie Michelle Lawston and Ashley Lucas (2011), little attention has been paid to such "insider" documents as prison newspapers. Helen Novek notes that "while the phenomenon of contemporary prison writing per se continues to be well established by scholars of literature, criminal justice, and sociology . . . , the surviving internal publications of prisoners—newspaper, magazines, newsletters—are largely overlooked" (2005b, 284).

Prison newspapers such as the *AKA* situated within a history of prison publication practices may be considered "outsider" publications. Novek defines "outsider" publications as " a form of alternative media created by groups that are not only overlooked by the mainstream media but also marginalized and despised by society" (2005b, 283). According to Scott McGrath Morris, prison journalism, a form of alternative discourse or counterdiscourse first begun in the 1800s, expanded in "the late nineteenth century" as part of the growing prison-reform movement, and became a "cultural institution" in the 1950s (2008, 6). Prison newspapers became an integral part of the prisoners' rights and prison arts movements in the 1960s and 1970s, according to Lee Bernstein (2010). Prison journalism, however, began to die out in the late 1980s and 1990s as the conservative, repressive political atmosphere and the growing prison population caused prisons to institute increasingly repressive security measures. The *AKA* ceased publication in 1989.

Publications such as the *AKA* are part of what Anne Ruggles Gere (1994) calls the "extracurriculum of composition" because they provide alternative literacy structures and spaces outside of school for incarcerated writers both to practice important literacy skills and to incorporate their own "home" languages into their writing. Kirpal Gordon observed that one of the goals of the *AKA* was to "make the culture of the streets speak to the culture of the classroom and vice versa," creating a unique collaboration between the classroom and the "extracurriculum" as well as a statement about the value of privileging languages outside of academic discourse. He explained that the goals for the *AKA* were communal:

> The vibe of the newsroom and the newspaper was that true authority was celebrated as power to join, whereas every manifestation of the prison system expressed its authority to us as power to prevent. Another way of saying this: these overachievers found their mother wit and skillful ju-jitsu, and by using their communication skills to elevate population, they experienced transcendence from the prison of ego and understood an identity larger than themselves. In short, they became writers, contributors to their culture, scribes to their tribe.

Scott Whiddon observes that the well-known, award-winning newspaper the *Angolite*, produced at Louisiana State Penitentiary, has similar goals: it also "recognizes the complex nature of power that marks their hours as writers and inmates, yet it continues to enact contemplation and potential social change from the unlikeliest of locations" (2010, 171).

The goal of the *AKA*, therefore, was not to provide literacy instruction in order to practice skills that might earn *AKA* writers and editors jobs in the future but to help the *AKA* writers and editors become part of the AKCF community and to understand they were part of "an identity larger than themselves," writers with important cultural contributions to make. Kirk Branch observes that the discourse of correctional education "explicitly holds out the successful socialization of its students as a central goal of the field" (2007, 55). Redemption or socialization, at least not in the manner defined by correctional education, was not Gordon's purpose.

"I Had Grown Narrow-Sighted Playing the Hero-Activist-Writer-Advocate": Kirpal Gordon's Transformation

This project is based on two interviews with Kirpal Gordon. I knew, through mutual friends, that Gordon had taught in prison during the 1970s and 1980s; I even had copies of *Empire!* that had been distributed in the correctional facility where I taught in a college program from 1984 to 1995. The face-to-face interviews were digitally recorded and then transcribed. In addition to participating in several hours of interviews, Gordon read and edited the interview transcripts, expanding some information and clarifying details. Portions of an interview conducted in a restaurant were difficult to hear because of background noise, exemplifying what Shannon Carter and James Conrad call the "messy process of 'capturing oral histories'" (2012, 98). I then worked from two data sets: my initial interview transcripts, interpreted as best I could despite the background noise, and Gordon's revision of these transcripts. These two data sets illustrate Carter and Conrad's observation that oral "records are partial, inadequate interpretations rather than reliable, complete, unbiased and unfiltered historical records" (2012, 98). Gordon also actively participated in the project by sharing time, personal property (copies of the *AKA* and *Empire!*), and information. His willingness to participate as a "coresearcher" reflects his commitment to the collaborative, equalitarian, and democratic principles reflected in his creation and guidance of *AKA*.

Gordon's transformative journey began in 1982 when he was hired as a full-time General Equivalency Diploma (GED) language arts teacher at AKCF, a medium-security men's prison in Staten Island, New York, that opened in 1976 and closed, under some controversy, in 2011. Gordon also taught college classes and established and edited *AKA* and *Empire!*. Although he had previously taught in prison writing workshops in Arizona, he "had no idea what went on during the day program," which may be true for many of us teaching in prison literacy programs; even though I have been engaged with such programs for thirty years, I have "no idea" what goes on in the prison during the day and am an "outsider" in many important ways. Gordon's full-time position provided him with a perspective most of us who teach in prison never get to experience.

During our conversations, Gordon detailed the process of this transformation as well as the path that brought him to AKCF. A native New Yorker, Gordon returned in 1979 to New York City from Arizona, where after completing an MFA program in poetry at Arizona State University, he had taught English composition, creative writing, and world religions at Arizona State Prison from 1977 to 1978. He had been a yoga and meditation teacher, had studied at Naropa with Allen Ginsburg, and had lived in an "intentional community," so he brought the ideals and political commitment of the 1960s and 1970s to his work at Arthur Kill. Even though Gordon made what can be considered radical changes to AKCF, he stressed that he should not be considered a "hero," a tempting narrative for prison educators to fall into. He reflected, "I had grown narrow-sighted playing the hero-activist-writer-advocate, but they [the incarcerated writers and editors] gave me new eyes that the revolution would not be televised." Like the basic-writing teachers Mina Shaughnessy describes in "Diving In" (1976), who underwent great transitions, Gordon was changed by his teaching. An examination of the founding and development of the AKA reveals his growth and transformation as he developed a communal space where incarcerated writers could become "scribes to their tribe."

"Square, White, Rote, . . . Boring":
Transforming the Terms of Prison Literacy

The AKA was established not as an isolated phenomena but as part of an environment of literacy that Gordon worked to create throughout the prison in order to facilitate collaborative conversation and to expand and redefine the prison's idea of "literacy." For example, he noted the inadequacy of the GED curriculum and test: at the time, the test consisted solely of multiple-choice questions and did not require students to write, which became a compelling reason for Gordon to undertake numerous literacy initiatives: "I think that if language arts had been learned in a more meaningful way, none of this might have happened. Students weren't asked to make sentences of their thoughts; they were asked, for example, where to put in (or take out) punctuation for other people's sentences." The language arts curriculum was, as Gordon noted, "square, rote, white, mainstream, boring, and irrelevant." Tobi Jacobi, twenty-some years later in her introduction to the special issue of *Reflections* on "prison literacies, narratives, and community connections," remarks on the continued inadequacy of the GED, which is, as she notes, "federally mandated" in many prisons and jails: "literacy work is limited to this kind of basic training" (2004, 5). Jacobi reflects that "access to GED training and curriculum is vital to many low level literacy students" (2004, 5), but additional literacy efforts such as prison newspapers can offer important access points to literacy and literacy support.

One of the first moves Gordon made, even though the prison administration told him to "do nothing" when he was first hired, was to collect almost a thousand donated books from bookstores throughout New York City and to make the collection available to the entire facility. He stated, "I invited teachers and their students to come to my room, browse, find a book or two and take it. I also invited the guards, counselors and shrinks, recreation staff and front office staff to come by. . . . Many friendships were forged. A room full of free books was excellent common ground, a great way to meet colleagues." In addition, the free "lending library" was a way for him to meet inmates who were not "programmed into my class" and to invite them to become part of the newspaper staff. Gordon curated an eclectic collection of literature beyond the "harlequin romances, self-help dumb-downs and celebrity bios" common to the limited resources of many prison libraries (Sweeney 2010). Gordon's "lending library" included works by Coleridge, Whitman, London, Hughes, Hurston, Borges, Salinger, Ginsberg, Burroughs, Baraka, Pinero, and Vonnegut as well as by Malcolm X, Eldridge Cleaver, and Angela Davis. This library was intended for serious intellectual engagement and became both a hub of literacy for the entire prison and an example of how Gordon consciously worked to became part of the AKCF community in an effort to create "intercultural conversations" that supported "social change." The library was a radical move to cross the strict boundaries and borders separating inmates from corrections officers, civilians from prison staff, and administrators from teachers according to the "us" and "them" mentality that defines the prison community. Gordon undertook additional literacy initiatives, such as developing a post-GED, precollege writing group, implementing a reading series with writers from groups such as the Poetry Society of America, and creating a position for a part-time writing and journalism teacher. Branch points out that Stephen Duguid describes a similar "alternative educational space," in which "inmates see themselves as being treated as subjects rather than objects" (2007, 88), with an emphasis on communal decision making and the arts. Whiddon notes that the writers and editors of the *Angolite* likewise created a similar space, "a 'third space' . . . between the institution of the prison and the various literacies of the 'free world'" (2010, 169). Gordon understood the need for these literacy efforts to be both metaphorically and literally throughout the facility; he stated that he, "unlike the other teachers who stayed in their classrooms, . . . moved around the facility a lot." That "movement" throughout Arthur Kill provided him with a deep understanding of the prison environment and the multiple perspectives of the many people who were part of AKCF.

"What Better Use of Literacy Than to Make Culture of It?": Establishing AKA and Subversion

Asked by the AKCF superintendent to establish a newspaper, Gordon used this moment as an important "outreach opportunity" for the incarcerated writers to "apply communication skills and to develop literacy outside of school settings." The newspaper became a foundational part of a culture of literacy with a purpose beyond disseminating information. Gordon commented, "What better use of literacy than to make culture of it? What better use of a newspaper than to advance the value of education to inmates?" The newspaper writers and editors used literacy for their own purposes and developed literacy practices to help them understand their own communities. Gordon explained that "we argued that it was our responsibility as educators to make their language arts meaningful by giving them forums and outlets for self-expression. . . . Our idea was to let the culture of the streets speak to the culture of the classroom and vice versa," a revolutionary idea about literacy in the carceral environment and a reminder that even in a site of composition where literacy is highly regulated, it is possible for writing to become a means of subversion. James Berlin notes that "while language indeed serves as a means for control and domination, it can also serve as an instrument of liberation and growth" (2003, 106). Agency is obviously limited within the razor-wire confines of the correctional environment, but Gordon understood the power of language Berlin describes: "So, we changed the language. Three C's—*care*, *custody*, and *control*. In other words, we're not you, and you're not us. And my experience in the shop was 'You are me, and I am you.' In other words, stop thinking like an inmate and start thinking like an owner." By changing the language used by the institution to name and define the incarcerated writers, Gordon was able to allow those writers to become "agents of action," thus subverting the institution's purpose of defining them as objects to be acted upon.

Gordon was able to obtain official prison newspaper status for the *AKA* as well as a small budget under a New York Department of Corrections directive. Beginning in the fall of 1984, 800 copies were distributed to the prison population, 250 to prison staff, and an additional 50 to magazines and writers "on the outside." The *AKA* defined itself as "a community service news magazine published bi-monthly under the direction of the Education Department." The newspaper published issues on special topics such as sports, education, and Black History Month and regularly included such typical features of newspapers as editorials, news stories, and feature stories on issues of concern to the AKCF community. *AKA* also included some features not typically found in newspapers "on the outside," such as a "legal corner," poetry, artwork, and articles written in Spanish. The *AKA* staff worked to appeal to both "inside" and "outside" readers. The *AKA* writers took seriously Gordon's injunction to "stop thinking like an inmate and start thinking like an owner" in articles such as an editorial titled "Of Pen and Paper," in which the writer encourages incarcerated writers and students in the facility's GED and college programs to "take your studies seriously" and to keep in mind that "communication skills have to be attained and maintained through practice, in order for us to compete on campus or in the job market." The writer of this editorial imagines his incarcerated readers as citizens of a broader world beyond facility confines, in which they are students and people seeking jobs, identities beyond that of "prison inmate." Whiddon notes that the writers and editors of the *Angolite* employed similarly "appropriate rhetorical strategies that are common in mainstream texts and discussions in order to position their own resistance and to provide a counteridentity that challenges contemporary notions of prisoners and prison cultural; for these writers, literacy is a sociopolitical practice" (2010, 170). The *AKA* staff assumed a rhetorical stance that afforded them the opportunity to participate in public discussions as part of a "sociopolitical" practice of literacy.

The *AKA* was intended, from the inaugural issue, as a text the AKCF teachers could use in their classrooms but also was distributed to prison literacy classrooms "throughout the state," thus justifying the cost to the Department of Corrections. Even though censorship is a pressing issue for prison newspapers (Morris 2008; Novek 2005a), Gordon noted that the *AKA* staff never had to confront such questions because he made sure that "censorship never came up as an issue to divide us," emphasizing the collaborative nature of the newspaper staff. He explained that "to each of the news teams I made it clear that the paper is a voice for the incarcerated, not a voice for the people who were incarcerating them. Therefore, we could not give 'them' [prison officials] call to take it away. Censorship was a discussion and debate within our own circle." However, even though censorship of the *AKA* was not a problem, every issue of the paper had to have, as Gordon stated, "the dep [deputy] of programs . . . look[] over each issue before we went to press, but he never had a problem with content," testament to the editorial team's collaborative skill in anticipating censorship issues.

Gordon's comment that the *AKA* existed "for them," the incarcerated writers and editors, marks the publication as an act of resistance, as perhaps all prison writing is. As such, the *AKA* is part not only of the history of journalism behind bars outlined by Morris but also of a long tradition of work by incarcerated writers. Prison literacy researchers have noted the potential for prison writing as an act of resistance in a totalizing institution

(Chevigny 1999; Franklin 1998; Jacobi and Stanford 2014; Stanford 2004; Whiddon 2010). Whiddon observes that even though Michel Foucault characterizes a carceral space as subject to the "totalizing power of discourse," he nevertheless "locates a space for the invention and even resistance" to this power of discourse (2010, 171).

"What More Democratic Use of Literacy Could There Be?": Material Consequences

Conflicts around the AKA were not limited to questions from the staff about appropriate content. Prison staff also often asked Gordon why he was "trying so hard with these animals" and "why they deserve[d] self-expression and free college." These questions emphasize Branch's observation that there are "tensions produced by promoting an educational mission within a correctional setting" (2007, 73). Gordon's response to these questions is crucial in understanding his conception of his place in this prison and the point of view he was able to provide. He responded that he, too,

> was a subhuman mongrel, with an alias (a.k.a.), who had been arrested as an eighteen-year-old, and instead of going to college on a scholarship, I could have gone to state prison except for the fact that the judge and my dad and uncle stood up for me. So now I was standing up for my hand-picked news team, who were standing up for the whole population and had the good sense to make reportage, art, photography, cartoon, op-ed, and feature writing that revealed one another's humanity. What more democratic use of literacy could there be?

Gordon's comment about "the democratic use of literacy" is an example of Berlin's belief that "all citizens" should participate in democracy (2003, 85), even if that participation is within the limited confines of a carceral setting.

The AKA had other material consequences. As Gordon noted, the purpose of the AKA was to facilitate conversations in all readers and in the facility itself. Early in 1986, he said, the newspaper staff ran an interview with the new warden, which, according to Gordon, was "an insightful conversation with a candid and brilliant human." However, "what people talked about" was a quote that ran beneath the photograph of him: "If it were not for inmates, some staff members might be pumping gas or selling hamburgers at McDonald's." This quote was "the start of a thousand conversations . . . up front with the staff and down back with the inmates. While most acknowledged that the quote was true, the corrections officers union took it personally, staged a protest and held a big whoop-de-doo. . . . [T]he morale was so poor among the guards that their union built a quality-of-life building next to the parking lot. I'm glad *AKA* helped stir it up." In addition, *AKA* sponsored an inmate committee on AIDS that Gordon characterized as "under the radar, usually a one-to-one inmate counseling," because AIDS at that time was "the really scary and unspoken thing about [New York State] prison life in the '80s." According to a study done in 1993, AIDs was indeed a concern in New York State prisons and city jails: at the time of the study, 17 to 20 percent of incarcerated people in the state were AIDS positive, as were 25 percent of those incarcerated in New York City jails (Jonsen and Stryker 1993, 7). Gordon characterized the *AKA*-sponsored AIDS-counseling group as a "stealth-style example" of the newspaper's engagement with an emerging issue because he and the newspaper staff assessed that they could not participate in a public discussion of this issue at the time. Their decision illustrates the complexity and limitations of participation in civic discourse in a carceral setting. The AIDS initiative as well as other actions not only provoked conversations but also allowed the newspaper to make some material changes that resulted in improved quality of life for corrections officers and incarcerated people alike.

Gordon eventually left his position at AKCF and prison teaching to pursue other opportunities, but he maintained connections with many of the inmate newspaper "krewe." He commented that "it was a long and wonderful run whose final chapter I'm still living because when these guys got out, I became involved in their lives, which taught me to straddle two Americas: the one we live in and the one they live in." Gordon even noted that at the time of our interview he still saw a few of the men who had been involved in the *AKA* but that "almost all of those guys are dead now," a sad example of the "two Americas" Gordon observed. Beyond the material changes to the facility that AKA contributed to, Gordon felt that he himself was transformed by the experience. Perhaps the most important lesson he learned is that he had to acknowledge the expertise of the incarcerated staff and writers: he could not "represent the experience of that everyday guy in jail," but his staff could. Gordon further understood that the incarcerated writers he worked with taught him "how to appreciate the everyday inmate, not as a guy who needed educational services but as a human being, a brother in pain."

"The Larger Dialogue about Democracy" in a Prison Setting

Even though Gordon and his staff experienced many difficulties in the production of the AKA and in the creation of a literacy environment at AKCF, they persisted because they understood the importance of establishing a space for dialogue and collaboration in the restrictive environment. Their experience reflects Berlin's claim that social-epistemic rhetoric "contains within it a utopian moment, a conception of the good democratic society" (2003, 88). Remarkably, this is what Gordon and AKA coeditors Jody Swilky and Darrah Cloud were able to achieve in a small way in the contained, constrained, and regulated world of Arthur Kill. Although the period in which the AKA was issued was obviously not a "utopian moment" within a society that is anything but "democratic," its editors provided a space for expression, agency, literacy, and autonomy in a place where literacy is highly regulated. An examination of the history of the AKA provides an opportunity to open our profession to these voices, which Berlin says are "yearning for freedom, for possibility, transparency, equality" (2003, 108).

Although the AKA staff could not literally take part in "the good democratic society," they were able, with the work of committed teachers and activists such as Gordon, to learn to write various types of news articles, become informed about their world, make rhetorical choices, and create networks in the prison community and with the outside literary world. (Many of these writers went on to successfully submit their work to "outside" literary journals, publications, and contests.) Because the AKA staff presented themselves as serious journalists and engaged in the discourse of journalism, they participated in public discourse as concerned and responsible citizens. Gordon's ultimate goal for the paper was to help his staff achieve parole and really engage with "the larger dialogue" as much as former inmates can and to give them what he called "the power to join" by providing them with the tools to participate in civic discourse through the use of their own voices. Tobi Jacobi also notes the potential for prison literacy initiatives to provide participants with "civic skills necessary for success upon release from institutional care." She is aware of the limitations of "civic participation in most areas of carceral life" but at the same time observes that participation in a literacy program can "model the benefits and challenges of civic participation that prisoners can experience when transitioning to new communities and experiences post-incarceration" (2009, 55; see also Jacobi 2008).

Berlin notes that the political movements in which Gordon was immersed in the 1960s and 1970s were responses to racial injustice and resulted in "a rhetoric of public discourse that demanded communal participation in decision making" (2003, 85). In the interviews, Gordon noted this racial injustice, observing that the majority of the newspaper staff were African American men. He chronicled the depressing list of reasons that brought many of these men into the prison system: "Some were in there because on the street their jones was out of control—coke, heroin, pills, alcohol, sex, violence—prison saved them from themselves. Some belonged in a mental-care facility. Some had developmental problems or very low IQs. Some had already been too long in the system; [had] incarcerated or addicted parents, family break-ups; [had been in] foster care, JD jail, adult prison; [had incurred] parole violation and return." The racial imbalance Gordon noted remains disturbingly unchanged; Patrick Berry observes that "as Angela Davis and others have noted, the predominance of African Americans in the prison-industrial complex has intensified over the years" (2014, 144).

Gordon also incorporated the ideals of the 1960s by creating the newspaper as a communal space. Although this is now a common workshop strategy (Jacobi 2008, 2009), at the time he was practicing something new in not only allowing but encouraging the writers and editorial staff to make "communal" decisions. For example, he noted the importance of "getting out of the way" of newspaper writers and editors and allowing them to make their own editorial choices and decisions: "I wanted to be their adviser, not its [the *AKA*'s] ghostwriter, managing editor, and conflict resolver." Gordon's commitment to "communal decision making" was intended to provide a voice to perhaps the most voiceless members of our society.

"Hope Is a Hard Thing to Find Inside"

Despite winning several prizes for prison newspapers and being widely circulated, the *AKA* was a relatively small publication that lasted only a few years. So why should we pay attention to the history of this long-defunct prison newspaper, whose existence is relegated to the small collection of copies Gordon has saved? As I listened to Gordon tell his story and reviewed the transcripts of those conversations, three clear reasons to pay attention to this history emerged. First, *AKA* was an early precursor of such contemporary prison writing groups as SpeakOut! (Jacobi 2008, 2009) and can provide a vision for how such groups can be established and maintained as collaborative, equalitarian spaces. Second, Gordon's story can provide a way of thinking about literacy in prison beyond functional and redemptive views of it—for instance, Berry's "contextual now," in which writers engage in writing for its own sake. And last, such a space can be transformative not only for the incarcerated writers but for the teacher as well.

The *AKA* staff and writers, although a very different kind of group than SpeakOut! (Jacobi 2008, 2009), formed an important foundation for many of today's prison literacy groups. The SpeakOut! writing workshops are only one example of contemporary prison literacy programs, but their emphasis on participatory democracy, their foregrounding and honoring of the voices of their participants, and their emphasis on publication and distribution of these marginalized voices places them in a lineage of prison writing workshops that began with the workshops Celes Tisdale began in Attica following the deadly riot in 1971 and that the *AKA* developed. Although most of us are not full-time literacy teachers in carceral spaces, we can reflect on how our literacy programs can serve not only the incarcerated writers in our classrooms but the entire prison facility as well, despite, as Branch points out, the institution's conflicting goals for literacy programs (2007, 73). Can we collaborate with prison administrators, corrections officers, and other teachers? Although it may seem impossible to think about enacting collaborative, equalitarian goals in an institution whose very existence defies these goals, Gordon's experience demonstrates that this type of collaboration and consequent participation in public discourse might indeed be possible, even if in very small ways.

Robert Yagelski recounts his experience of teaching in a college-in-prison program and reflects on what potential literacies in carceral spaces might look like in such a space:

> I began to realize how important the writing class was for most of them—not because they were enrolled in a college equivalency program . . . but because the class was a genuine escape from that depressing place, a few hours of respite from the inhumanity and degradation they experienced the rest of the week, a few moments where they were treated as students rather than as inmates—treated, that is, as human beings. Writing class was a way for them to be human again. (2011, 109)

Gordon stated at the beginning of the first interview that "the whole purpose was to humanize the situation." Beyond this primary intent, the production of the *AKA* also served as a catalyst for the transformation of Gordon himself and the entire facility. What better use of literacy, indeed?

References

Berlin, James. 2003. *Rhetoric, Poetic, and Culture.* Anderson, SC: Parlor Press.

Bernstein, Lee. 2010. *America Is the Prison: Arts and Politics in the 1970s.* Chapel Hill: Univ. of North Carolina Press.

Berry, Patrick. 2014. "Doing Time with Literacy Narratives." *Pedagogy* 14, no. 1: 137–60.

Branch, Kirk. 2007. *Eyes on the Ought to Be: What We Teach When We Teach about Literacy.* New York: Hampton Press.

Carter, Shannon, and James H. Conrad. 2012. "In Possession of Community: Toward a More Sustainable Local." *College Composition and Communication* 64, no. 1: 82–106.

Chevigny, Bell Gale, ed. 1998. *Doing Time: 25 Years of Prison Writing*. New York: Arcade.

Foucault, Michel. 1979. *Discipline and Punish: The Birth of the Prison*. New York: Vintage.

Franklin, H. Bruce, ed. 1998. *Prison Writing in 20th Century America*. New York: Penguin.

Gere, Ann Ruggles. 1994. "Kitchen Tables and Rented Rooms: The Extracurriculum of Composition." *College Composition and Communication* 45, no. 1: 75–97.

Jacobi, Tobi. 2004. Foreword to "Prison Writing, Narratives, and Literacies." Special issue of *Reflections* 4, no. 1: 1–11.

———. 2008. "Slipping Pages through Razor Wire: Literacy Action Projects in Jail." *Community Literacy Journal* 2, no. 2: 67–86.

———. 2009. "Writing Workshops as Alternative Literacy Education for Women." *Corrections Today* 71, no. 1: 52–57.

Jacobi, Tobi, and Anne Folwell Stanford, eds. 2014. *Women Writing: Activists, Scholars, and Writers Speak Out*. Lanham, MD: Rowman and Littlefield.

Jonson, A. R., and J. Stryker, eds. 1993. *National Review Council (US) Panel on Monitoring the Social Impact of the AIDS Epidemic*. Washington, DC: National Academics Press.

Lawston, Jodie Michelle, and Ashley Lucas, eds. 2011. *Razor Wire Women: Prisoners, Activists, Scholars, and Artists*. Albany: State Univ. of New York Press.

Morris, Scott McGrath. 2008. *Jailhouse Journalism: The Fourth Estate behind Bars*. Piscataway, NJ: Transaction Press.

Novek, Helen. 2005a. "The Devil's Bargain: Censorship, Identity, and the Promise of Empowerment in a Prison Newspaper." *Journalism: Theory, Practice, and Criticism* 6, no. 1: 5–23.

———. 2005b. "Heaven, Hell, and Here: Understanding the Impact of Incarceration through a Prison Newspaper." *Critical Studies in Mass Communication* 22, no. 4: 281–301.

Shaughnessy, Mina. 1976. "Diving In: An Introduction to Basic Writing." *College Composition and Communication* 27, no. 3: 234–39.

Stanford, Anne Folwell. 2004. "More Than Just Words: Women's Poetry and Resistance at Cook County Jail." *Feminist Studies* 30, no. 2: 277–301.

Sweeney, Megan. 2010. *Reading Is My Window: Books and the Art of Narrative in Women's Prisons.* Chapel Hill: Univ. of North Carolina Press.

Whiddon, Scott. 2010. "'To Live outside the Law, You Must Be Honest': Words, Walls, and the Rhetorical Practices of *The Angolite.*" In *Agency in the Margins: Stories of Outsider Rhetoric,* edited by Anne Meade Stockdell-Geisler, 165–96. Madison, NJ: Fairleigh Dickinson Univ. Press.

Yagelski, Robert P. 2011. *Writing as a Way of Being: Writing Instruction, Nonduality, and the Crisis of Sustainability.* New York: Hampton Press.

11

Prison Writing Instruction and the American Prison Writing Archive

SEAN MOXLEY-KELLY

Prior to the mass-incarceration state, visibility was a key component of state punishment. Stockades, whippings, and public executions discouraged criminal behavior by making the violent repercussions of such behavior visible to the public. In contrast, the modern American prison renders state punishment invisible behind towering concrete walls. This shift has given rise to a tradition of testamentary prison writing, a collective effort to make the corporeal realities of the prison experience visible through texts. Prisoners today who wish to contribute to this effort have a variety of venues for doing so, including an array of literary journals and projects such as the PEN American Center.

One new avenue for prisoners to speak to the world outside is the American Prison Writing Archive (APWA). This chapter argues for the value of the APWA for teachers of prison writing and their students. This value is found in two ways: (1) the archive as a source of readings for both teacher and students and (2) the archive as a location for "publishing" student writing. These benefits are particular to the exigency of prison writing and the functionality of the archive. When mined for classroom reading material, the APWA can provide samples of considerable artistic merit that demand an interpretive stance founded on the rhetorical principle of "listening" to a text. More importantly, these readings offer students an opportunity to recognize the variety of politically engaged prisoner writing that comes out of our mass-incarceration state and how they connect to that writing. Submitting writing to the APWA gives students the opportunity to participate in that project and creates opportunities for meaningful student engagement.

The American Prison Writing Archive

The APWA is a digital archive of prison writing. It accepts and makes public nonfiction writing from prisoners, staff, teachers, and others with firsthand experience inside prison walls. Fiction and poetry are not included. The archive is growing rapidly: from approximately one hundred submissions in 2015 to more than eleven hundred in 2017, with forty to sixty additional submissions arriving monthly (Larson 2015b). Submissions are solicited by prison volunteers, teachers, and others who interact with prisoners and by notices in hard-copy prison newsletters (Larson 2015a). The APWA most often presents collected works on its website in two forms: the original submission scanned as a pdf file and a searchable transcription (if the original is handwritten). In addition, submitted items are tagged with author attributes optionally provided by the submitter, including state/location, age at sentencing, gender, parental and veteran status, race, and so on. For instance, if a researcher wanted to locate a collection of writings by Hispanic fathers in California, the archive provides the capability to perform that search. In addition, the full contents of the archive can be browsed.

As the archive's introductory material states, it "is intended for researchers and for the general public, to help them understand American prison conditions and the prison's practical effects and place in society" (APWA Editors n.d.). Its organizer, Doran Larson, elaborates that he hopes the archive, as a digital resource for exclusively firsthand accounts of life behind bars, will someday represent a key component of the body of literature attesting to the realities of American mass incarceration (personal communication, 2015). Thus, the APWA is not explicitly designed for pedagogical purposes. However, students as well as researchers can benefit from the way its contents "testify" to life behind bars.

The value of archives for writing pedagogy has been discussed in what scholars call the *archival turn* in rhetoric and composition. Such work explores the opportunities that archives present for student research and writing and establishes valuable practices for incorporating archives in the classroom. Specifically, work in archival pedagogy emphasizes that critically examining archival material can form a foundation for students' analytical and creative work both within and beyond the archive (Blackwell and Martin 2009; Comer and Harker 2015; VanHaitsma 2015). Because the archival turn has focused on higher education, this work must be adapted to suit the particular challenges and needs of prison writing pedagogy, implications I explore in this section.

The Digital Archive of Literacy Narratives (DALN) is frequently used in writing and other college courses and makes an excellent reference for teachers interested in the APWA. Like the APWA, the DALN contains firsthand accounts of transformative experience in a variety of formats. Also like the APWA, the DALN is a living, growing archive in which contributors play a role in defining the archive and constructing the history it contains (Palmer 2009; Selfe and DALN Consortium 2012). However, the DALN has more than six thousand submissions (and counting) as well as a longer history, including an established record of classroom use. This record provides valuable guidelines for incorporating the archives into teaching. Kathryn Comer and Michael Harker surveyed teachers to explore the pedagogical uses of the DALN, uncovering a variety of what they call "promising practices." They found many instructors used the archive as "site for student publication" (2015, 72). However, submitting material is not the first action students take. According to Comer and Harker, the DALN "deserves and rewards sustained engagement" (2015, 78) and is best incorporated into a sequence of coursework where students are first tasked to read existing narratives for analysis and invention purposes and then subsequently invited to contribute to the archive.

Others echo this approach to using archives in teaching. Pamela VanHaitsma considers specifically digital archives and advocates that students "simultaneously examine traditional archival materials from the past and create new online archives of related materials from their lives" (2015, 35). She argues that by analyzing and contributing simultaneously, students are moved to consider the relevance of what they are reading to their own lives and develop curiosity and engagement. Megan Norcia asks students to engage with "I Remain: The Digital Archive of Letters, Manuscripts, and Ephemera" by transcribing, annotating, researching, and contextualizing a letter for inclusion in the archive. Although not submitting original primary material of their own to the archive, these students are engaging with an ongoing critical discourse by contributing original analysis grounded in their understanding of the archive's function (2008, 105). Similarly, Christopher Blackwell and Thomas Martin describe undergraduate students engaging with digital archives by doing research as well as annotating and organizing materials—in other words, taking a hand in creating the archive. Students, feeling they have contributed something valuable, demonstrate considerable "dedication and excitement" (2009, paras. 5–6). Such research indicates how archival pedagogy incorporates a critical analytical approach as a way for students to understand the function of the archive and create deep, meaningful engagement.

The approach to incorporating an archive must be driven by the content of that archive, a particular challenge in the case of a prison writing archive because prison writing is qualitatively different from other forms of autobiographical writing. A model for reading the APWA grounded in archival, rhetorical, and literary scholarship is helpful. Once again, the DALN provides an excellent starting point. The DALN is distinct from most archives because it contains contemporary, audiovisual records that are "not only narratives of literacy-in-development but also examples of literacy-in-practice" (Comer and Harker 2015, 67). Cynthia Selfe and the DALN Consortium argue that teachers have a moral obligation to DALN contributors because those contributors are putting themselves in a revealing position and have the reasonable expectation that "someone is out there listening to one's messages, reading them, and composing meaning from them" (2012, "Rhetorical Responsiveness" sec.). Contributors are using the space to perform at least somewhat efficacious political and social action. Selfe and the DALN Consortium insist we thus engage in rhetorical responsiveness, which means we read not to verify but with a "responsibility logic" and an active response. These narratives are not just data; they are an opportunity to reflect and change our practices. This understanding has significant implications for us as teachers, who can use "this important information to reconsider and re-shape our instruction in light of what we learn about the role that literacy has played in the lived experiences of individuals" (Selfe and DALN Consortium 2012, "Rhetorical Responsiveness" sec.). As teachers of prison writing, we have a similar obligation to consider material produced by our students and other prison writers as "serious communications" about prison and its practices and to use this information to "reconsider and re-shape our instruction." In fact, the ethical responsibility is considerably stronger in this case because contributors to the APWA face risks for witnessing the reality of their life behind bars.

Selfe and the DALN Consortium are concerned primarily with teacher's practices, but the "responsibility logic" that can guide work in the DALN is not exclusive to teachers and scholars. A similar productive approach is provided by rhetorical scholarship and the work literary scholars do with survivor testimony and witness literature. D. G. Myers argues that survivor testimony should not just be heard or empathized with, a purely emotional response. It also should not be exclusively subjected to academic interpretation that "is founded on the principle of meaning-concealed-beneath-the-surface" (1999, 268) and is thus suspicious and harmful to those who bravely submit themselves to the trauma of reliving their experiences by writing them. An appropriate response to such a text, Myers explains, is instead one that is "neither arbitrary nor predetermined, but self-willed and adjusted to circumstance. . . . [W]hen we act responsibly we do not ask what such experiences mean, but how they are to be acknowledged" (269). This approach does not preclude analysis but instead forms the foundation of analysis. Readers can—indeed, should—interpret or analyze because that is an ethical and responsible acknowledgment of the text. Similarly, Krista Ratcliffe models *rhetorical listening* as a trope for the active interpretation of texts. Like Myers, Ratcliffe asks us to "not read simply for what we can agree with or challenge" (1999, 203). Listeners should instead

> invoke both their capacity and their willingness (1) to promote an *understanding* of self and other that informs our culture's politics and ethics, (2) to proceed from within a *responsibility* logic, not from within a defensive guilt/blame one, (3) to locate identification in discursive spaces

of both *commonalities* and *differences,* and (4) to accentuate commonalities and differences not only in claims but in *cultural logics* within
which those claims function. (204)

Once again, this approach encourages readers to come to a text in an actively responsible, ethical way and to use that stance as a basis for further
analysis of the text. Such a method "has the potential to generate more
productive discourses about and across both commonalities and differences" (Ratcliffe 1999, 221).

We can consider the question of veracity in APWA submissions as
an example of how a rhetorically responsive approach to these texts can
be beneficial. Texts in the APWA make assertions that some readers
may doubt, including claims about gross institutional mistreatment. We
should keep in mind that it is not our primary goal to verify truth or
untruth or to determine whether "these narratives are verifiable data"
(Selfe and DALN Consortium 2012, "Rhetorical Responsiveness" sec.).
Archives, the APWA included, are always a constructed, partial view of
history (Palmer 2009; Ramsey et al. 2010). If the texts in the APWA are
approached with a rhetorically responsive attitude, it becomes evident
that the writers have written not so much to present their personal experiences as to contribute to an alternative view of the mass-incarceration
state, one that highlights the experiences of those supposedly protected
but simultaneously silenced by law.

A rhetorically responsive approach can have particularly profound
effect for incarcerated students who are reading material in the APWA.
"Listening" for understanding, seeking identification, and attending to
commonalities and differences and the cultural logics that underlie commonalities and differences are important elements to reading archival
material. For the incarcerated, these elements can form the foundation
of a transformational writing experience grounded in what Doran Larson calls "prison poetics." Larson argues for the existence of "recurrent,
internal, formal traits" of prison writing that emerge from the material
realities of the prison writer's incarceration, realities that the prison writer
is both within and resisting (2010, 144). In particular, Larson argues that
the dynamics of isolation (of the prisoner from the world and from other

prisoners) and control (often exerted in an extralegal manner with no over-sight) affect prison writing and lead to two recurring tropes. The first is the dissociative trope, in which the "I" of the prison writer becomes divorced from the individual self and comes to represent larger communities; the second is the associative trope in which the writer "names the contemporary communities among which s/he numbers him- or herself, and/or names an ancestry in the history of prison writing" (Larson 2010, 145–46). Prison writers do not place pen to paper with the immediate ability to articulate their political position and deploy the features of prison poetics. Although Larson discusses examples of prison testimony in which the authorial voice comes to us fully formed, he also identifies in *Soledad Brother: The Prison Letters of George Jackson* (1970) the catalyzing of the voice from biography, a genre in which the "I" of the prison writer has not undergone dissociation, to testament. He claims that in the case of the common criminal, who is likely to come to prison without political awareness or writing expertise, "documenting the dissociative–associative trope as one achieved not only by labor, but by labor that the prison it-self engenders . . . offers a material continuum from the biography of the street, to autobiography that opens the penal apparatus to public scrutiny, to testament" (2010, 157). In other words, testamentary prison writing is grounded in the writer's ability to speak for and about the larger community and history of prisoners and prison writers, and the prisoner's ability to produce this writing is developed (not innate). The commonalities and differences (Ratcliffe 1999) identified by an incarcerated reader of the APWA can foster the dissociative–associative trope Larson discusses. The APWA provides an avenue through which *prisoners* can become *testifiers*.

Norcia states that "the vitality of the archive is in its usefulness and usability for communities of learners. An archive should be a forum where the past and the present not only meet but engage and interact" (2008, 101). With the APWA, the opportunity is not for individuals divided by time to engage and interact but instead for individuals divided by multiple layers of concrete, iron bars, and barbed wire to do so. Larson identifies a set of recurring themes in the work presented in the APWA, including real and effective oversight of staff behavior, educational and other rehabilitative opportunities, medical treatment, public-policy issues that have led to mass incarceration (including mandatory sentencing), and the writers' personal experience with all of these things (personal communication, 2015). By reading submissions to the APWA, identifying themes, and thereby identifying what they have in common with other prisoners, students can gain the knowledge to help them move along the path toward expressing prison poetics. Prisoners' awareness that they are part of a 2.3-million-strong community can help prepare them to enter the conversation around disciplinary practices and speak there with authority.

Many of these same benefits can be accrued by providing students with prison writing from other venues, including the published collection *Fourth City: Essays from the Prison in America* (Larson 2013) and established classics of the genre, such as Eldridge Cleaver's memoir *Soul on Ice* (1968). However, unlike traditional publications, the APWA provides all writings in both original and transcribed versions. Prison writers make do with the facilities they have access to, which can vary greatly with level of prison security, location, and the whims of administration. The APWA speaks to this reality by making submissions available in their original format, which often bears the marks of that context in the form of crossouts, marginal comments, and so on. Archived content that preserves the material reality of writing can "add another layer to the life of the text and invite discussion about the function and utility of the archive" (Norcia 2008, 97). This layer provides another opportunity for students to identify with the text they are reading and explore their connections with the text, an opportunity that is not offered by most sources of prison writing.

There are material challenges associated with using the APWA as a source of reading for incarcerated students. The first is that prisoners obviously cannot access the digital archive directly and must rely on the teacher to locate and provide copies of selections to students. However, the APWA reduces this impediment as much as possible by making all material free and easily accessible, which is valuable for any prison writing instructor facing budgetary restrictions. Anyone with access to the Internet as well as a printer and copier can acquire and reproduce readings. The second potential challenge is that submissions to the APWA vary in quality in just about every aspect imaginable—a natural result of the project accepting submissions from any source, publishing anonymously (if the writer desires), and making only the most general requirements regarding content. However, this can be a productive challenge. As part of an archive rather than a literary journal or published book, texts in the APWA represent the work of contributors with varying amounts of writing experience. Furthermore, many records in the archive are of high quality and demonstrate principles of effective writing, as the following section demonstrates.

Samples from the APWA

How do APWA writings create opportunities for appropriate rhetorical response and for students to engage in the process of dissociation–association? Because these readings would be used in a writing class, I highlight some features of these texts that could form the basis of class discussion. Most instructors of prison writing are well aware that prison writers can produce hugely affecting art, and the following samples are representative of that ability. In reality, many submissions to the APWA are closer to political screed—abstract discussions of political issues related to mass incarceration without strong reliance on personal experience or other forms of evidence. These items are more likely to be useful for a researcher than for a teacher or writer, however, so I discuss two samples that incorporate personal experience and narrative. Although less common, this type of writing is not unrepresentative of the writing that can be found on the APWA.

In an argumentative essay based on his personal experience as a hard-of-hearing prisoner in the Washington State prison system, Martin G. Gann (2013) describes arbitrary rules and a general refusal to respond to his particular human needs. For example, he is not allowed to keep spare hearing aid batteries, and his batteries go dead without warning, leaving him sometimes unable to hear and respond to warnings and alerts. Gann's experiences are unlikely to be shared by prisoners with normal hearing. This text invites students to identify similarities and shared cultural logics while respectfully attending to differences in specific contexts. After "listening" to Gann, students may respond with similar situations when they felt a particular medical or personal need that the institution disregarded in favor of a one-size-fits-all approach. Recognition of this binding force represents Larson's dissociative trope. Thereafter, students may feel prepared to speak with or for disabled prisoners based on a similar cultural logic. They can add hard-of-hearing prisoners to the "contemporary communities among which s/he numbers him- or herself" (Larson 2010, 145) when applying the associative trope in their own writing.

As a persuasive essay, Gann's text makes a number of effective decisions that merit attention, particularly for a class interested in principles of rhetoric. His essay begins with a clear statement of purpose—"In this writing I hope to convey my experiences as they relate to two things" (2013, 1)—and follows it with a roadmap. He describes his military employment as well as his volunteer and marriage history and claims, "I had always been an upstanding citizen and contributing part of society" (1). He neither denies nor describes the crime that sent him to prison and refers to it somewhat poetically as his "fall." In other words, Gann makes tactical decisions about what to disclose and what not and constructs a credible ethos likely to resonate with readers outside of prison. That ethos is synergistic with his use of logos, which he relies on heavily to make his claims about institutional neglect. He describes how sitting in a secluded portion of the visitor area makes it easier for him to hear his wife of eighteen years during her regular visits. He then lays out in a matter-of-fact manner the laborious process of arranging this seating situation by spending five months working through a complex bureaucracy (4).

In "Food for Thought" (n.d.), B. G. Jacobs offers an essay that is closer to memoir and would be a natural fit as a writing sample for a creative-writing class. Jacobs begins his narrative in his maximum-security prison cell, thinking about food, before traveling back into his personal history and a description of the role food played in his Puerto Rican family. There are some recurring motifs, such as a need to avoid the wasting of food—a need shared by both Jacobs and his grandmother. He includes sight, smell, and touch imagery in describing his grandmother's kitchen. Most striking are the specific details he includes about the process and product of his prison cooking efforts. Some of these details are about ingredients and methods, similar to descriptions one might find in traditional food writing, as when he describes how powdered Cheez-Its added to a soggy noodle paste gave this ersatz dough both a pliable consistency and a slightly cheesy flavor.

Other details, no less intriguing and revealing to those on the outside, are about the logistics of prison life, such as the chain of illicit contacts Jacobs had to make to smuggle a large tin can into his cell to use as a cooking pot. This material provides affect to Jacobs's familiar complaints of institutional neglect and struggles with despair. They ground his work in the realm of the material and the relatable and broaden it by exploring the challenges incarcerated people face in accomplishing a simple task—cooking dinner—that others take for granted. In discussing this story, one of my students responded strongly to Jacobs's make-do approach to cooking tools and referred to Jacobs's prison yard as "MacGuyver-Land" for the ingenuity shown by prisoners—a response that suggests a nascent move toward prison poetics.

Writing to the APWA

The American Prison Writing Archive can help students understand their place in the pantheon of prison writing. It can also help them contribute to that pantheon. I have already discussed the power of the APWA to help students engage with what Larson calls the associative and dissociative tropes. This section extends the argument that APWA submission is a form of publication that allows students to contribute to public dialogue and develop their identity as writers, and it expounds on the pedagogical benefits of submitting to the APWA. Self-identification as a writer is particularly important for incarcerated students because feelings of writing self-efficacy are the strongest predictor of prisoner participation in education programs (Jonesa et al. 2013, 54). Descriptions of the enthusiasm students feel in developing such an identity commonly appear in narratives of prison teaching (e.g., Shelton 2007, 62; Smitherman and Thompson 2002; Zimmerman and Zimmerman 2012, 223). The APWA makes that opportunity accessible to every prisoner.

Incarcerated writers view "the publication of their work . . . as a kind of liberation (Freire). Through their words, they become present in the free world" (Appleman 2013, 28). Submitting their writing to the APWA gives prisoners that presence: meaningful access to the public sphere and the opportunity to participate in the public dialogue on disciplinary practices. By submitting their writing to the archive, students write to a specific rhetoric situation, "an in-progress, internet-based [sic], digital archive of non-fiction essays that will offer the public first-hand testimony to the living and working conditions experienced by prisoners, prison employees, and prison volunteers" (APWA Editors n.d.). The audience for the APWA includes academics, college undergraduates, legal activists, public-policy makers, and anyone with an interest in making changes in institutions. Writing to the APWA invites discussion about the kinds of research projects that might rely on APWA material and how to use ethos, pathos, and logos to make an argument that is effective for these audiences. Comer and Harker (2015) similarly argue that submitting material for inclusion in the DALN is beneficial because the archive represents a real and public rhetorical situation. They found that submission led to positive outcomes for students, such as increased confidence in their literacy skills and an appreciation for the diversity of ways to learn and communicate.

The task of achieving publication can be particularly challenging and dispiriting for incarcerated writers for reasons that are beyond their control. Publishing in a journal may require familiarity with the journal's guidelines and a process of editing and revision by correspondence, a logistical challenge when prisoners are moved among units unexpectedly and the prison system provides no mail forwarding. This is not an issue with the APWA, which is responsive to the material institutional constraints that incarcerated writers face. The APWA publishes most submissions regardless of content and format (excepting items that refer to ongoing legal cases, advocate for violence, or raise similar issues [Larson, personal communication, 2015]), and back-and-forth correspondence is not required. Students can submit handwritten material or submit anonymously to protect themselves from retaliation by prison staff or administration. Students may also appreciate the ability to contribute artwork with their writing. The archive's open nature is also responsive to less material constraints. Incarcerated writers are likely confronting a history of educational inequality simply by putting pen to paper. Facing these challenges is clearly an important part of building their identities as writers. Some students lack the expertise and skills to publish in traditional venues but have much to say. The APWA represents an opportunity for students to contribute to public dialogue on American prisons and to offer their perspective immediately. It gives them the opportunity to develop an identity as a writer, a witness, and a participant in the tradition of prison poetics. They can define themselves by something other than their crime, "even if they are writing about the crime and the circumstances that led to their crime" (Larson, personal communication, 2015).

Arguably, the APWA's policy to publish all material removes the challenge and corresponding accomplishment associated with meeting a publication's standards. However, the lack of editorial policy for APWA submissions does not mean that quality is not a factor in APWA-bound material but rather that quality is measured in different ways and has different effects. Polished and effective pieces in the archive will likely receive the greatest amount of attention from researchers and other readers. Nevertheless, students may not feel the same sense of accomplishment submitting to the APWA as they would if their work were accepted for a journal or magazine. A focus on attitudes, in particular self-esteem and self-confidence, is an extremely important component of any prison curricular offering in comparison to education in a noncorrectional venue (Gehring 1988; Zaro 2000), so this is a significant loss. Prison writing instructors should certainly encourage students to contribute their work to publications, including the *Journal of Prisoners on Prisons*, which offers essays and analysis by current and former prisoners, and *PEN America: A Journal for Writers and Readers*, which emphasizes free expression. Incarcerated youth can submit writing and art to the biweekly magazine *The Beat Within.*[1] Prison writing groups may collect their work into self-published chapbooks or zines. And, of course, writers can submit material

---

1. For more on the *Journal of Prisoners on Prisons, PEN America: A Journal for Writers and Readers,* and *The Beat Within,* visit their websites at http://jpp.org/Articles .html, https://pen.org/pen-america-a-journal-for-writers-and-readers/, and http://www.the beatwithin.org/about-us/.

to any number of general literary journals, magazines, and other publications. Fortunately, work submitted to the archive can be freely published elsewhere (Larson, personal communication, 2015), so the APWA can be used as a complement to or initial foray into public writing, one that is structured to be as accessible as possible for prison writers.

Submitting to the APWA thus gives students a chance to testify; it is a venue that is responsive to the challenges they face and provides the opportunity to write to a concrete and meaningful rhetorical situation. As discussed in the previous section, all of these outcomes are best realized when students first work "in" the archive as readers. Dennis Zaro argues that it is incumbent upon the correctional educator to have access to a "repertoire of teaching strategies that can be immediately implemented" in a variety of contexts without need of material assets (2000, 192). The APWA can meet that need.

Conclusion

There are risks associated with the pedagogical approach advocated here. Many of the submissions to the APWA deal with sensitive issues, including sexuality, and so readings should be selected carefully. Some prison administrators may veto the use and submission of these materials, perhaps on the grounds that prisoners are not generally allowed to exchange correspondence. In truth, work that even implicitly suggests to prisoners that they are part of a collective or community runs counter to the basic precepts of prisons, which depend on isolation to maintain security. Becoming politicized is a potentially dangerous act for prisoners, and teachers risk engendering that politicization with explicit discussions of prison poetics. The submission of writing to the archive to expose prison conditions incurs another set of risks, which are not fully offset by the ability to submit anonymously.

Nevertheless, the American Prison Writing Archive presents a unique opportunity for prison teachers and their students. For a teacher of prison writing, the power of the APWA is in part related to the material affordances it provides—those elements of its design that respond to the peculiar challenges of prison writing by emphasizing accessibility, simplicity, and anonymity. These qualities facilitate the opportunities for engagement and transformation presented by the APWA. Existing scholarship on archival pedagogy suggests that to truly realize these opportunities, the prison educator should use the APWA as both a site of publication and a site for research and analysis. Reading archival material can evoke critical thought and creative invention, but it can also entail significant challenges. A focus on rhetorical responsiveness, which emphasizes listening for similarities and differences in a text to foster intercultural communication, can help overcome these challenges for both teachers and students. For incarcerated students, the understanding and respect fostered by a rhetorically responsive approach have additional value. The APWA can connect students to the larger community of prison writers, giving them an opportunity to make use of what Larson (2010) calls politically powerful "prison poetics." Furthermore, the artistic merits of the material in the APWA should not be discounted. As the selections by Gann and Jacobs indicate, the APWA contains a diverse array of texts that exemplify commonly discussed writing principles, such as attending to audience and creative use of sense imagery.

By submitting their own writing to the APWA, students are producing writing with real personal and political stakes. They can contribute to a project that is making pressing incarceration-related issues visible and, it can be hoped, facilitating positive changes, and they can apply prison poetics in their own work. They can join the community of contributors who write with the expectation that they will be heard. Most of all, the APWA offers our students a way to produce texts that have huge positive impacts on their personal identity. Writing for publication is rewarding, and the APWA helps introduce students to that reward.

References

American Prison Writing Archive (APWA) Editors. n.d. "The American Prison Writing Archive Questionnaire." APWA. At http://www.dhinitiative.org/files /APWA-Questionnaire.pdf. Accessed July 28, 2016.

Appleman, Deborah. 2013. "Teaching in the Dark: The Promise and Pedagogy of Creative Writing in Prison." *English Journal* 102, no. 4: 24–30.

Blackwell, Christopher, and Thomas Martin. 2009. "Technology, Collaboration, and Undergraduate Research." *DHQ: Digital Humanities Quarterly* 3, no. 1. At http://www.digitalhumanities.org/dhq/vol/3/1/000024/000024.html.

Cleaver, Eldridge. 1968. *Soul on Ice.* 1st ed. New York: McGraw-Hill.

Comer, Kathryn B., and Michael Harker. 2015. "The Pedagogy of the Digital Archive of Literacy Narratives: A Survey." *Computers and Composition* 35 (Mar.): 65–85.

Gann, Martin G. 2013. "One Small Voice through the Wall." Digital Humanities Initiative, American Prison Writing Archive. At http://apw.dhinitiative.org/islandora/object/apw%3A265.

Gehring, Thom. 1988. "Five Principles of Correctional Education." *Journal of Correctional Education* 39, no. 4: 164–69.

Jackson, George. 1970. *Soledad Brother: The Prison Letters of George Jackson.* New York: Coward-McCann.

Jacobs, B. G. n.d. "Food for Thought." Digital Humanities Initiative, American Prison Writing Archive. At http://apw.dhinitiative.org/islandora/object/apw%3A181. Accessed July 28, 2016.

Jonesa, Lise Øen, Terje Mangerb, Ole-Johan Eikeland, and Arve Asbjørnsen. 2013. "Participation in Prison Education: Is It a Question of Reading and Writing Self-Efficacy Rather Than Actual Skills?" *Journal of Correctional Education* 64, no. 2: 41–62.

Larson, Doran. 2010. "Toward a Prison Poetics." *College Literature* 37, no. 3: 143–66.

———, ed. 2013. *Fourth City: Essays from the Prison in America.* East Lansing: Michigan State Univ. Press.

———. 2015a. "Building the Archive." From ENG412x: Incarceration's Witnesses, Mar. At https://courses.edx.org/courses/HamiltonX/ENG142x/2015_T1/courseware/e21b9fea7ad44790b5ec0d5ea3b7a06d/f3leee9f8abb4f7594b68e0726d11829/3.

———. 2015b. "Searching the Archive." From ENG412x: Incarceration's Witnesses, Mar. At https://courses.edx.org/courses/HamiltonX/ENG142x/2015_T1/courseware/e21b9fea7ad44790b5ec0d5ea3b7a06d/f3leee9f8abb4f7594b68e0726d11829/2.

Myers, D. G. 1999. "Responsible for Every Single Pain: Holocaust Literature and the Ethics of Interpretation." *Comparative Literature* 51, no. 4: 266–88.

Norcia, Megan A. 2008. "Out of the Ivory Tower Endlessly Rocking: Collaborating across Disciplines and Professions to Promote Student Learning in the Digital Archive." *Pedagogy* 8, no. 1: 91–114.

Palmer, Joy. 2009. "Archives 2.0: If We Build It, Will They Come?" *Ariadne*, no. 60 (July). At http://www.ariadne.ac.uk/issue60/palmer.

Ramsey, Alexis E., Wendy B. Sharer, Barbara L'Eplattenier, and Lisa S. Mastrangelo. 2010. Introduction to *Working in the Archives: Practical Research Methods for Rhetoric and Composition*, edited by Alexis E. Ramsey, 1–8. Carbondale: Southern Illinois Univ. Press.

Ratcliffe, Krista. 1999. "Rhetorical Listening: A Trope for Interpretive Invention and a 'Code of Cross-Cultural Conduct.'" *College Composition and Communication* 51, no. 2: 195–224.

Selfe, Cynthia L., and Digital Archive of Literacy Narratives (DALN) Consortium. 2012. "Rhetorical Responsiveness: Responding to Literacy Narratives as Teachers of Composition." In *Stories That Speak to Us: Exhibits from the Digital Archive of Literacy Narratives*, edited by H. Lewis Ulman, Scott Lloyd DeWitt, and Cynthia L. Selfe. Logan, UT: Computers and Composition Digital Press. At http://ccdigitalpress.org/stories/daln1.html.

Shelton, Richard. 2007. *Crossing the Yard: Thirty Years as a Prison Volunteer.* Tucson: Univ. of Arizona Press.

Smitherman, Tracy, and Jeanie Thompson. 2002. "'Writing Our Stories': An Anti-violence Creative Writing Program." *Journal of Correctional Education* 53, no. 2: 77–83.

VanHaitsma, Pamela. 2015. "New Pedagogical Engagements with Archives: Student Inquiry and Composing in Digital Spaces." *College English* 78, no. 1: 34–55.

Zaro, Dennis. 2000. "The Self Actualized Correctional Educator." *Journal of Correctional Education* 51, no. 1: 191–93.

Zimmerman, Keith, and Kent Zimmerman. 2012. *H Unit: A Story of Writing and Redemption behind the Walls of San Quentin*. Nashville: Turner.

12

Writing-about-Writing Pedagogies in Prison

KIMBERLEY BENEDICT

Why are writing-about-writing (WAW) pedagogies worth using in prison settings, and what can they accomplish there? Here is one imprisoned writer's eloquent and impassioned response to that question:

> The Department of Corrections is what sociologists refer to as a "total institution." The goal of this kind of institution is to control most aspects of the incarcerated citizen's life. As a total institution, therefore, the D.O.C. is rule-oriented. It deemphasizes choice, offers no explanation for orders barked, rigidly applies its rules, will not keep incarcerated residents in the loop, and requires residents to just "do as you're told." We are stripped of all meaningful identity, reduced to a number, and stamped with the non-authoritative label "felon." Moreover, it is no secret that one goal of the system is to perpetuate the existence of a non-dominant group. Prison is a dehumanizing environment, to say the least. The WAW curriculum, on the other hand, sets out to achieve the exact opposite. It is a humanizing curriculum and thus a potentially potent tool of rehabilitation and restoration within a prison context.[1]

This powerful passage highlights the main premise of this study: that WAW pedagogies can play a meaningful role in prison classrooms because they run counter to key aspects of prison culture, thereby opening

1. All imprisoned writers' comments in this chapter were obtained through the Institutional Review Board process.

up new possibilities and experiences for student writers. I focus here on four ways in which WAW pedagogies resist and revise institutional scripts. First, the WAW approach downplays rules and emphasizes choices. Second, it shares expertise by giving students access to the same "insider" information as their instructors have. Third, it equips students to construct authoritative identities and voices. Finally and perhaps most importantly, it seeks to empower students. To understand how WAW achieves these ends, it is important to first clarify the term WAW *pedagogy* and to review WAW scholarship that is relevant to prison writing.

Defining "Writing about Writing"

WAW is an increasingly important approach to teaching college writing that uses composition scholarship as course content. Students read academic studies of writing theories and practices, most of them written for professionals in the fields of composition and rhetoric. Some instructors who employ a WAW approach use the textbook developed by Elizabeth Wardle and Douglas Downs, *Writing about Writing: A College Reader* (2014d). Other instructors compile their own selection of readings. WAW pedagogies have been implemented in diverse ways to meet the needs of various student groups, programs, and institutions (Bird 2013, 70; Downs and Wardle 2012, 139–43). Common to most WAW pedagogies, however, is an emphasis on helping students develop "declarative and procedural knowledge" about writing (Bird 2013, 70; Downs 2010, 20; Wardle and Downs 2014a, 280). This two-part goal sets WAW apart from other approaches to teaching and learning academic writing. Most pedagogies focus on procedural knowledge—namely, concrete practices and processes for producing texts. However, fewer pedagogies aim to help students develop declarative knowledge—that is, an understanding of key research that constitutes core knowledge in writing studies. WAW's emphasis on both forms of knowledge makes it unique.

In a prison setting, what is noteworthy about WAW's dual emphasis on declarative and procedural knowledge is that it runs contrary to the ethos of prison culture. Incarcerated individuals must follow numerous procedures but are by definition excluded from the declarative body of knowledge that prison officials typically wield as an instrument of power. In contrast, WAW pedagogies say to imprisoned students: You are welcome to know not just what is expected of you in various writing situations but also where those expectations come from, whose priorities they serve, how others have dealt with them in the past, and what range of responses are available to you now. You are welcome to have access to the same information that writing authorities and experts have, information that is constructed less like a rulebook and more like a dialogue in which contributors build on, critique, and revise each other's ideas. The power of declarative knowledge is explored later in this essay; the point here is simply to recognize that WAW's fundamental commitments set the stage for unique learning experiences in prison settings.

In terms of previous scholarship, we do not yet have a body of published research on WAW and imprisoned writers, but we do have substantial research on how WAW has affected students from another institutionally marginalized group: basic writers. WAW studies of basic writers can provide insights relevant to the experiences of imprisoned writers. This is not to compare or equate the abilities of these two groups of students; on the contrary, the imprisoned writers I have worked with have strong writing skills. Rather, this study compares the two groups' institutional identities. Both basic writers and imprisoned writers are members of "nondominant" groups, a term used by Kris Gutierrez, P. Zitlali Morales, and Danny Martinez (2009) to call attention to power relations and to refer to persons who wield little or no institutional power. Those who do wield power—the college admissions committee, the corrections system—assign identities to basic writers and imprisoned writers that too often diminish and circumscribe these writers' real and perceived agency as well as their sense of worth. Glynda Hull and her colleagues (1991) argue that these diminished identities are institutionally constructed, not essential or intrinsic. Their claim that we live in a "culture in the grips of deficit thinking" (324) rings true not only in their intended context of remedial education but also in the context of contemporary mass incarceration because both systems tend to define people in terms of their failures. Given this commonality, it is worth examining how WAW has empowered basic writers to construct more positive and authoritative identities and to explore how WAW can work similarly among writers in prison. In the discussion that follows, I draw on studies of WAW in general and with respect to basic-writing populations and interpret them based on my experience with incorporating WAW pedagogy into a prison writing course. More importantly, I draw on the perspectives of imprisoned writers who were in the class, which provide critical insights into WAW's significance.[2]

From Rules to Choices

To establish a context for the discussion, a brief overview of how WAW pedagogy was used in our prison class is necessary. The class was an introductory college writing course. It met for one semester and was the first part of a two-semester sequence. In the first term, students focused on composition and rhetoric, and in the second term they focused on research-based writing. Our readings came mainly from Wardle and Downs's collection *Writing about Writing: A College Reader* (2014d) but included other texts as well. We began with essays on the transition to college writing and the importance of feedback. Then we divided our time between studies of composing processes, studies of rhetoric and rhetorical analysis, and studies of literacy. For each assigned reading, students wrote informal responses. Over the course of the semester, they also wrote three essays. In the first essay, students analyzed experienced writers' composing processes;[3] in the second essay, they used rhetorical concepts to analyze

2. I am grateful to all the students who contributed time, energy, and insight to this study: Amari, Arthur, the Bruiser, Daniel, Elad, Jason, John, Juvenile Lifer, Martiniano, Nathaniel, Nicodemus, Sam, Student Number One, and the Theologian. I thank them for joining in the conversation and sharing their expertise.

3. The idea of studying experienced writers' composing processes comes from Wardle and Downs 2014b. However, the project had to be adapted to make it work in a prison setting. Wardle and Downs suggest that students read online interviews with published authors, such as the interviews in the *Paris Review* and in the "Writers on Writing" column in the *New York Times*. Since our prison class did not have access to the Internet, we turned to professors in the English Department at our main campus. They filled out surveys about their composing processes, and the surveys were photocopied and distributed in the prison classroom, so students could draw on them for data.

a piece of their own writing; and in the third essay, they used the same rhetorical concepts to analyze a published piece of writing.

The first thing students usually notice about WAW is that it is less prescriptive than writing instruction they have received in the past. Students using the *Writing about Writing* textbook realize this as soon as they read the introduction, where a striking contrast is made between rules and choices. The editors claim that students are typically taught that "what makes good writing is following all the rules and avoiding errors: *Just don't do anything wrong* and your writing will be okay" (Wardle and Downs 2014c, 2, emphasis in original). Read in a prison context, this injunction sounds similar to the institutional scripts that imprisoned writers encounter each day: the stress on regulatory compliance echoes the language and philosophy of corrections. But the editors make it clear that this is not their preferred outlook, and what they advocate instead has intriguing implications for prison classrooms.

Wardle and Downs go on to offer an alternative script in which authorities are less invested in rules and more interested in writers' successes and lived experiences: "But there's more than one story about writing. You'll find the college writing instructor who assigned this book probably believes a very different story, one based not on teachers' rulebooks but rather on observation of successful writers and how writing, reading, language, and texts actually work—how people actually experience them" (2014c, 3). In this script, students are invited into a "fuller and richer" world that encourages inquiry—"What transfers is not *how to write*, but *what to ask about writing*"—and creates agency—"Writing is about communicating in ways that work, that *do something* in the world" (3, emphasis in original). The editors sum up their alternative vision by explaining that WAW is not about obeying simple directives but about understanding complex processes and making choices: "This book doesn't give you easy, quick, or limited advice about how to write, but instead shows you ways of thinking about how writing works, and how to make informed and effective choices for yourself in each new writing situation" (3).

For most imprisoned writers, the invitation to "make choices for yourself" is a striking departure from the institutional narratives they usually hear. Several members of our class affirmed this point. One student appreciated the fact that WAW curriculum did not give directives; as he put it, "Never does WAW tell me something has to be done a certain way and only that way. It gives me options." Another student appreciated WAW's emphasis on understanding as opposed to compliance, explaining that "in a prison setting, we are laden with rules, but the emphasis in the WAW approach is on helping us understand how writing works, not just learning rules." A third student commented on how WAW cared less about rules than about writers' well-being; he felt the main difference between WAW and other curricula was that "WAW put the rules of writing to the back burner and allowed me, as a writer, to just write. The emphasis seemed to be on the writer's comfort and not on rigid rules." And a fourth student noticed how WAW minimized rules in order to maximize communication and understanding, both scarce commodities within prison systems. He felt that WAW "didn't present writing as a rule-encumbered endeavor; instead, it introduced the concept of understanding the meaning and purpose of writing as communication."

As students discussed rules and choices, they sometimes used striking prison metaphors to describe how and why WAW pedagogy had a positive effect on their writing. One student invoked the notion of constraint, saying, "WAW can be very effective in a prison setting, because we are so constrained by rules that it is refreshing to be taught in a way that does not teach with rigid inflexible rules."

Another student took the concept of confinement and infused it with a dose of humor: "I've suffered through many English classes, including college ones. Before my class with WAW, the classes I had taken seemed rigid and mechanical. I found my creativity and enjoyment blocked by inflexible approaches to writing. I found other curricula to be confining (I'm a prisoner, so the pun is intended). However, that wasn't the case with WAW." Taking a more serious tone, a student used contrasting images of chains and freedom to describe his writing. He explained that "WAW was both insightful and freeing. It was insightful because I was able to learn about the writing process, like rigid rules versus heuristic rules, and see where I am at and why, and what I can do differently. It was freeing because like the heuristic rules, I am not chained to a specific rule, but am free to experiment without stress." Likewise, a student used liberation language to characterize his experiences with WAW pedagogy, stating that "because choices were emphasized more than rules, I was liberated to write. I did not feel shackled by my perfectionism, but instead found that through the process of writing, I was able to find my voice."

Taken together, these statements suggest that WAW's preference for inquiry-based learning over rule-based learning can be particularly meaningful in prison settings and may resonate deeply with imprisoned writers. Although seemingly simple, WAW's shift from rules to choices lays the groundwork for more complex activities that contribute to student empowerment, activities explored in more detail in the next section.

Reconfiguring Hierarchies through Sharing of Expertise

One such activity is the sharing of professional knowledge. In an early debate about the pros and cons of WAW pedagogy, one of the most memorable points in favor of WAW was made by Barbara Bird, who highlighted the way WAW makes teachers' sources of expertise available to students. Addressing other scholars, she pointed out that writing studies "have helped *us* become better writers," and asked, "Why deprive our students of writing content, content that has made such a difference for us as writers?" At the same time that she called for sharing of expertise, she also identified with students' experiences of being excluded from expertise, explaining, "It is this point that impassions me the most. I was a basic writer, and I was never *taught* writing. I was assigned writing in my freshman writing class and was told about purpose and context and thesis statements, but these lessons were not helpful. I never knew *how* writers wrote . . . until I read writing studies articles" (2008, 169, emphasis in original).

This commitment to sharing information and wanting students to be "in the know" stands in sharp contrast to the boundaries surrounding authoritative knowledge in prison culture. Prisons are predicated on hierarchies where only those in charge have access to important information, and inmates are systematically excluded from knowledge that circulates among persons of power. In addition to withholding institutional knowledge, correctional systems restrict inmates' access to other sources of knowledge, limiting their contact with outside individuals and organizations. By contrast, WAW pedagogies work to deconstruct such barriers, inviting imprisoned writers to come alongside their instructors and read the texts that shape the instructors' thinking and research. One student in our class noted this sense of invitation and interpersonal connection: "It was as if I was put into contact with professional writers and given a behind-the-scenes look at the tools which facilitate success, and was shown how to use those tools." Another student highlighted WAW's commitment to shared knowledge by describing it as "more of a writing apprenticeship than a standard curriculum." The term *apprenticeship* is an excellent characterization of the learning that Bird (2008) hoped to facilitate by giving students access to the same body of research that their professors studied.

Bird's later research takes a closer look at how WAW pedagogies aim to level the playing field between those who already have access to knowledge and those who have yet to gain access. She describes a WAW curriculum she developed for basic-writing courses that stresses "the critical importance of understanding academic discourse's conceptual meta-knowledge" (2013, 64). Here, metaknowledge is equivalent to the declarative knowledge mentioned earlier, a defining feature of WAW pedagogies. One of the texts Bird assigns is David Bartholomae's essay "Inventing the University" (1986), which makes a strong case that without meta- or declarative knowledge students are effectively shut out from full participation in authoritative conversations. Bartholomae describes this problem using an "inside/osutside" metaphor, noting that it is difficult for a student writer to "get inside a discourse he can only partially imagine" (19). Building on this metaphor, Bird explains how WAW ushers students into more authoritative spaces: "Our students don't have to try to *imagine* the inside, or purposes of academic discourse if we *teach* them core concepts that drive academic writing" (2013, 64, emphasis in original). She reinforces this point by drawing on the work of Amy Burgess and Rosalind Ivanič, who have studied writer identity extensively; they claim that "when students work to acquire the social identity of academia, holistically engaging it, they can be 'positioned' as insiders" (quoted in Bird 2013, 65). This goal of expanding "insider" spaces to include those who would otherwise be shut out has important implications, particularly in prison classrooms.

The most obvious implication is a shift in traditional power relationships. This shift is documented in Jonnika Charlton's study of WAW in a basic-writing program, where one teacher reports that "writing studies changes the dynamic of the classroom in the sense that the instructor is not an authoritative figure telling students what to do, but a facilitator helping students make sense of what's going on in college and in their brains as they read and write, a process they never considered" (2012, quoted on 109). We have seen how WAW invites students to read alongside their instructors; here, we see how WAW invites instructors to come out from behind the lectern, further evidence of movement away from hierarchies toward shared expertise. The move to redefine authority so that it is no longer understood as giving orders but as facilitating understanding can be meaningful in prison settings insofar as it temporarily disrupts institutional dynamics and bears witness to the possibility of changing those dynamics long term through the presence of critically informed pedagogies and programs. Members of our prison class commented on WAW's ability to reconfigure power relationships and confirmed its importance in their classroom experience. For example, one student appreciated how WAW "allowed for open communication between student and professor." For another student, this open communication was transformative insofar as it "changed the way I viewed the student/instructor relationship." Other students appreciated the respect and dignity they experienced in the classroom, where they were "treated more like a peer and less like a pupil." As one student put it, "WAW was helpful because it treated me as an equal." One of the most powerful testimonies came from a student who argued that "the greatest feature of WAW, within the prison culture, is the paradigm shift from a hierarchy where the instructor is an authoritative figure, to having an equal partner in the creating of meaning through shared texts. Prisoners live in a structured society where everything, including instruction about writing, is dominated by the perceived necessity of exercising and establishing authority. WAW breaks down that dynamic from the onset."

The more students are given access to declarative knowledge, the more their roles are redefined, sometimes to the extent that they become teachers in their own right. This role reversal is illustrated in a basic-writing study by Brisa Galindo and her coauthors (2014), all of them student writers who were labeled remedial. They describe what they learned from WAW pedagogy and how they put WAW ideas into practice. As they tell it, WAW can invert traditional classroom hierarchies to the extent that students are functioning as researchers and teachers, and teachers are learning from students' work. According to their narrative, their instructor set the learning process in motion by assigning readings about literacy and power. But at the end of the first term, Galindo and four other students still had questions about these issues and were not satisfied with their teacher's answers, so the teacher encouraged them to do further research (11). The students pursued their questions in a second-term project that involved extensive primary research, and their work heightened their teacher's awareness of campus policies and politics of remediation. As Galindo and her coauthors put it, the project was educational not only for them but "for our professors, class TAs, and writing center tutors, pushing us all . . . to stretch our own ideas about labeled writing populations" (5).

This example reinforces and extends points made earlier about shared expertise. Not only does WAW enable students to learn alongside teachers, but it equips them to become experts in their own right and to make significant contributions to their academic communities. In prison environments, WAW's capacity to invert power hierarchies can make the classroom a radically different space than the rest of the prison complex—a place where imprisoned writers are encouraged to develop real expertise by exploring beyond the boundaries of what their instructors know. For example, in the research study discussed in this chapter, students contributed primary insights that went well beyond their instructor's secondary knowledge; they also provided feedback that pushed the instructor to develop deeper insights into the dynamics of writing in prison.

Authoritative Identities and Voices

Another reason WAW is worth using in prison classes is that it taps into writing's potential to shape identity. Scholars have commented on this potential, delineating the ways that "writing enacts and creates identities and ideologies" (Adler-Kassner and Wardle 2015, concept 3, 48–58). In explaining this threshold concept, Kevin Roozen highlights "the roles writing plays in the construction of self" (2015, 50). He argues that writing is primarily "about becoming a particular kind of person, about developing a sense of who we are," and thus he encourages teachers and students to "approach writing not simply as a means of learning and using a set of skills, but rather as a means of engaging with the possibilities for selfhood available in a given community" (51). WAW lends itself well to such engagement because as learners develop declarative and procedural knowledge and gain access to professional discourse, they learn to see themselves less as hapless novices and more as active scholars. Bird intentionally fosters this kind of identity development in her basic-writing class by choosing WAW readings centered on social identity theory. She believes that such a curriculum "effectively equips students to develop an academic writer identity" (2013, 64). She goes on to say that "students construct academic affiliation once they understand academic purposes and dispositions, that is, the *whys* behind discourse practice. This understanding gives students the power to choose how they want to negotiate their academic selves in connection with their non-academic lives" (65–66, emphasis in original). This claim is fascinating when read in the context of prison education. What might it mean to negotiate one's academic identity with one's identity as an inmate? How might WAW pedagogies empower imprisoned writers to create strong academic identities that supersede or redefine the identities assigned to them by correctional systems?

Some potential answers can be found in the study by Galindo and her coauthors (2014), where student authors used WAW pedagogies to resist reductive identities assigned by their institution and to construct more authoritative identities for themselves. Upon entering college, the students were designated as needing extra academic support and encountered various forms of institutional stereotyping, even though the university did not officially endorse or practice remediation. The stereotyping, which was negative and often demeaning, made the students feel alternately ashamed, afraid, angry, and despondent. In their writing class, however, they were introduced to WAW and developed declarative knowledge that gradually helped them reframe their identities. The students attributed the process specifically to WAW pedagogy, explaining, "Elizabeth Wardle and Doug Downs' *Writing about Writing* unmasked the language of re-mediation for us" (Galindo et al. 2014, 5). They could pinpoint which parts of the WAW curriculum empowered them and why:

> As we read Deborah Brandt's [1998] work on literacy sponsorship and Jean Anyon's descriptions of socioeconomic-status (SES) differenti-ated high school curricula and pedagogy, we began to challenge CSU's [California State University's] administrative labeling practices, show-ing how these labels isolate and limit students. This has come to matter enormously to us, and thus we offer the following narratives, which have helped us to better understand the importance of language and labels. We hope to challenge others to think about how the language they use each day shapes writers and the writing that takes place in their spaces. (Galindo et al. 2014, 5–6)

These insights into how WAW can help students construct strong scholarly identities and avoid internalizing negative labels were echoed by students in our prison writing class. One member of the class explained that "prison often dehumanizes prisoners and makes them feel inferior, inadequate, and hopeless. After spending decades in prison, we tend to lose our identity. WAW allows us to regain our sense of self and agency, by understanding that these identities are institutionally constructed and not intrinsically who we are." For some students, the process of building authorial identity was facilitated by reading accounts of experienced writ-ers' composing processes. For example, one student explained that "WAW revealed the vulnerabilities and struggles that even expert writers face early on in their development; this gave me a sense of belief in myself. Just knowing that they became much better writers after all their struggles, made me think, why can't I?" He went on to say, "At one point, I had an 'ah-ha' moment when I realized that I too could write like the experts, have written like the experts, and will continue to write like them because of the WAW curriculum." For other students, study of rhetoric enhanced the process of building identity. One student said that "the part of the class that dealt with rhetorical situations and rhetorical analysis allowed me to begin to construct an authoritative identity." Another student made similar connections between rhetorical awareness and the development of authority, saying that WAW challenged him to "think rhetorically, critically, and authoritatively." Others felt that the curriculum as a whole "encouraged and equipped [them] to construct an authoritative identity" because WAW "helps students understand that they *can* do things they didn't know they could do" (emphasis in original). These kinds of insights expanded imprisoned writers' sense of their abilities and potential.

For learners who have been institutionally marginalized, one of the most important parts of constructing an authoritative identity is developing a voice. Lauren Rosenberg has noted this phenomenon among adult learners who attain basic literacy skills later in life, observing that "for people who have been marked as socially voiceless, acquiring new literacies can open up a space where they can achieve something they have wanted for a long time: to inscribe their views" (2015, 112). WAW pedagogies can help students achieve this kind of fluency, as demonstrated in Bird's research about how WAW builds students' "confidence in themselves as thinker-writers who have authority to speak their ideas into academic conversations" (2013, 68). WAW similarly led students described in the study by Galindo and her coauthors to develop more authoritative voices. One student recounts, "As we began to read John Swales, James Paul Gee, Deborah Brandt, Ann Johns, Sherman Alexie, bell hooks, Mike Rose, and others, I noticed that Professor Hanson believed in us, saw us as normal and challenged us. One way she did this—beyond having us read difficult, 'real' work—was by asking us, surprisingly, what we would say back to them, and how they might speak to us in response" (Galindo et al. 2014, 9). For these students, "speaking back" was not merely a classroom exercise; they went on to publish their research findings in the journal *Young Scholars in Writing*.

Rosenberg's insight about adult learners can be extended to imprisoned writers; they, too, are "socially voiceless" in several respects, so gaining fluency in academic discourse opens up new venues where they can speak, write, and have their ideas taken seriously. For them, WAW's invitation to speak out and speak back affords possibilities that are radically different from conventional prison discourse. More than any other part of WAW pedagogy, this issue of voice was deemed important by students in our prison class. They appreciated how WAW allowed them "to be part of a discourse community" and "to join conversations about writing." One student commented on how unusual it felt to exercise his voice, saying, "I had never before participated in a curriculum that allowed me to feel as though I was participating in a conversation." Another student made a similar observation: "When our professor said that through writing, we would dialogue and contribute to academic discourse, I don't think any of us had ever heard that before." Yet another student noted that WAW invited everyone into scholarly discussions, regardless of expertise or lack thereof; as he put it, "The curriculum prodded me into entering the broader academic conversation, despite the fact that I possessed insufficient domain knowledge." And one student developed further the notion of "prodding," characterizing the authors of the WAW readings as colleagues who expected him to speak out; he envisioned the curriculum as a forum where "each expert essentially pushes us onto the academic stage, encouraging us to add our individual voices to the academic conversation."

As the semester progressed, students in the prison writing class became accustomed not only to the idea of using their voices but also to speaking with power. As one of them put it, "WAW showed me how important it is to be able to . . . take my part in the academic conversation with authority." For another student, the key to developing an authoritative voice was understanding intertextuality. He explained, "WAW opened my eyes to the interconnectedness that exists between texts. This helped me realize that if I looked closely enough, I could see this huge conversation waiting for me to join in, with my voice and claims of my own." Yet another student was struck by the fact that the scholarly conversations engendered by WAW were open and dynamic, remarking, "WAW showed me that I can insert my opinion and that I have an authoritative voice. I no longer have to regurgitate information or write in one particular process or style." One student succinctly summed up the significance of finding and using one's voice: "WAW gives us back our voice and recognizes that we have something important to say."

Seeking Student Empowerment

In light of the issues examined thus far—making choices, developing expertise, and constructing authoritative identities and voices—it is hardly

surprising that student empowerment is a recurring theme in WAW studies. In the early phase of the WAW movement, Wardle explicitly spoke
about empowerment, declaring that "the goal of the curriculum . . . is to
*empower students to understand better how writing works in the world and
in their lives*" (2008, 176, emphasis in original). As the movement grew
and WAW pedagogies were implemented in a variety of different contexts,
the goal of empowerment remained constant (Downs and Wardle 2012).
Based on their survey data, Downs and Wardle reported,

> WAW proponents as a group seem greatly concerned with student em-
> powerment. They want students to have what Barbara Bird, director of
> the Writing Center at Taylor University, describes as "greater control
> over and investment in their learning/knowledge construction," and
> they want students to be what Heidi Estrem calls "the primary knowl-
> edge-makers and contributors." Most of those who responded to our sur-
> vey see their WAW approaches as ways of helping students draw from
> their own literacy and writing experiences and research to generate real
> writerly authority. (2012, 135)

Taking the notion of empowerment a step further, Shannon Carter argues
that there is an "activist stance . . . embedded in a writing-about-writing
approach," particularly when WAW is used with basic writers (2009–10, 1).
Carter celebrates WAW's "activist potential" (2) and characterizes her use
of WAW in basic-writing classrooms as "practical activism" (5) because
of the way the curriculum offers marginalized students conceptual and
discursive tools they can use to write their way into authority.

Most members of our prison class agreed that WAW was empowering.
On a practical level, they gained skills they could transfer to other classes,
which instilled confidence about their ability to write across disciplines
and to wider audiences. For instance, when faced with a complex writing
project in a theology course, one student used a nonlinear composing
process that he had developed in our English class; he also experimented
with different voices, eventually settling on one that was both personable
and authoritative. These choices proved so effective that the student's
instructor encouraged him to expand the final version for publication.
Members of our class defined empowerment not only in practical terms

but in abstract terms, too. One student emphasized the gains he had made in motivation: he felt the WAW curriculum was transformative "because it encouraged me to want to do more, to improve, and to help others." Others said they had been empowered through the process of constructing an authoritative identity and voice (discussed earlier in this essay). For one student, that process opened up previously unimaginable possibilities; he explained that "'being heard' is not something that seems possible [for a prisoner], but WAW challenges that position." Another student found strength in self-discovery, saying, "I felt empowered as I found my voice and my own distinct identity as a writer."

Interestingly, some members of the class discussed empowerment in political terms, stating that WAW had equipped them to critique established truths and to work for change. For instance, one student explained that he found rhetorical analysis empowering because it allowed him to see texts as claims that could be questioned and challenged rather than as indisputable facts: "The curriculum encouraged me to critically challenge authority. This challenge is not the product of hyper-skepticism or rebellion. It is rather the intelligent, fair, clear, logical, unbiased rhetorical analysis of truth claims. The key here is that no claim enjoys immunity from potential critical analysis, whether we are talking about a dictionary definition, a scholarly essay, or the Constitution of the United States." Another student felt that WAW equipped him not only to critique truth claims but also to put his critiques in writing. He explained his political motivations for wanting to write more effectively: "I'm a lifer. I'll never get out. Therefore, I've turned my attention to activism against mass incarceration and the spoilage of human potential in these prisons. That requires becoming a better writer. WAW helps me to address the forces of social engineering that shape mass incarceration. It helps me to read materials like *The New Jim Crow*, and to take those ideas to the next level, by writing about and building on those arguments." This example echoes other students' comments about writing to "join a conversation," but here the conversation is not merely academic; it is explicitly social and political, and the student characterized his writing as a form of activism.

These examples help confirm Carter's (2009–10) claims about WAW's activist potential. In seeking student empowerment, WAW pedagogies are similar to critical and cultural studies pedagogies (Downs and Wardle 2012, 136). The similarity holds significance for prison educators committed to modes of teaching that are socially and politically conscious. At the same time, it is worth noting some of differences in these two pedagogies and the implications of those differences for prison contexts. Downs and Wardle offer the following comparison:

> WAW and CCS [critical and cultural studies] have common ends, though they might be viewed as in opposition due to their differing sense of the source of student empowerment. The CCS approach tends to work toward empowerment by having the teacher instruct students to write through and write about issues of empowerment. In the WAW approach, the content and methodology of the course itself are seen as the sources of empowerment; in other words, students are empowered to better understand themselves as writers and users of language because the course treats them as authoritative speakers and asks them to own and take control of their own literate experiences, expertise, and questions. (2012, 136)

Instructors using CCS pedagogies may see this characterization as inaccurate; surely the "content and methodology" of the CCS course are meant to serve as a "source of empowerment." Although some aspects of Downs and Wardle's comparison can be questioned, it does raise a useful inquiry about how visible issues of empowerment are in each pedagogical approach. Curriculum in WAW tends to be less obviously political than curriculum in CCS, a difference that matters if classroom materials are subject to close scrutiny by prison administration. This is not to say that WAW is apolitical; it is deeply political for reasons already outlined here. But it facilitates student empowerment through complex rhetorical activities that create meaning and knowledge on multiple levels, which makes it less likely to be identified and pigeonholed as problematic by administrators. Some teachers may feel this difference makes WAW a less genuinely activist pedagogy than CCS, but in prison settings the subtlety and complexity of WAW's activist energies are not so much a weakness as a strength. Ultimately, the point is not to set CCS and WAW against each other but to highlight their shared goals and to note how WAW as a newer pedagogy can broaden existing possibilities for critically informed work with imprisoned writers.

Looking Ahead

Though there is good reason to believe strongly in WAW's potential as a prison pedagogy, we must acknowledge with Carter that "WAW is not magic. No single approach will work everywhere and all the time for all programs, and even those of us willing to call ourselves staunch advocates of WAW disagree on the specifics of its implementation. Like most things of course, local contexts matter" (2009–10, 8). Thus, the study described in this chapter does not provide a template for teaching WAW in prison but instead offers a starting point for instructors and students to consider how WAW might enrich their classroom endeavors and how they might shape WAW concepts to fit their particular educational contexts. Several areas are particularly promising for future research on WAW in prison classrooms.

The first area has to do with how imprisoned writers bring unique perspectives to WAW material, teaching their instructors to look at it in new ways. Students in the prison class regularly call attention to themes that I have missed and that on-campus students have never mentioned. For instance, one imprisoned writer was intrigued by the fact that the composition scholars we studied—Margaret Kantz (1990), Mike Rose (1980, [1989] 2005, 2015), Nancy Sommers (1984, 2006), and so on—genuinely cared about students and wanted them to succeed. I had never noticed this theme before, but to the student it was both apparent and transformative. He explained, "WAW introduced me to the idea that there is a community of writers and writing instructors who are deeply concerned with the development of new writers and improved writing curriculum. That was eye-opening. After realizing that, I was able to commit to learning how to express myself through the written word." These kinds of comments can be eye-opening for teachers as well, providing greater insight into imprisoned learners' needs and values.

A second area worth studying is imprisoned writers' ideas for incorporating WAW pedagogies into primary and secondary education. Time after time, students in our prison writing class asked, "Why weren't we taught these concepts earlier?" As adult learners who were benefiting from WAW in numerous ways, they felt strongly that WAW pedagogies should not be restricted to college-level courses. Some speculated that if they had developed declarative and procedural knowledge about writing during their K–12 years, their educational and personal histories might have been much different. Their proposals for improving public schools' writing curriculum, especially for students at risk, deserve further study by educational researchers and policy makers.

A third area that needs to be taken seriously is imprisoned writers' request for greater representation in WAW curriculum. Although students in our class appreciated many aspects of WAW, they wished that the curriculum had included essays by imprisoned writers as well as research related to writing in prison. They felt that this change would make WAW material even more relevant to imprisoned writers and would broaden all readers' understanding of what it means to write in a prison setting. One student observed that Wardle and Downs's textbook *Writing about Writing* already has a precedent of listening to marginalized writers and examining writers' constraints, so, given this precedent, it is easy to envision how studies by and about incarcerated writers could strengthen and enrich future editions of the textbook.

A fourth area worth watching is how imprisoned writers who have studied WAW concepts pass those concepts on to other incarcerated students, effectively taking on teaching roles within the prison system and setting cycles of empowerment in motion with minimal input from an outside teacher. There is evidence of this process in our campus's college-degree program in prison, where last year's students are designing and facilitating a preparatory course for incoming students. In their curriculum, they are including several WAW articles that they consider essential reading for college writers, with topics ranging from feedback to composing-process heuristics to rhetorical situations.

The example of the preparatory course suggests that WAW pedagogies could eventually engender prison learning communities such as the one described by Andrea Olinger and her colleagues (2012), where the roles of teacher and learner are dynamic and interdependent. In that prison class, teachers from the outside stand on the sidelines and serve as "volunteer teacher-trainers" (81), while imprisoned students assume leadership roles as head teachers. Members of the class say this arrangement creates "an unusual atmosphere of collaboration and trust that empowers all involved" and where "the gains are uniquely reciprocal" (81). Growth occurs on multiple levels. On the one hand, outside teachers "have learned to become resources, not experts," given the fact that they are "novices in a prison classroom." On the other hand, prison students doing the teaching are already "attuned to learners' needs" but are deepening their understanding of course content and are "developing expertise in the field" (81). Collaboration, trust, and reciprocity are exciting goals for prison education, and WAW holds strong promise for enabling students and teachers to realize such goals.

References

Adler-Kassner, Linda, and Elizabeth Wardle, eds. 2015. *Naming What We Know: Threshold Concepts of Writing Studies.* Boulder: Univ. Press of Colorado.

Bartholomae, David. 1986. "Inventing the University." *Journal of Basic Writing* 5, no. 1: 4–23.

Bird, Barbara. 2008. "Writing about Writing as the Heart of a Writing Studies Approach to FYC: Response to Douglas Downs and Elizabeth Wardle, 'Teaching about Writing, Writing Misconceptions' and to Libby Miles et al., 'Thinking Vertically.'" *College Composition and Communication* 60, no. 1: 165–71.

———. 2013. "A Basic Writing Course Design to Promote Writer Identity: Three Analyses of Student Papers." *Journal of Basic Writing* 32, no. 1: 62–95.

Brandt, Deborah. 1998. "Sponsors of Literacy." *College Composition and Communication* 49, no. 2: 165–85.

Carter, Shannon. 2009–10. "Writing about Writing in Basic Writing: A Teacher/Researcher/Activist Narrative." *Basic Writing e-Journal* 8–9:1–16. At https://bwe.ccny.cuny.edu/Issue%208_9%20home.html.

Charlton, Jonnika. 2012. "Seeing Is Believing: Writing Studies with 'Basic Writing' Students." In *Teaching Developmental Writing: Background Readings*, edited by Susan Naomi Bernstein, 102–12. Boston: Bedford St. Martin's.

Downs, Doug. 2010. "Teaching First-Year Writers to Use Texts: Scholarly Readings in Writing-about-Writing in First-Year Comp." *Reader: Essays in Reader-Oriented Theory, Criticism, and Pedagogy* 60:19–50.

Downs, Doug, and Elizabeth Wardle. 2012. "Reimagining the Nature of FYC: Trends in Writing-about-Writing Pedagogies." In *Exploring Composition Studies: Sites, Issues, and Perspectives*, edited by Kelly Ritter and Paul Kei Matsuda, 123–44. Logan: Utah State Univ. Press.

Galindo, Brisa, Sonia Castenada, Esther Gutierrez, Arturo Tejada Jr., and De-Shonna Wallace. 2014. "Challenging Our Labels: Rejecting the Language of Remediation." *Young Scholars in Writing* 11:5–16. At https://arc.lib.montana.edu/ojs/index.php/Young-Scholars-In-Writing/article/view/272.

Gutierrez, Kris, P. Zitlali Morales, and Danny Martinez. 2009. "Remediating Literacy: Culture, Difference, and Learning for Students from Nondominant Communities." *Review of Research in Education* 33:212–45. doi:10.3102/0091732X08328267.

Hull, Glynda, Mike Rose, Kay Losey Fraser, and Marisa Castellano. 1991. "Remediation as Social Construct: Perspectives from an Analysis of Classroom Discourse." *College Composition and Communication* 42, no. 3: 299–329.

Kantz, Margaret. 1990. "Helping Students Use Textual Sources Persuasively." *College English* 52, no. 1: 74–91.

Olinger, Andrea, Hugh Bishop, Jose Cabrales, Rebecca Ginsburg, Joseph Mapp, Orlando Mayorga, Erick Nava, et al. 2012. "Prisoners Teaching ESL: A Learning Community among 'Language Partners.'" *Teaching English in the Two Year College* 40, no. 1: 68–83.

Roozen, Kevin. 2015. "Writing Is Linked to Identity." In *Naming What We Know: Threshold Concepts of Writing Studies*, edited by Linda Adler-Kassner and Elizabeth Wardle, 50–52. Boulder: Univ. Press of Colorado.

Rose, Mike. 1980. "Rigid Rules, Inflexible Plans, and the Stifling of Language: A Cognitivist Analysis of Writer's Block." *College Composition and Communication* 31, no. 4: 389–401.

———. [1989] 2005. *Lives on the Boundary: A Moving Account of the Struggles and Achievements of America's Educationally Underprepared.* New York: Penguin Books.

———. 2015. *Back to School: Why Everyone Deserves a Second Chance at Education.* New York: New Press.

Rosenberg, Lauren. 2015. *The Desire for Literacy: Writing in the Lives of Adult Learners.* Conference on College Composition and Communication Studies in Writing and Rhetoric. Urbana, IL: Conference on College Composition and Communication of the National Council of Teachers of English.

Sommers, Nancy. 1984. "Revision Strategies of Student Writers and Experienced Adult Writers." *College Composition and Communication* 31, no. 4: 378–88.

———. 2006. "Across the Drafts." *College Composition and Communication* 58, no. 2: 248–57.

Wardle, Elizabeth. 2008. "Continuing the Dialogue: Follow-Up Comments on 'Teaching about Writing, Righting Misconceptions.'" *College Composition and Communication* 60, no. 1: 175–81.

Wardle, Elizabeth, and Doug Downs. 2014a. "Looking into Writing-about-Writing Classrooms." In *First-Year Composition: From Theory to Practice*, edited by Deborah Coxwell-Teague and Ronald Lunsford, 276–320. Anderson, SC: Parlor Press.

———. 2014b. "Processes: How Are Texts Composed?" In *Writing about Writing: A College Reader*, 2nd ed., edited by Elizabeth Wardle and Doug Downs, 677–82. Boston: Bedford St. Martin's.

———. 2014c. "Threshold Concepts: Why Do Your Ideas about Writing Matter?" In *Writing about Writing: A College Reader*, 2nd ed., edited by Elizabeth Wardle and Doug Downs, 1–11. Boston: Bedford St. Martin's.

———, eds. 2014d. *Writing about Writing: A College Reader*. 2nd ed. Boston: Bedford St. Martin's.

Contributors

Index

Contributors

Kimberley Benedict earned her MA from the University of Chicago and her PhD from Stanford University. She also studied at the Bread Loaf School of English in Middlebury, Vermont. She is the author of *Empowering Collaborations: Writing Partnerships between Religious Women and Scribes in the Middle Ages* (2nd ed., 2014). She teaches writing courses at Calvin College and works with students in the Calvin Prison Initiative.

Tasha Golden is a doctoral student in public health at the University of Louisville. She researches the impact of creative writing and the arts on stigma, discourse, and community health; she also leads writing workshops for incarcerated teen women. Golden is the frontwoman and songwriter for the critically acclaimed band Ellery. Her songs have been heard in major motion pictures, in TV dramas, and on radio. Her prose and research have been published in *Ploughshares, Pleiades,* and *Ethos Journal,* among others. Her debut book of poetry, *Once You Had Hands* (2015) was a finalist for the Ohioana Book Award in poetry for 2016. See her website at http://www.tashagolden.com.

Tobi Jacobi is associate professor of English at Colorado State University, where she teaches courses on writing and literacy theory with a specialization in the work of incarcerated women writers. She directs the university's Community Literacy Center and trains student and community volunteers to facilitate writing workshops with incarcerated adults and at-risk youth in northern Colorado, a program that has been publishing and circulating writings from confined populations for ten years. She has published on community literacy and prison writing in book collections and journals such as *Community Literacy Journal, Corrections Today, Feminist Formations,* and the *Journal of Correctional Education.* Her edited collection *Women, Writing, and Prison: Activists, Scholars, and Writers Speak Out* (with Ann Folwell Stanford) was published in 2014. Her current research, along with Laura Rogers and Ed Lessor, focuses on examining narratives of representation from a girls' training school in Hudson, New York, in the 1920s and 1930s.

Joe Lockard is associate professor of English at Arizona State University. He is an Americanist specializing in the nineteenth century and the literature of US slavery. He founded the Arizona State University Prison English project in 2009 and continues to teach weekly poetry workshops at Florence State Prison.

Ashwin J. Manthripragada is visiting assistant professor of German at Hobart and William Smith Colleges. He received his doctorate from the University of California at Berkeley in 2014. His current research focuses on the work of Stefan Zweig in global contexts. Manthripragada teaches courses in literature, film, writing, and German. He brings his concern for social justice education into his courses both on the college campus and within a correctional facility. He created and now serves as the director of the writing tutorial in that facility.

Meghan G. McDowell is an assistant professor in the Department of History, Politics, and Social Justice at Winston Salem State University. A proud first-generation college student, McDowell received her doctoral degree in justice studies from Arizona State University. Her research focuses on abolitionist alternatives to the carceral state. McDowell's published work has appeared most recently in *Social Justice: A Journal of Crime, Conflict, and World Order* and *Contemporary Justice Review*. She is currently at work on a book-length manuscript tentatively titled "'Block Parties Not Jails!' (Re)Imagining Public Safety in a Carceral State."

Sean Moxley-Kelly is a PhD candidate at Arizona State University, where he studies writing, rhetoric, and literacies. His research considers the overlap of composition, technology, and social categories, including gender and race. In particular, he focuses on how underrepresented or silenced groups make a case for themselves as participants in collective enterprises through the transformative act of writing. He teaches composition courses that incorporate student archival research and writing.

Juan Pablo Parchuc holds a PhD in literature from the University of Buenos Aires. He teaches literary theory in the Philosophy and Literature Faculty of the University of Buenos Aires and teaches in the university's program of higher studies in federal penitentiaries. Founded in 1985, this university program in prison is the first of its kind in Argentina. He has been responsible for academic activities and university extension programs in prison since 2005. He also directs the Prison Extension Program, which organizes workshops and courses in rights, education, and writing in jails located in both the Federal District and the Province of Buenos Aires as well as teacher training, research, and dissemination activities. As head of this program, he organizes the annual National Conference on Writing in Prison. He has published in edited collections and journals in literary theory, Argentine literature, cultural studies, human rights, and prison education.

Anna Plemons is the College of Arts and Sciences director of the Critical Literacies Achievement and Success Program at Washington State University and a faculty member of the Department of English, where she teaches courses in composition, rhetoric, and digital culture. Since 2009, Plemons has taught writing in the California prison system through the Arts in Corrections program at the California State Prison–Sacramento and in the Lake Tahoe Community College's Incarcerated Students Program. She has published in *Teaching Artist Journal* and *Community Literacy Journal*, and she has a coauthored chapter in the book *Overcoming Writers' Block: Retention, Persistence, and Writing Programs* (2017).

Julie Rada has done theater for almost twenty-seven years and has worked on more than eighty theatrical projects. In recent years, she has concentrated on prison-based theater and has facilitated creative and educational work in four prisons. She recently concluded a workshop with women at Draper Prison in Utah using autoethnographic writing and theater practices to explore issues related to intimacy, relationships, and diversity. Rada attended the Experimental Theatre Wing at New York University/Tisch and Naropa University for undergraduate studies; she holds an MFA from Arizona State University and most recently had a faculty appointment as the Raymond C. Morales Fellow in the College of Fine Arts at the University of Utah.

Sherry Rankins-Robertson is associate professor of rhetoric and writing at the University of Arkansas at Little Rock. While a faculty member at Arizona State University, she and Joe Lockard established the PEN Project in partnership with Penitentiary of New Mexico. Her scholarship has appeared in *Kairos*,

Computers and Composition, Journal of Basic Writing, and *Academe* as well as in diverse edited collections. Rankins-Robertson served as a coeditor of *WPA: Writing Program Administration,* the journal of the Council of Writing Program Administrators, from 2014 to 2016. She is a coeditor with Nicholas Behm and Duane Roen of *The Framework for Success in Postsecondary Writing: Scholarship and Applications* (2017). She continues to teach writing in Arkansas prisons.

Alison Reed is an organizer of opposition to California prison-expansion projects. Her teaching and activism remain grounded in collaboratively developing alternative visions of collective social life without cages. Reed is a newly appointed assistant professor of African American literature and studies of race and ethnicity in the Department of English at Old Dominion University. Her research on performance cultures and social movements has appeared most recently in *Text and Performance Quarterly* and *Lateral: The Journal of the Cultural Studies Association.* In addition to a collection of poetry, she is completing two book projects: "Love and Abolition," on the social life of black queer performance from James Baldwin to #BlackLivesMatter, and "Black Sound, White Masks," on the racial and sexual politics of sonic embodiment from minimalist classical music to jazz metal.

Rivka Rocchio is a community cultural development specialist interested in theater as a means of cross-cultural communication. Since graduating from Emerson College with a BA in theater education and a BA in writing, literature, and publishing, Rocchio has taught theater and English in prisons, high schools, and middle schools and has worked with the Peace Corps in Samoa and Liberia. Recently graduated from Arizona State University's MFA Theatre for Youth program, Rocchio works throughout Arizona with people who are incarcerated or homeless, focusing on creating spaces in which artistic communities can flourish. Samples of her work can be found at http://www.rivkarocchio.com/.

Laura Rogers is the Writing Center director and assistant professor of composition and rhetoric at the Albany College of Pharmacy and Health Sciences, where she teaches writing, literature, and film classes. She has been involved in prison literacy programs since 1984. Her current work focuses on archival documents from the New York State Training School for Girls.

Bidhan Chandra Roy is associate professor of English literature at California State University at Los Angeles. Roy received his PhD from Goldsmiths College, University of London, and has published widely in the fields of postcolonial studies, community engagement, and critical pedagogy. He is the founder of WordsUncaged, a platform for men with life sentences in California prisons to converse and critically engage with the world beyond the prison walls. He is also a founding member of the Paws for Life dog program at Lancaster State Prison and currently serves as the faculty director for California State University's BA program at Lancaster State Prison.

Caleb Smith is professor of English and American studies at Yale University. He is the author of *The Oracle and the Curse* (2013) and *The Prison and the American Imagination* (2009) as well as the editor of *The Life and Adventures of a Haunted Convict*, a prison memoir by Austin Reed ([1858] 2016). Smith has written about contemporary media and the arts for *Avidly, Bomb, Paper Monument, Yale Review,* and other venues, and he is a contributing editor at the *Los Angeles Review of Books.*

Index

Page numbers in italics denote photographs, figures, and tables.

dramatic arts bridging relations between, 187–88; education as freedom for, xiv, 6, 11, 71, 75, 204; education shared between, 75–76, 77; as ESL teachers, 97; fear of, 27–28; grammatical proficiency of, 36; incarceration reasons for, 202; ingenuity of, 217; as literacy mentors, 101; LWOP status and education for, 90; motivations for student, 3, 4, 122, 123, 239; prison education shared among, 75–76, 77, 242; self-determination of, 79; social death of, 155–56; social justice potential for, 86, 158. *See also* juvenile inmate writers and writing
inscription modes, 72
inside–outside relationships: dramatic arts' impact on, 174, 176–77, 178–79, 188–89; in fugitive counter-ethics, 165; prison newspapers transforming, 196, 197; with teachers, 28; in WAW, 231–32
Inside Prison Podcast, 154
institutionalized prejudice, 78–79, 152
Internet. *See* website publications
intimacy, 176–79
"Inventing the University" (Bartholomae), 231
Irani, Kayhan, 122
Irwin, Katherine, 130
Ivanič, Rosalind, 231

Jackson, George, 3, 213
Jacobs, B. G., 216–17, 221
jail classrooms, 6–7; environmental challenges of, 148–49, 156; fugitive counter-ethics practiced in, 150–51,

158–60, 165; guards' presence in, 148–49, 159
jail reading group: false teaching theory origins in, 151–52; *The Hunger Games* analysis in, 156–59; racism inquiry in, 150, 160, 163–64
jail–university partnerships, 112–16
jail writing/literature, 6–7; civility exploration with, 112–16; political engagement with, 123–24; prison writing compared to, 40–41; social engagement with, 111n2, 111–12, 115, 116; university student response to, 113–15. *See also* SpeakOut!
James, Joy, 26
JanMohamed, Abdul, 155n6
job training, 89
Journal of Prisoners on Prisons, 219
juggling program, 101–2
justice. *See* social justice/injustice
justice/penal system, 6, 207; democracy and, 13; flaws of, xv, 52, 57, 63; freedom of speech in, 51; prison writing on, 53, 56–57, 66. *See also* carceral system; juvenile justice system
juvenile inmate writers and writing: collaborative approach with, 138–39; humor importance with, 139; impact of DOs on, 129, 129n2; insecurities with, 127; lesson plans for, 139–41; literacy of, 139n9; logistics and implementation for instruction of, 138–45; prompts for, 132–33, 139, 140; publishing/production of, 143–44, 144n12; social engagement benefit with, 6, 133; theories for instruction of, 130–38; trauma-informed curriculum for, 6, 128, 129, 131–32

11, 70, 70n1; by released prisoners,
55, 100. *See also specific topics*
prison educational board, 75, 76
Prison English Program/Prison Education Program, 2
prisoner discourse: direct engagement
for, 44–45; Foucault approach to,
33–36, 41, 43; listening to, 39, 52,
111, 131, 210, 242; reciprocal benefits
of, 39, 41, 46–47, 88, 203, 233. *See
also* voice
prison newspapers: budgets and funding
for, 197, 198; censorship of, 7, 192,
198; challenges and consequences
for, 199–201; facility changes aided
by, 200–201; goals of, 192–93; history
of, 191–92; inside–outside relationships transformed with, 196, 197;
literacy aided with, 194–95, 196–97,
198; publishing/production of, 7, 190,
191–93. *See also Arthur Kill Alliance*
prison reform, 74, 74n5
prisons: aesthetic deprivation of, 179–80;
APWA highlighting logistics and
conditions of, 213–14, 215, 217, 218;
democracy in, 201–3; funding of,
162n10, 162–63; humanizing rhetoric
about, 151–56; in labor economy,
16–17, 20, 21; privatization of, 2,
162n10; working-class writing relationship with, 5, 15–16, 19. *See also
specific topics*
prisons abolition movement, 7, 125, 152,
153–54, 161, 165n12
prison–university partnerships, 7–8, 191;
BA degree program through, 32–33,
40–47; dramatic arts under, 172–73,
178–79, 186–87; with relational
curriculum focus, 96–97; voice
empowerment with, 43–46

prison writers, 191; activist potential
with, 238–40; alienation of, 13; citizenship claim of, 12, 13; marginalization of, 21, 24; motivation for, 3, 4,
122, 123; after 1971, 26; prison writing course on, 83, 85–86; self-growth
of, 5; self-identification as writers,
217–18, 219; WAW empowerment of,
225–30, 232–41; WAW study of, 242;
working-class scholarship on, 19–20,
21. *See also* poets and poetry
prison writing instruction: APWA used
in, 209–15, 217–21; challenges with,
xvi, 7; DALN used in, 209–11, 218;
freedom of expression with, xvi, 11,
36; humanizing impact with, 204;
inmates' writing informing, 211;
peer-organized, 32; on prison writers,
83, 85–86; process-based over rule-based, 227–30; by released prisoners,
55; resources for, 3–4, 33, 207, 208,
214, 218, 221; satisfaction in, 5; social
justice impact with, 2, 67; transparency with, 79–81; voice and rhetorical analysis in, 37–38, 40–41; voice
empowered with, 36
prison writing/literature: carceral system
failures highlighted in, 62; censorship and control of, 7, 26, 35–36, 38;
on citizenship standing, 12, 14; class
consciousness transformation with,
18–19; community building with, 67,
125; as coping method, 54–55, 64,
66; dissociative–associative trope in,
212–13, 216, 217; for dramatic arts,
177–79, 184–87; editorial control of,
26, 35–36, 38; human rights awareness and promotion with, 49–50,
53, 67; isolation themes in, 212–13;
jail writing compared with, 40–41;

social engagement, 49, 67; critical-
thinking skills aiding, 70, 82, 86; with
drama and performance, 142–43,
174–75; jail writing/literature im-
pacting, 111n2, 111–12, 115, 116;
juvenile detention writing impact-
ing, 6, 133; with letterpress project,
117, 119; prison education impact
on, 92–93; prosocial compared to
antisocial, 133n5
social justice/injustice, 49–50, 53; civic
participation for, 202; inmate students'
potential for, 86, 158; neoliberal logic
contradictions on, 151, 152, 153, 160,
162n10; prison funding in place of,
162n10, 162–63; prison writing instruction impact on, 2, 67; prison writing
on, 56, 60; teacher awareness of, 79
social media, 44, 72
social movements, 20, 151, 152, 165
socioeconomic status, 235; as incarceration factor, 2, 5, 15, 16, 17, 50, 50n3,
72; juvenile justice system and, 134
Soledad Brother (Jackson), 213
Solinger, Rickie, 122
Solzhenitsyn, Aleksandr, 3
Soul on Ice (Cleaver), 214
SpeakOut!, 6, 97, 191, 203; archival
prison artifacts project of, 119, *120–
21*, 122; civility group writing project
of, 112–16; collaborative approach
of, 110–17, 119; format and focus of,
109, 110–11; letterpress project of,
116–17, *118*, 119; participant motivations in, 122, 123
SpeakOut! Journal, 111, 111n2, *118*, 123
state punishment, 207
state violence: in Argentinian prisons,
6, 51n5, 51–52, 58, 61–62, 66; coded
language for, 159

Steely, Robyn, 88
stereotypes, 175, 234
strengths-based approach, 130–38
students. *See* inmates; *specific topics*
Students at the Center, 160n9
student–teacher hierarchies, 39, 81, 157;
collaborative approach for addressing, 174; expertise sharing impact on,
230–33; GIP's impact on, 38; in prison
compared to "free" classrooms, 28
Support Me, Period (*Bancame y punto*)
(Cabrera), 55
Swilky, Jody, 201

teachers, 7, 26; activist, 28, 110, 171;
class awareness of, 18, 24–25, 28;
and ESL, 97; expertise sharing of,
230–33; facility familiarity of, 196;
fear of inmates, 27–28; human
rights violations response from, 52;
inside–outside relationship with,
28; lending library established by,
195–96; modeling behavior of,
141–42; motivations of, 24–25; in political resistance with oppressed, 79;
prison educational board relationship
with, 75; race awareness of, 24–25;
reciprocal benefits for, 39, 41, 46–47,
88, 141–42, 203, 233; respect from,
139; social justice/injustice awareness
of, 79; as "teacher-students," 141,
141n10, 145, 182
Teach for America, 154–55
technology, 71–75, 74nn4–5, 227n3
Telling Stories to Change the World
(Solinger, Fox, and Irani), 122
testimony: prison writing as, xv, 53, 58,
207, 208, 213, 218, 220; responsibility
logic in reading, 211